T0329457

AMERICA THE GREAT AND
ITS SELF-DESTRUCTION

AMERICA THE GREAT AND ITS SELF-DESTRUCTION

Viewing the Superpower through the Lenses of Ancient Confucianism and Chaos Theory

Wei-Bin Zhang

Algora Publishing
New York

Library of Congress Cataloging-in-Publication Data

Names: Zhang, Wei-Bin, 1961- author.
Title: America the great and its self-destruction : viewing the superpower
    through the lenses of ancient Confucianism and Chaos Theory / Wei-Bin
    Zhang.
Description: New York : Algora Publishing, [2021] | Summary: "This book
    explores how the basic concepts of the yin-yang vision, and
    socioeconomic chaos theory, shed light on American civilization, what it
    represents, and the natural cycles it is going through. Zhang aims to
    "find the equations, the mechanisms, of historical evolution...I
    systematically compare the basic ideas related to virtue and
    non-government intervention between Confucius (a rationalist and sober
    ethical system), and Adam Smith.""— Provided by publisher.
Identifiers: LCCN 2021042479 (print) | LCCN 2021042480 (ebook) | ISBN
    9781628944761 (trade paperback) | ISBN 9781628944778 (hardcover) | ISBN
    9781628944785 (pdf)
Subjects: LCSH: United States—Civilization.
Classification: LCC E169.1 .Z43 2021 (print) | LCC E169.1 (ebook) | DDC
    973—dc23
LC record available at https://lccn.loc.gov/2021042479
LC ebook record available at https://lccn.loc.gov/2021042480

Printed in the United States

Selected works by Wei Bin Zhang

Synergetic Economics
Japan versus China in the Industrial Race
Confucianism and Industrialization
Adam Smith and Confucius –The Theory of Moral Sentiments and The
    Analects.
Singapore's Modernization
The American Civilization Portrayed in Ancient Confucianism
Fukuzawa Yukichi: The Pioneer of East Asia's Westernization with
    Ancient Confucianism
The General Economic Theory: An Integrative Approach
The Butterfly Effect in China's Economic Growth – From Socialist
    Penury towards Marx's Progressive Capitalism

Human nature is evil, and goodness is caused by intentional activity.
  Xun Zi (298–238 BC)

The rulers of the state are the only persons who ought to have the privilege of lying, either at home or abroad.
    Plato (424–348 BC)

For a man to sacrifice to a spirit which does not belong to him is flattery.
    Confucius (551–479 BC, 2:24)

If the people be led by the laws, and uniformity sought to be given them by punishments, they will try to avoid the punishment, but have no sense of shame.
    Confucius (551–479 BC)

A petty thief is put in jail. A great brigand becomes a ruler of a Nation.
    Zhuangzi (369–295 BC)

TABLE OF CONTENTS

PREFACE AND ACKNOWLEDGEMENTS   1

1. THE SUPERPOWER AFTER WORLD WAR II AND ITS FOUNDATION   5

1.1 America as the Global Superpower after WWII   8

1.2 Early America with Immigrants and Multiple Cultures   13

1.3 Love of Freedom with Abundant Land and Slaves   17

1.4 Cultural Formation Based on Religious Spirits and British Rationality   24

1.5 The Declaration of Independence, the Constitution, and the Government
Structure   28

1.6 Anti-British and Slave-Owning Founding Fathers   32
    George Washington (1732–1799)   34
    Alexander Hamilton (1755?–1804)   34
    Benjamin Franklin (1706–1790)   35
    John Adams (1735–1826)   35
    Samuel Adams (1722–1803)   36
    Thomas Jefferson (1743–1826)   36
    James Madison (1751–1836)   36

1.7 The Civil War and Abolishing Slavery   37

1.8 Pondering America Through the Lens of Ancient Confucianism   43

2. WEALTH WITH CAPITALISM   51

2.1 Adam Smith, Keynes, and America's Market Economy   52
2.2 Economic Growth and Improved Living Conditions   56
2.3 The U.S. Stock Exchange   59
2.4 Household Income and Wealth Inequalities   62
2.5 Dynamics of the Productivity and Wage Gaps   69
2.6 Poverty and Distribution of Social Welfare   72
2.7 Growth, Consumption, and Saving   76
2.8 Education and Its Role in Enriching and Empowering People   81
2.9 Science and Technology in National Development   88

3. POWER WITH DEMOCRACY   95

3.1 The Political Game Between the Democratic and the Republican Party   98
3.2 Converging Political Ideas Between the Parties   102
3.3 Law and Social Justice   105
3.4 Political Power   109
3.5 Trump Elected as the President   114

4. GENDER AND RACIAL RELATIONS WITH INDIVIDUALISM   119

4.1 Individualism and Gender Relations   121
4.2 Romantic Playfulness and the Dynamics of Family   127
4.3 Gender Games and Broken Families   135
4.4 Criminals in America   139
4.5 Multiculturalism with Immigrants   142
4.6 Racial Assimilation with Economic Development and Education   148
4.7 The Slovenian-American as First Lady and the American Dream   153
4.8 The South-African-Canadian-American as the Richest in America 155
4.9 Indian CEOs in American Multinational Corporations   156
4.10 Chinese Restaurants in America   159
4.11 Costs of Social Parasites   163

5. THE END OF LINEARIZED AND SIMPLIFIED IDEOLOGIES   169

5.1 Ancient Greek Democracy Based on Slavery and America's Democracy   170
5.2 Daniel Bell's End of Ideology   172
5.3 Fukuyama's Last Man and the End of History   174
5.4 Huntington's Clash of Civilizations   177
5.5 Mutually Debilitating American Core Values   182
5.6 The End of Rational Simplicity and Colonization-Convenient Thinking   190

6. AMERICA'S DEEPENING DESTRUCTIVENESS IN THE GLOBAL VILLAGE   195

   6.1 Self-Organization of Human Societies with Creation and Destruction   196

   6.2 America's Declining Relative Economic Power   197

   6.3 America of the People, for the Rich, and by the Rich   200

   6.4 A Thucydides Trap Between America and Other Powers?   206

   6.5 People of Color as the Principal New Immigrants, and Global
      Respectability   212

   6.6 The Average IQ Population in the Global Village   221

   6.7 On Spengler's The Decline of the West   225

   6.8 America's Deepening Self-Destructiveness   229

REFERENCES   243

Figures and Tables

Figure 1.1 GDP per Capita in the USA, 1878–2012, in 1990 dollars 10

Figure 1.2 US and Some Selected Countries' GDP Growth 10

Table 1.1 Some Indicators in Singapore and America 15

Map 1.1 Contemporary Map of the United States 19

Map 1.2 Landscape of the United States 19

Table 1.2 The Population Growth in America from 1610 to 1780, m for million 20

Photo 1.1 Symbols of American, Japanese and Mainland Chinese Cultures 33

Photo 1.1 Moses, Confucius (left), and Solon at the U.S. Supreme Court 43

Figure 2.1 U.S. GDP Growth Rate, 1961–2019, in 2010 U.S. 57

Figure 2.2 Dynamics of American Income Distribution from 1968 to 2018 65

Figure 2.3 Household Income Distribution due to Education Degree 66

Figure 2.4 Ethnicity-Based Household Income Distribution 66

Figure 2.5. The Dynamics of Wealth in American Economy, 1989–2016 67

Figure 2.6 U.S. Has Highest Level of Inequality Among G7 Countries 68

Figure 2.7 Shares of Aggregated Income by Top 1% in G7 Countries 69

Figure 2.7 Growth Rates (%) of Productivity and Worker's Hourly
 Compensation 71

Figure 2.8 The Compensation Ratio of CEO and Worker, 1965–2019 72

Figure 2.9 Poverty and Poverty Rate of America, 1959–2016 76

Figure 2.10 Gross National Saving Rates of U.S., Japan, and China, 1980–2018 80

Figure 2.11 Dynamics of Personal Saving Behavior in America, 1960–2019 81

Figure 2.13 The Government Budget for R&D in the United States, 1953–2013 91

Figure 2.14 Convergences of R&D Structure Between America and China 92

Figure 3.1 The Eligible Voter Turnout Rate in the US Presidential Elections   112

Figure 4.1 Dynamics of Marriage, Selected Countries   130

Figure 4.2 Dynamics of Divorce, Selected Countries   132

Figure 4.3 Share of Marriages Ending in America   133

Figure 4.4 Dynamics of US Births Outside of Wedlock in Percentage, 1964–2014   138

Figure 4.6 Incarceration Rates of the World May 1, 2018   142

Figure 4.7 Maslow's Hierarchy of Needs   151

Figure 4.8 Median Household Income by Ethnicity in US in 2018, US$ 157

Figure 6.1 Falling Share of U.S. Economy in the Global Economy   199

Figure 6.2 Falling Share of U.S. Economy in Global Purchasing Power   199

Figure 6.3 U.S. Arms Exports, 2000 to 2019, in 1990 million US$ 210

Figure 6.4 The Top 6 of Average Annual Arms Exports, 2007 to 2017   212

Figure 6.5 Original Countries of American Immigrants   215

Figure 6.6 Ethnic Population Components across Ages   216

Figure 6.7 Dynamics of American Population Components   218

Figure 6.8 Origins of the U.S. Immigrant Population, 1960–2016   219

Table 6.1. Average IQs, GDP per Capita, Happiness Indexes, and Frequency of Sex   225

Table 6.2 Dynamics of Europeans' Distrust of the U.S. Government   238

Preface and Acknowledgements

Mankind is in the middle of historical transformation after the bifurcation point of the ending of the Cold War. Global digitalization connects the entire world like a single tiny vacant room, as far as verbal communication capacity is concerned. Time and space are losing their traditional role in the formation of civilizations. Rumination over possible relations between civilizations is not only intellectually interesting but also practically significant. The world is closely connected by digital technologies, low-cost transportation, global education, globally diffused rational knowledge, (relatively) free diffusion of religions, global inter-marriage, global migration, global environmental concerns, global trade, global criminals, and global nuclear powers.

A modern rational civilization is bolstered by its ideology. The role of rational ideology is to provide a structure for the creation, distribution, and consumption of wealth, power, and sex (and its associated products such as family and children). For instance, American ideology says that in the United States wealth is determined by free market mechanisms, political power by democracy, and sex by individualism (and romanticism). The modern conception of professionalism in the market economy is essential for order and the efficient division of labor. But professionalism might lead to personal behavior not necessarily socially desirable, such as, a soldier kills for the sake of killing; a lawyer protects the customer for the sake of protection; a professor publishes for the sake of publishing even with faked data; a financier invests for the sake of gambling.

Adam Smith (1726–1790) and Karl Marx (1818–1832), for instance, provide different structures for wealth, but they have little insight into power and sex. Many philosophers (and the creators of some religions often are shallow philosophers, by modern standards) give interesting opinions on sex and power but have little insight into the complexity of the economic world. In the Chinese bible, *Yi Jing*, (or I Ching) everything is — consciously or unconsciously, objectively or subjectively, material or immaterial, legally or illegally, fairly or unfairly, and directly or indirectly — related to everything else over time and space. Constructiveness incites destructiveness, and vice versa.

America, as the greatest country on the earth, attracts attention daily on billions of screens across the tiny globe. It is simultaneously watched, examined, imitated, learned, appreciated, targeted (for miscellaneous motivations), criticized, loved, mocked, and hated by someone, somewhere. The lenses through which people study America are many and varied.

The intention of this book is to ruminate on American civilization using the *yin-yang* vision, socioeconomic chaos theory (Zhang, 1991) and general economic theory (Zhang, 2020). I have been interested in American civilization for many decades. I am especially interested in examining American civilization through the lens of ancient Confucianism. This is perhaps no accident. I have long been interested in German philosophy and thought. A great thinker of Western civilization, known as the last universal genius, Gottfried Wilhelm Leibniz (1646–1716), extensively studied things Chinese and perceived himself as a follower of Confucianism. He predicted:

> It is in my view a unique disposition of fate which has placed the highest civilizations the human race has achieved as it were at the two extremities of our continent, that is in Europe and China, which adorns the opposite end of the earth as a kind of oriental Europe. And the highest providence is also at work in the fortunate circumstance that, while the nations which are most highly developed and at the same time the furthest separated reach out their arms to one another, everything that lies between them is gradually brought to a higher way of life. (Myers, 1982: 160)

The central position of European civilization has been replaced by America after WWII. The center of East Asian modernization had been Japan for many years before Chinese and Korean regions have sped up Westernization after WWII. If one considers America as an extension of Europe and Japan as that of China, the great thinker's view is still structurally correct. Greatest thinkers in human race are more often mis-interpreted and forgotten than correctly appreciated. This is owing to the natural law of human race evolution — collectively repeating certain stupidities. I have applied modern Western value and ancient Confucianism to examine different societies. I started to be concerned with dynamics of American civilization more than 20 years ago when I happened to read *The Clash of Civilizations and the Remaking of the World Order* by Huntington (1996). When reading the provocative book, I had an idea about why not seeing American civilization with ancient Confucianism. The idea resulted in my 2003 book: *The American Civilization Portrayed in Ancient Confucianism.* This book is a still protracted endeavor.

This book reflects on American civilization with recent advances in science and empirical evidence. It shows that increasingly deepening destructiveness in American economic, political, cultural and social subsystems tends to weaken America's relative position in global division of labor and consumption. Destructiveness is deepening because the three core rules — free market, democracy, and individualism (+ romanticism) — which have bolstered America's greatness — are no more healthily synergetic in the American organ. It is also based on ancient Confucianism (Zhang, 1999, 2013). I quote extensively from the Confucian classics. Some of quotes from Confucius and Mencius are from https://quotes.thefamouspeople.com/confucius-84.php. Other quotes are from https://www.brainyquote.com, and https://www.azquotes.com, with a few exceptions which can be identified by googling. I am deeply grateful to these websites.

I am thankful to my Publisher Dr. Claudiu A. Secara and Editor Dr. Martin DeMers for many important comments and suggestions for improving the manuscript and effective co-operation.

It is a great fortune for me to have the opportunity to work in a small and beautiful tourist coastal city with about 100,000 habitants in Japan over years. Beppu city, colored by flowers and leaves over the four seasons, has 2,300 hot springs personalized by the seven types among the verified ten types in the world. I completed this book at the Ritsumeikan Asia Pacific University. The campus, facing the ocean, overlooking Beppu City, standing by the deep valley, and relying on the beautiful mountains, tranquilizes me with flowers and birds in the four seasons. I am grateful to the intellectual and cultural campus life sustained collectively by the colleagues, students, and staff members from over 100 countries. I am grateful for the university's supportive environment in research.

1. The Superpower After World War II and Its Foundation

> Opportunities of time vouchsafed by Heaven are not equal to advantages of situation afforded by the Earth, and advantages of situation afforded by the Earth are not equal to the union arising from the accord of Men.
>
> Mencius (372–289 BC, 4:1)

Social life is full of games. Game needs rules such as laws, customs, implicit or explicit rules. In modern times, national rule in some countries is ideology. A society is characterized by its creation, distribution, and consumption of wealth, power, and sex under different rules, based on self-interest, sympathy, and justice. The international games played between capitalism and socialism might look immature to future generations but they are a step in the process towards a newfangled global world order with rationalized co-existence among humans (in the process of evolving from group-based monkey societies to global human society).

Civilization refers to intellectual, emotional, spiritual, technological, and physical stocks accumulated over perhaps a few hundred years, for the Americas (if we omit the aboriginal American cultures), for Europe, China, India, and other cultural areas over some thousand years. When Huntington (1996) was setting up his clashes of civilizations, China, as a modern society, was too young to know about being civilized, or too old to correctly remember the high parts of its own civilization. Chinese Communism, which is the current dominant ideology of China, has little to do with the high parts of Chinese civilization. Uneducated and uncultivated Chinese generations picked up a Western ideology that even Western civilization centers did not care much about. China added miserable memories to Chinese civilization during the two hundred years before the economic reform in 1978. As I wrote in the Preface to *The Butterfly Effect in China's Economic Growth*, the point of studying history is to solve high dimensional partial differential equations with initial conditions. The fundamental job of research of history to find the equations, i.e., [formulas or] mechanisms, of historical evolution. Rational civilizations should have the same equations, but diversified paths of movement. A historian who applies wrong equations even with correct historical factors will lead to, almost certainly, wrong conclusions. New knowledge and new perspectives, not to say new facts and new biases, will change the history. Occurrence is invariant but the history of the occurrence changes with time.

Physicist Stephen Hawking (1942—2018) talks about the time of the universe: "The past, like the future, is indefinite and exists only as a spectrum of possibilities." An individual historian may be honest, but the data available may be faked. Hermann Hesse, with his literate precision, observes: "To study history means submitting to chaos and nevertheless retaining faith in order and meaning."

In the last few years, the mantra "make America great again" was daily dispersed over the world. The phrase had been popularized by Donald Trump since his 2016 presidential campaign. People across the world initially had no idea what this slogan really meant as they already took it for granted that America was the greatest superpower. However, the tirelessly repeated slogan and no progress seen in the last few years has made the world aware that America might be in a quagmire. Edgar Allan Poe (1809–1949) hints at why such a slogan would become a global fad: "The death of a beautiful woman, is unquestionably the most poetical topic in the world."

In fact, Ronald Reagan (1911—2004) promoted "Let's make America great again" as the key phrase in his 1980 presidential campaign. This did not provoke global attention as the world was not instantly connected, as it is today, but few foreigners thought about it seriously. At that time, America was behaving relatively freely, fairly, energetically, and generously, as far as most outsiders could tell. No important index hinted that America was about to become "not great." Moreover, Reagan's phrase was too long. Trump shortened it to satisfy a 4-word golden rule of propaganda. But the phrase was not too long for the American masses to remember; and that creates a dichotomy between America and non-America.

A society can be characterized by the creation, distribution, and consumption of wealth, power, and sex with various combinations of self-interest, sympathy, and justice. Wealth is accumulated, owned, and applied in diverse cultures under different institutions. "Nation" is a grand game composed of various levels of sub-games. The national game may be, for instance, governed by religion or ideology. America's ideology is capitalism (for wealth), democracy (for political power), and individualism and liberty (for sex and its associated products such as family, and other relations). Adam Smith is known for his theory about ownership and its application in a fixed power structure and non-accumulating economy (e.g., Ross, 1995). Karl Marx studies capital accumulation in a capitalist economy. America's wealth issue (and later, knowledge and technology) is solved by Adam Smith's market mechanism. Its political power is mainly determined by what it calls democracy. America's gender issues were solved with traditional values before WWII and since then have mainly followed individualism (expressed in a great variety of manifestations of sexuality and family instability). In America, wealth, power, and sex are ruled by uncoupled, at best loosely interwoven, rules (and religions). National ideology and games in the form of family, associations, religious groups, and institutions have varying relations with wealth, power, and sex.

In his 1859 *On the Origin of Species*, Charles Darwin (1809–1882) argued that natural selection favors the highest forms of life over the lesser. He referred to this process as "the survival of the fittest." He applied this idea to social change and pointed out that it is due to natural selection that one nation expands more powerfully than another, develops industries, becomes wealthy, and wins colonies. Zinke (1868:29) bolstered the theory: "There is apparently much truth in the belief that the wonderful progress of the United States as well as the character of the people, are the results of natural selection; the more energetic, restless, and courageous men from all parts of Europe having emigrated during the last ten or twelve generations to that great country, and having there succeeded best.... All other series of events — as that which resulted in the culture of mind in Greece, and that which resulted in the empire of America Rome — only appear to have purpose and value when viewed in connection with, or rather as subsidiary to ... the great stream of Anglo-Saxon emigration to the west."

The global game after WWII has been played with two fuzzy ideologies, communism and capitalism. America has been the main player on the side of capitalism.

Capitalism, like communism, includes self-destructive inclinations. According to the *yin-yang* vision of world, socialism will move towards capitalism and vice versa. Almost all main socialist economies have already moved towards capitalism either through quick collapses or gradual economic reforms. America has been cyclically oriented towards socialism. Its economy has been characterized by Keynesianism, something between communism and capitalism. Keynesianism justifies strong government intervention in the market economy. America has prolonged its global super-power status with its unimpeded glory under Keynesianism. But capitalist economies are now troubled with Keynesianism and have no clear and solid ideas about where to place their ideologically loyalties.

Globalized education in rational thinking, the widely available internet, reduced costs of transportation, and the erosion of ideologies (partly owing to advances in knowledge in social sciences) have connected the world. But in tandem with its decades of prosperity and success in global competition, many American achievements have recently turned out to be "destructive" to America's relative position in the world. For instance, Americanized global education plus the U.S. America-created internet have empowered almost every corner of the world to appreciate properly, understand correctly, learn quickly, and imitate (legally or illegally) whatever happens in America (with the exception, so far, of a few high-tech products). For now, America is still the superpower and, considered in the short run, it is not apparent that it will be losing this position anytime soon. But if one looks at its relative position in various fields compared to its golden period of the 1960s–1990s, America has already declined significantly.

1.1 America as the Global Superpower after WWII

> Some labor with their minds, and some labor with their strength. Those who labor with their minds govern others; those who labor with their strength are governed by others. ... This is a principle universally recognized.
>
> Mencius (372–289 BC)

The elation expressed by Hermann Hesse (1877–1962) can be applied to describe America at the ending of WWII: "It was morning: through the high window I saw the pure, bright blue of the sky as it hovered cheerfully over the long roofs of the neighboring houses. It too seemed full of joy, as if it had special plans, and had put on its finest clothes for the occasion." English poet Oscar Wilde (1854–1900) described America from the Irish perspective: "America is the only country that went from barbarism to decadence without civilization between." Perhaps, China's speed has been much faster than America's. Interesting history starts from a singular bifurcation point. For America, this point happened with the occurrence of WWII (1939–1945). For modern China, the point was the rise of Deng Xiaoping to the top position in China. America benefited nationally from the war, in net terms. Europe, the center of Western civilization, experienced self-destruction from the internal conflicts.

Geography, ideas (rational ideology or religion), science and technology are necessary for understanding societies, organizations, institutions, productions, and consumption. Values sustain efforts and distribute costs and benefits of efforts. The initial conditions of colonial America included vast territory, abundant ideas, multiple cultures, small population, and profit-oriented behavior. Competition and innovation in the economy were advanced with passions, energies, and progressiveness. Tocqueville (1835:215) commented: "I think that nations like men, in their youth almost always give indications of the main features of their destiny." Seeing how energetically the Anglo-Americans conducted trade, using their natural advantages and achievements, he foretold that the United States would emerge as the leading naval power. He was certain that America was born to rule the seas long before that became a reality.

The devastation of Europe during WWII enabled the once British colony to become the outstanding power among the global civilizations, as Russia did not seem to have the cultural stock to play the role of the center of modern civilizations, irrespective of its excellent achievements in literature, arts, science, and technology.

WWII also allowed America to establish the spiritual foundation for becoming a great country. In late 1944 when WWII was ending, President Roosevelt (1944: 405) exulted: "At the end of this war this country will have the greatest material power of any Nation in the world. It will be a clean, shining America." As Michel de Montaigne had already observed in the 16th century, "Fortune, seeing that she could not make fools wise, has made them lucky." The 35th president of the United States, John F. Kennedy (1917–1963) expressed American self-confidence: "We have the power to make this the best generation of mankind in the history of the world or make it the last." Figure 1.1 testifies how this has been realized by the linear economic expansion never before experienced in human history. The slope of growth after WWII was steeper than all the earlier economic history. America has been a great attractor of people from around the world, due in large measure to the trend in per capita incomes.

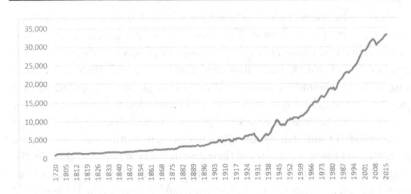

Figure 1.1 GDP per Capita in the USA, 1878–2012, in 1990 dollars

America has been the largest economy by nominal GDP and net wealth for many years, as plotted in Figure 1.2 (Brunozzi, 2018). Its per capita income for 2020 was estimated at $63,051. Its GDP per capita ranked at 7th (nominal) and 10th (PPP) in 2019. It is the world's largest importer and second largest exporter. The share of the services sector in the GDP was 80.2%, the industrial sector 18.9 %, and agricultural sector only 0.9% in 2017. The services sector employed 80% of the labor force, the industrial sector 19%, and the agricultural sector only 1%. It is an advanced and mixed economy. It is the most technologically powerful economy in the world. Its large companies dominate global business. Its companies are at the forefront in technological advances, in fields such as computers, pharmaceuticals, medical, military equipment, and aerospace. The U.S. dollar is the world's foremost reserve currency and is most traded in international transactions. Some foreign countries also use it as their official currency.

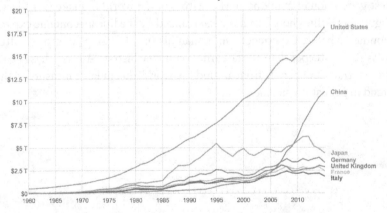

Figure 1.2 US and Some Selected Countries' GDP Growth

After WWII, America grew rapidly. Many positive factors combined to create the great epoch. Except for obvious reasons such as the unprecedented scale and scope of advances in applied sciences and technology, a wave of immigration was the unique determinant.

The U.S. population is now the third largest in the world. During and soon after WWII, armies of the best brains and well-known intellectuals were recruited by Washington from various parts of the world, and German experts were given incentives to join the Americans. America was enjoying an epoch of increasing returns to scale, during which one talented individual could produce more value than one thousand workers could do. Many earlier immigrants were adventurous, talented, well-educated and diligent; they contributed to building and maintaining the country and they played a determining role in America's leading position in various fields of science and technology. Many of these new immigrants saw some reward for their ingenuity and hard work. Meanwhile, they did not hinder the upward mobility of those born in America because they had expanded opportunities for everyone.

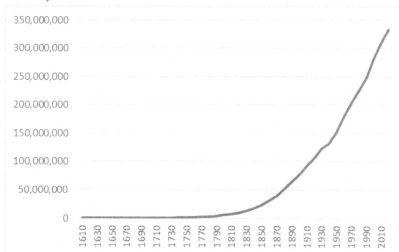

Figure 1.3 The Dynamics of Population of the United States, 1610—2020

America, equipped with the widely-spoken English language, upbeat British spirit, and unself-conscious way of empire building, thus moved ahead of the rest. In his Inaugural Address, January 20, 1961, President Kennedy told the American people: "United, there is little we cannot do in a host of cooperative ventures. Divided, there is little we can do — for we dare not meet a powerful challenge at odds and split asunder.... And so, my fellow

Americans: ask not what your country can do for you — ask what you can do for your country." In the 1960s, America was not only to be economically rich but also had confidence in creating the best generation of mankind. A progressive, energetic, talented young man eager to learn has time to prove what he claims. America did not fail in the great expectation.

In his *Day of Affirmation Address* at the University of Cape Town, on June 6, 1966, the president's brother Robert F. Kennedy (1925–1968) expressed this American confidence:

> For the fortunate among us, the fourth danger is comfort; the temptation to follow the easy and familiar path of personal ambition and financial success so gradually spread before those who have the privilege of an education. But that is not the road history has marked out for us. There is a Chinese curse which says "May he live in interesting times." Like it or not, we live in interesting times. They are times of danger and uncertainty; but they are also the most creative of any time in the history of mankind. And everyone here will ultimately be judged — will ultimately judge himself — on the effort he has contributed to building a new world society and the extent to which his ideas and goals have shaped that effort.

This is the spirit, confidence, and mindset of an intelligent man living in the middle of the rising America, aware of potential risks even while collectively moving upwards as a nation. The risk he referred to is perhaps nothing but a sign of being great. It is only in greatness that powerful politicians could so confidently and honestly reveal future national problems in public. Another kind of man, living at the center of the greatest country, could see the rest of the world as nothing more than worthless enemies or smiling servants. More than half a century later, the President Trump encouraged Americans to be great again, without referring to how that might be achieved. This time it was no longer an energetic, linearly progressive, dream-driven man in his prime that was representative of America. Jimmy Carter, the 39th president of the United States (1977–1981) expressed the point well: "A strong nation, like a strong person, can afford to be gentle, firm, thoughtful, and restrained. It can afford to extend a helping hand to others. It's a weak nation, like a weak person, that must behave with bluster and boasting and rashness and other signs of insecurity."

In the global village, all developed economies are alike (in a visionary and structural sense); each undeveloped economy is poor in its own way. A civilized society innovates to enhance its comparative advantage in competitive global markets, improves itself through education and public investment, and opens and limits its trade swiftly in a beneficial manner. Nevertheless, developed economies are not easily sustainable in the long term. In *Catas-*

trophe Theory, Vladimir Arnold (1992, 31-32), alleges that good things tend to be fragile as a good system incorporates simultaneously a number of qualities and it falls apart if one of these qualities fails: "[F]or systems belonging to the singular part of the stability boundary a small change of the parameters is more likely to send the system into the unstable region than into the stable region. This is a manifestation of a general principle stating that all good things (e.g., stability) are more fragile than bad things. It seems that in good situations a number of requirements must hold simultaneously, while to call a situation bad even one failure suffices." This also implies that for rationally civilized societies there are only limited structures or patterns, given historical conditions. The law of the jungle does not sustain a highly civilized society with a large number of people. Aristotle (2009: Book 2) reasons: "[I]t is possible to fail in many ways (for evil belongs to the class of the unlimited, as the Pythagoreans conjectured, and good to that of the limited), while to succeed is possible only in one way (for which reason also one is easy and the other difficult — to miss the mark easy, to hit it difficult); for these reasons also, then, excess and defect are characteristic of vice, and the mean of virtue; For men are good in but one way, but bad in many."

As America has been the superpower for many years, now is the time to examine the mechanisms underlying its greatness and the possible predicaments and disasters in association with the greatness. As no great empire or dynasty lasts very long in history, it is also the time to see whether America can prove to be the exception. The *yin-yang* vision might be mulishly dismal, but Blaise Pascal (1623–1662) brightly yet rationally noted: "Continuous eloquence wearies. Grandeur must be abandoned to be appreciated. Continuity in everything is unpleasant. Cold is agreeable, that we may get warm."

1.2 Early America with Immigrants and Multiple Cultures

> A person is born with a liking for profit.
>
> Xun Zi (298–238 BC)

Amy Bloom (1953–) reminds us: "People tend to forget in our country, we'd pretty much be immigrants, except for the Native Americans." "When asked by an anthropologist what the Indians called America before the white man came, an Indian said simply 'Ours'." (Vine Deloria, Jr., 1933–2005). America is composed of aboriginal Americans and immigrants of diverse cultures. Native Americans (people before Europeans discovered America) are strangely referred to as aboriginal Americans in the American national language. Almost all the political and economic fundamental prin-ciples accepted in America were basically created in Europe. America effec-tively applied these principles according to changed circumstances. It has continued to use the English language as the national language. The colony (or colonies) of the British Empire would "replicate" many aspects of its (or their) master to dominate the world, upholding the master's global posi-tion with its political ideas as well as its language. An imported culture has the advantage of improving the principles, customs, and institutions of the original culture(s) in a foreign environment. Undesirable elements of the original cultures can be selectively avoided, replaced with new technologies and playing on natural conditions.

Successful economies built mainly by immigrants of multiple races are not only European-derived, like the U.S., Canada, and Australia. Singapore is an example in Asia (see, Zhang, 2002). Prosperous regions like Hong Kong and Taiwan were built by immigrants with Chinese cultural backgrounds, although they were poverty-stricken, mostly illiterate and with no social status (in China).

The destruction and ruin of so many other nations in World War II, including Great Britain, left a great opportunity for Americans to build a country with great universities, great projects, great companies, to create global superstars in the sports and arts, and to become a great collector of Nobel prizes.

In Asia, the tiny island economy of Singapore has similar elements for sustainable development as in America, even though their population sizes and economic structures are different. Singapore, lacking almost any natural resources, is mainly composed of Chinese, Indian, and Malay Singaporeans. There was little resistance to the building of alternative cultural and institu-tional constructs, and the cost in loss of tradition was negligible compared to the gains in the new country. Singapore, originally a British colony like the U.S., was built by poor immigrants with the British as the master. Currently, its per capita ratings according to important variable values are very close to those in America as listed in Table 1.1.

It is interesting to note that in the U.S. the household average incomes of Chinese Americans and Indian Americans are higher than that of white Americans. The per-household income of Indian Americans is the highest among all ethnic groups in the United States. This implies that it is ideas, diligence, and geography, and not only skin, that matter in economic prog-ress.

Table 1.1 Some Indicators in Singapore and America

Country	IQ rank (IQ)	GDP per capita (US$) in 2017	Happiness Rank in 2018	Population in 2018	Top 100 Universities in 2019
Singapore	1 (108)	57,713	34	5.6 mil.	2
America	27 (98)	59,532	18	327 mil.	27

Voltaire (1694–1778) broached the question of how America could be united, given its population of mixed white people would have been enemies in Europe: "When it is a question of money, everyone is of the same religion." This is especially true of poor and low-education European immigrants whose original countries had repeatedly conquered or been conquered by other European countries. Early Americans were largely British. Naturally, they created a White, Anglo-American, protestant-dominant culture (Mauk and Oakland, 1997). Many of the political, social, constitutional, and religious institutions were established on the basis of this culture. For most of the 19th century, over two-thirds of US immigration was from Northwestern Europe. From the early 20th century, the proportion of the new arrivals was more diversified. There were more differences in appearance and heritage. The trend has increased till now. America has received families from all over the world. It is now a global society with a hybrid population composed of Native American, European, Latino, African, and Asian ancestry.

Michael Lind (1996) divides American history into three stages: Anglo-America (1600–1865); Euro-America (1860s–1960s) and Multicultural America (1960s–today). American historian George Bancroft (1855:508) describes the early racial variety:

> Italy and Spain, in the persons of Columbus and Isabella, joined together for the great discovery that opened America to emigration and commerce; France contributed to its independence; the search for the origin of the language we speak carries us to India; our religion is from Palestine; of the hymns sung in our churches, some were first heard in Italy, some in the deserts of Arabia, some on the banks of the Euphrates; our arts come from Greece; our jurisprudence from Rome; our maritime code from Russia; England taught us the system of Representative Government; the noble Republic of the United Provinces [the Netherlands] bequeathed to us, in the world of thought, the great idea of the toleration of all opinions; in the world of action, the prolific principle of federal union.

All these sources of ideas and thought were adopted, mixed or neglected as time passed. Hudson (1981:3) concludes that it is the European elements that are the main components of American civilization: "After a long period in which historians have emphasized the uniqueness of almost everything American, it is becoming increasingly clear that the United States can properly be understood only as an integral part of a larger European society." Americans imported the language, the tables of weights and measures, the most characteristic proverbs, and most of the nursery rhymes from the British and other parts of Europe. America adopted the European concept of trial by jury and the European structure of the legal system with its guarantees of liberty. American culture has been equipped with Europe's great classical writers and painters, dominant philosophical thought, the music of European composers, and the discoveries of European scientists. America's most salient aspects of religion, literature, law, philosophy, art, or science are applications and extensions of European civilization. They are not simple imitations and extensions of Europe. As it became increasingly sophisticated, America created its own features, too, along the way. With regards to democracy in Europe, DiNunzio (1987: vii) scrutinized the differences and noted: "[T]he modern European tradition of governance since the seventeenth century has been authoritarian and, until well into the 19th century, deeply hostile to democratization."

Figure 1.4 plots the dynamics of population in America till 1830. The census numbers of do not include Native Americans until 1860. American immigration history can be divided into the colonial period, the mid-19th century, the start of the 20th century, and post-1965. During the 17th century, about 0.4 million English people, which was about 90% of white immigrants, came to colonial America and half stayed permanently. From 1770 to 1775, the number from Europe was estimated between 0.35 to 0.5 million. They were English, Scotts, Irish, Germans, Swish, and French. Additionally, there were 300,000 African who immigrated involuntarily. By 1790 the population was estimated 4 million. The Naturalization Act of 1790 allowed only free white people to be naturalized American. By the early 1830s, immigration slowed to an annual rate for the most part under 10,000.

The Naturalization Act included blacks in the 1860s and Asians in the 1950s. Such racial distinctions made by immigrants themselves were unique in the world. During the period of 1836 to 1914, over 30 million Europeans migrated to America.

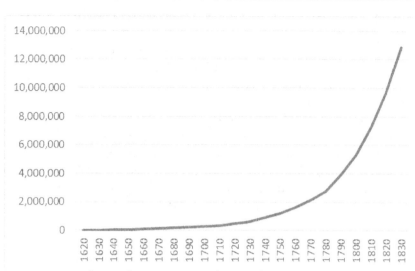

Figure 1.4 The Population, 1610–1830 (a part of Figure 1.3)

1.3 Love of Freedom with Abundant Land and Slaves

> It is the inborn nature of human beings that it is impossible for them not to form societies. If they form a society in which there are no class divisions, strife will develop. If there is strife, then there will be social disorder; if there is social disorder, there will be hardship for all.

Xun Zi (298–238 BC, 10:5)

Man is concretized by cultural soil. Tocqueville contradistinguished the American culture with that of his motherland, saying that Americans did not understand Pascal. This tradition is reflected in elite education (Deresiewicz, 2015). There is no such thing as a genius who is independent of his cultural soil. Tocqueville (1835:149) epitomizes the early American cultural traits: "The passions that stir the Americans most deeply are commercial and not political ones, or rather they carry a trader's habits over into the business of politics. They like order, without which affairs do not prosper, and they set an especial value on regularity of mores, which are the foundation of a sound business; they prefer the good sense which creates fortunes to the genius which often dissipates them; their minds, accustomed to definite calculations, are frightened by general ideas; and they hold practice in greater honor than history."

Why has America been so attractive to many types of people across races? If one can choose only one reason among numerous possibilities, it would be freedom. Freedom to accumulate wealth and to consume, freedom to gain power, freedom to wield it over other people (under law), freedom to sexually empower oneself, freedom to make exchanges, and freedom of beliefs; this is the most elementary amenity for human happiness. Man loves freedom to control other humans and the environment for his own emotional and physical needs. One may find pleasure in brain washing others with thought or religion, or in plying others for sympathy or empathy or love, or in taking advantage of others as slaves or servants, and so on. Man benefits personally or collectively from assorted combinations of love, hate, co-operation, and discrimination, depending on the circumstances and environment.

Tommy Hilfiger sums up what the combined conditions imply: "The road to success is not easy to navigate, but with hard work, drive and passion, it's possible to achieve the American dream." Adam Smith detailed an economic institution he called the free market under law. He argued that such a set up would create a prosperous society in harmony with selfish human nature. Early American immigrants would maximize the freedom to pursue one's own interest with or without the law.

The geography of the United States varies across its immense area, as illustrated in Map 1.1 and Map 1.2. Much of the central United States is relatively flat and arable land. Agricultural land was, for instance, about 45% of the total land area in 2016. (Here, agricultural land refers to the share of land area that is arable under permanent crops and pastures.) The climate is varied, from tropical Florida and Hawaii to Arctic in Alaska, but most of the land is temperate. The nation has many areas set aside for the public use.

The West Coast of the continental United States is located on the Pacific Ring of Fire, which is the source of 90% of the world's earthquakes. The Great Plains and Midwest experience frequent severe thunderstorms and tornado outbreaks during spring and summer. Hurricanes also cause disasters in numerous parts of the country.

Although America has rich natural resources and a vast land mass, the early population was small, as listed in Table 1.2 (which does not include Native Americans). The population of China in 1780 was about 300 million, while America's population was less than 3 million. It is reasonable to expect that early immigrants, poor and low-class, arriving from their original countries to see the new vast and "empty" land exalted in and cultivated a taste for freedom.

Map 1.1 Contemporary Map of the United States

Map 1.2 Landscape of the United States

The economic history of America started in the 17th and 18th centuries. The colonies focused on farming. Vast land areas occupied by a small population imply that a centralized power would not be ineffective in controlling the territory. It is difficult to know in detail the human capital, values, customs, and habits of all these immigrants, but Europe was in the Age of Enlightenment and the Scientific Revolution. Open land combined with an emphasis on scientific ideas and rational thought would naturally lead immigrants to appreciate freedom.

Table 1.2 The Population Growth in America from 1610 to 1780, m for million

1610	1630	1650	1670	1690	1710	1730	1750	1770	1780
350	4,646	0.05m	0.11m	0.21m	0.33m	0.63m	1.17m	2.15m	2.78m

As he travelled in the United States in 1831–32, Tocqueville (1805–1859) was struck by the significant equality of conditions in the country. His two-volume book *Democracy in America*, published in 1835 and 1840, is still influential today. He remarked that as Americans were mainly immigrants, there were no traditional institutions, such as feudal traditions, to dominate life. American society was thus, socially, economically as well as politically, highly mobile. The people could work as entrepreneurs and accumulate wealth through diligence with few constraints. They could strive to be politically powerful, perhaps rising in a short period from obscurity to leadership, as parentage was not a significant barrier. Americans were geographically mobile, as they searched for fortune in one form or another; these immigrants had no special attachment to any given place. Due to this mobility and other conditions such as the laws, self-interest, voluntary associations, and vigorous local government, Americans did enjoy a high level of liberty and equality.

These were mainly people who had no hereditary wealth. Rather than the aristocratic ethic, America respected hard work and money-making. As ordinary people had power and a voice in the public sphere, American equality tended to lead to mediocrity. Men with superior talent and intelligence did not necessarily enjoy much political power. Men with virtue and talent but without the ruthlessness to climb over others were left with limited choices. They limited themselves to intellectual circles to explore complex social puzzles. They might also be engaged in amassing fortunes in the private sector.

Tocqueville famously said that no country, as far as he knew, had less independence of mind and true freedom of discussion. In Chapter 18 of *Democracy*, he castigated race differences in America: "The first who attracts the eye, the first in enlightenment, in power and in happiness, is the white man, the European, man *par excellence*; below him appear the Negro and the Indian. These two unfortunate races have neither birth, nor face, nor language, nor mores in common; only misfortunes look alike. The two occupy an equally inferior position in the country that they inhabit; both experience the effects of tyranny; and if their miseries are different, they can accuse the same author for them."

"The liberty of the individual is not a gift of civilization. It was greatest before there was any civilization," as Sigmund Freud (1856–1939) noted in wrapping up his analysis of the psychology of man. Each civilization has its own scope and degree of individual freedom. Freedom of society has historically been much shaped by geography. Rice-paddy, nomadic, desert-based, island, mountain and agrarian people have created, applied, and sustained different views on freedom, human relations, religions (or beliefs) and each developed varied customs in the processes of co-existence with nature and fighting their neighbors.

Geographical influences on races are imprinted in behavior and social organizations. For instance, nomadic culture is bolstered by respecting rule, kindness and democracy within the group, and cruelty with the outsider. This is due to the requirements for economic survival and the dynamics of group formation. Before the West opened up China, China knew two basic types of societies. One is rice-paddy-based. The typical image of such a society is immobile, connected by cultural customs, obedience, and cruelty within the group to enforce conformity. The other is nomadic. The image is mobile and connected with democratic-like sharing of benefits, and slaughtering the outsider without rule—not to mention law.

The development of the rice society is sustained by consciously or unconsciously creating and maintaining a set of cultural values by which it suppresses free expression of emotion, makes decisions on the basis of a detailed calculation of costs and benefits over the long term (costs and benefits are not only monetary but include multiple variables such as social status and family ties), has no freedom of sexuality, is extremely cautious in accepting the outsider, has no tradition of obeying a simple and well-developed law, has an advanced culture as the basis of class division, and has a dominant rational or irrational thought system as the principal basis of organization, accepts multiple religions and thought systems for co-existence with a well-cultivated minority, and has a fixed home territory with land as the lasting foundation.

The nomadic society, if its population is large, is united by targeting a common wealthy enemy. Wealth, women, abundant and luxurious food and drink, and a comfortable life are the goals for brave men with a fighting spirit; they look for the meaning of life in discipline and teamwork among men. Men would take unlimited pleasure in training for, planning, fighting and winning battles. Nomadic people of multiple groups hold some primary beliefs and boundless plateau. They don't suppress the expression of emotion, they make decisions based on a calculation of costs and benefits over a relatively short term, have less strict control on gender relations, are "quick" to recruit outsiders to form a stronger and larger team, follow simple and clear rules, establish a merit-based group order, and show mobility and flexibility. In such societies, might is the source of wealth and might is the source of sex. Any spirit can go as high as possible in nomadic or quasi-nomadic cultures.

America, as a part of the British Empire, has a typical way of doing business: the so-called rule of law. British civilization is largely an open society based on law. This tradition has facilitated America in its role as a global power. America evolved from its history and pioneers' ideals without cultural and traditional barriers. Other civilizations paid high costs to obtain freedom and accept equality among men in modern times, if they could do it. The (largely) unoccupied and uncultivated wilderness allowed immigrants a blank slate. They were free to write another chapter in the story of the human struggle to construct a new society with the knowledge and histories they brought from other civilizations. To European immigrants, who were once bound by chains of social class and custom, the American wilds granted an escape into a free life and greater well-being among the bounties of nature. "Never again," Turner (1861–1932, 1986:261–262) noted, "can such an opportunity come to the sons of men. It was unique." "Oh, how sweet," Turner (1986:262) cited from a European immigrant in the American forest, "is the quiet of these parts, freed from the troubles and perplexities of woeful Europe." America was a land of opportunity, of freedom, of democracy. They exhilarated in throwing away the bonds of social caste that had bound them in their original countries. They naturally prefer liberty to authority, freedom to responsibility, and rights to duties.

American freedom ensures that people (or groups of people defined in terms including skin color and religious adherence) can freely exploit their environment and society under law aimed to optimize profit. Ironically, America was able to be free also because of its slavery and institutional discrimination. The majority population in Early America was able to enjoy its freedom and prosper due to both the natural abundance and its acceptance of the institution of slavers. Once medieval England was assured of its safety from foreign invasion, the society evolved toward economic and political liberty. The English embraced the idea that individuals were born with rights. No one, not even the king, could take these rights away from individuals. The law played an important role in enabling the British ruler to control foreign lands in a "reliable" and "just" manner.

Before modern forms of transportation became widespread, nature played a far more important role in mind formation, social organization, ways of communication, daily human networks, clothes, food, habits, and attitudes towards foreign ideas and cultures. In what became the United States, South and North were differentiated in their attitudes to slaves more due to natural conditions than reasoning and rationality.

Man is naturally social — constantly desiring to be served and to serve society. Albert Einstein (1879–1955) imparted this thought: "Man can find meaning in life, short and perilous as it is, only through devoting himself to society."

With regard to the origin of the formation of communities, Freud (1951:59-60) asserted that:

> Human life in communities only becomes possible, when a number of men unite together in strength superior to any single individual and remain united against all single individuals. The strength of this united party is opposed as 'Right' against the strength of any individual, which is condemned as 'brute force.' The substitution of the power of a united number for the power of a single man is the decisive step toward civilization. The essence of it lies in the circumstance that the members of the community have restricted their possibilities of gratification, whereas the individual recognized no such restriction. The first requisite of culture, therefore, is justice — that is, the assurance that a law once made will not be broken in favor of any individual. The further course of cultural evolution tends toward ensuring that the law shall no longer represent the will of any small body — caste, tribe, section of the population — which may behave like a predatory individual toward other such groups perhaps containing larger numbers.... The liberty of the individual is not a benefit of culture. It was greatest before any culture, though indeed it had little value at that time, because the individual was hardly in a position to defend it.... The cry for freedom is directed either against particular demands of culture or else against culture itself."

Mongolians have called Genghis Khan the father of democracy. Nomadic cultures neighboring China had a free-wheeling life in the open environment under the rules of a nomadic lifestyle. In West and East Asia, Genghis Khan was the leader of the hordes who conquered many parts of the world accessible by their main, swift weapon, the horse. In modern times, Mongolians have called him the father of democracy, believing that democratic principles are inherent in the codes enacted by Genghis Khan. Like traditional Western democracy, Mongolian democracy is based first on a clear classification of insiders and outsiders. Genghis Khan established a vast empire with little cultural communication with the local cultures. The West established a great colonial empire due to similar rules of game, but with more civil components.

1.4 Cultural Formation Based on Religious Spirits and British Rationality

> The people are the most important element in a nation; the spirits of the land and grain are the next; and the sovereign is the least.
>
> Mencius (372–289 BC)
>
> Heaven did not create the people for the sake of the lord; Heaven established the lord for the sake of the people.
>
> Xun Zi (298–238 BC, 27:72)

Ralph Waldo Emerson (1803–1882) urged a focus on the development of American culture, saying: "We have listened too long to the courtly Muses of Europe." Nevertheless, I feel whatever he said is somehow similar to what some European thinkers had already said before him. One cannot easily escape the influence of the masters of the culture in which one was born. Original thinking about individual life is rare in a young civilization because previous civilizations have already accumulated a vast variety of experience as lived by heterogeneous types of personas.

American civilization has not actually come up with many interesting and original ideas about man and society, if one is familiar with Greek and modern European civilizations. It is in the spheres of technology and new ways of making money and social status that have been advanced on American cultural soil. Meaningful thought is repeatedly rediscovered, but frivolous ideas and emotions vary colorfully over time and space without any lasting force. European civilization was created by historical conflicts within, while America was started with imitation and learning. European writers have recorded how earlier Americans behaved with regards to copyrights, and their complaints about America's "indecent behavior" presaged the behavior of contemporary developing economies.

Voltaire justified the co-existence of the laws and religion, saying: "Wherever there is a settled society, religion is necessary; the laws cover manifest crimes, and religion covers secret crimes." Nevertheless, "With or without religion, you would have good people doing good things and evil people doing evil things. But for good people to do evil things, that takes religion." (Steven Weinberg, 1933–). Blaise Pascal (1623–1663) was straightforward: "Men never do evil so completely and cheerfully as when they do it from religious conviction." For modern men, the statement is still valid if "religious" is substituted with "ideological." The continuation of slavery was a case in point.

Rice-paddy East Asia did not have a tradition of obeying laws, for reasons in line with Michel de Montaigne's observation: "The way of the world is to make laws, but follow custom." While it's true that all European cultures were available and were mingled together through conflicts and communications during the formation stage of American civilization, North America started its civilization with British cultural stock, and British custom follows laws. The British cultural stocks accumulated through building and maintaining the last great empire encouraged the U.S. to disdainfully explore economies not only on the national but the global scale.

"Bigger things than the State will fall, all religion will fall" (Henrik Ibsen, 1828–1906). Os Guinness (1941–) pictured the modern religious influence this way: "The Christian Church in the U.S. is still strong numerically, but it has lost its decisive influence both in American public life and in American culture as a whole, especially in the major elite institutions of society." In earlier centuries, religions had a strong impact on American life (e.g., Butler, 1997; Schultz, 2006; Davenport, 2014), while the English philosopher John Locke (1689) exerted a lasting influence upon American political thought.

According to Locke, the fear of sedition on the part of religious minorities was without any logical basis. There was religious freedom under state protection, each religious group enjoys its own form of religious practice and the state will be in order. Nevertheless, the state must set some limits to the degree of religious toleration. Freedom might need to be limited so that the society and the state are not destroyed. A religion that asked for freedom so that it could seize the government and deny freedom to others ought not be tolerated (Grimes, 1983:55). In addition, the state should tolerate no religion if its adherents became bound to the protection and service of another prince (Locke, 1946:155). He also suggested that the state should not tolerate atheists because they could not be bound by oaths and promises that are essential to all organized society. Locke's ideas on the separation of the affairs of church and state also influenced the practice in America. The state and the church are separated and should exist in harmony if the state attends to the worldly welfare of the commonwealth and the church to the salvation of the souls. The Constitution determines that the government of the United States is secular. There is no state religion. The Constitution excludes the legal possibility of a civil religion. Kiely (1999:210) narrated this: "Americans tend to transfer for a unifying faith, a shareable reverence, onto the landscape or onto secular places and especially buildings associated with persons or events that we can all claim as our own." School textbooks in the United States, as shown by Vitz (1989), have been almost totally silent on the role that religion played in American history and society. There are no church taxes in the United States; the churches receive no state support.

Greenhouse (2006) analyzed the separation of church and state and wrapped up:

> The separation of church and state in the United States does not by itself create a secular state — and even less so, a secular public sphere. On the contrary, the constitutional requirement of separation can be (and is widely) read as a necessary connection between political legitimacy and religious pluralism — a proportion that carries significant if changeable cultural content in the United States today. Ethnographic and sociological accounts of civic, economic, and religious life among Americans return again and again to this connection as a fundamental principle of personal worth (in both the moral and economic sense of this term) and criterion of collective social value.

The Constitution and the first ten amendments (the Bill of Rights, 1791) enforce a separation between religion and state. The structure of religious life remains entirely distinct from the political organization. This has allowed the United States to change laws without destroying the foundations of ancient beliefs. The Constitution declares: "No religious test shall ever be required as a qualification to any office or public trust under the United States." People with different religions have thus equal access to national political power. The First Amendment to the Constitution states: "Congress shall make no law respecting an establishment of religion, or prohibiting the free exercise thereof." According to Fischer *et al.*, (1997: 261), the Amendment's first clause ("the Establishment Clause") seems to ask that no religious faith receive public support in order to dominate others, and the second clause ("the Free Exercise Clause") implies that all faiths should be free to strive to maintain themselves, to organize their worship, and to pursue their own religious truths free of public interference. Since the 1960s, the Supreme Court has explicitly forbidden government from aiding one religion over another or from aiding religion over non-religion.

"I doubt whether man can support complete religious independence and entire political liberty at the same time. I am led to think that if he has no faith he must obey, and if he is free he must believe." (Tocqueville, 1805–1859). In the same vein, George Washington (1732—799) related the significance of religion and morality in 1796 (Safire, 1992): "Of all the dispositions and habits which lead to political prosperity, religion and morality are indispensable supports. In vain would that man claim the tribute of patriotism who should labor to subvert these great pillars of human happiness, these firmest props of the duties of men and citizens.... And let us with caution indulge the supposition that morality can be maintained without religion. Whatever may be conceded to the influence of refined education on minds of peculiar structure, reason and experience both forbid us to expect that national morality can prevail in exclusion of religious principle."

European immigrants' ancestors had religions to warm their hearts and protect their territories in Europe. America's vast territories allowed immigrants to tolerate other people's religions and peacefully co-habit in the new world. Instead of religion, the new world had two great botherations to solve. They were respectively to get off the British tax rolls and to abolish slavery.

"Religion is an illusion and it derives its strength from the fact that it falls in with our instinctual desires." (Sigmund Freud, 1856–1939). Western movies of crimes and violence often are built on stories depicting crime bosses who are at the same time piously religious. Similarly, East Asian movies represent gangster leaders organizing robberies and simultaneously show exaggerated enthusiasm about building temples. For the *yin-yang* mind, the observation that the United States is the most market-driven and at the same time the most religious nation of modern times is not a paradox. The spirit of freedom is cultivated for progressing, advancing; the spirit of religion is maintained for placating, receding. The former fosters fairness, the latter avoids evilness. The balance is maintained through the co-existence of the calming force and violent destructiveness.

Tocqueville (1835: 21) was of the opinion that early American civilization was the product of the spirit of freedom plus the spirit of religion. As a free society begins losing the genuine spirit of freedom, the spirit of religion flies away. Americans' naked self-interest led to the need for religion in daily life. Religion applied a great restraint on the otherwise unrestrained pursuit of self-interest. Tocqueville saw that the spirit of freedom and the spirit of religion were often in conflict in European cultures, while they worked hand in hand in the United States. In the early history of America, religion and civil liberty were harmonious and mutually supportive. Religion treated civil liberty as an exercise of men's faculties and the world of politics as a sphere for displaying intelligence. For Tocqueville, the real school of republican virtue was the Church.

According to Huntington (1996), religion is a central defining characteristic of civilizations. So far, perhaps. His ideas deny the power of rationality in human history. In vast areas of East Asia, a region which has not been characterized by never-ending wars (except with nomads who had no interest in diffusing any "sophisticated" religion to their neighbors), religion is practiced but is not so important as Huntington' evaluation system assumes. Of course, if in his mind there was only one high civilization, he could perceive any other culture as uncivilized. Western civilization has been bolstered with religions, slavery, and racial discrimination. The Enlightenment started to weaken the influences of religions on its main evolutionary direction. We do not know yet the proportion of mankind who will prove to be genuinely "addicted" to religions when they are fully explored in the light of rational knowledge, freedom of choice, the variety of religious traditions, and decent living conditions.

China has never had a state religion, perhaps because China never used one religion to invade other people's lands, and there was no leisure to develop a sophisticated religion because of the neighboring brutal, smart, and non-religious nomads. All those who conquered China over the centuries had no state religion. While they were strong, Spain and Portugal were not strong enough to have any important influence on China. When Britain came to China it was a powerful country, but it had no strong interest in diffusing any religion.

Rationality and multiple religions co-existed over centuries in the East Asian race-paddy economies because spreading one religion as the state policy was not conducive to the co-existence of people living in isolation and harmony. When the West had become strong enough to conquer East Asia militarily, it had already abolished any state religion and hence it did not attempt to disseminate any religion to East Asia officially and systematically.

1.5 The Declaration of Independence, the Constitution, and the Government Structure

> When deeds and words are in accord, the whole world is transformed.
>
> Zhuangzi (369–295 BC)

Early immigrants came to America to search for freedom in making money, practicing their religion, or escaping European tyranny. Many of these people were naturally inclined to "neglect" their place of origin and leave it behind. On the other hand, the British master was unwilling to lose the colonists as a source of taxation, even though to collect taxes was a tortuous and tangled business. The game between master and servant would finally lead the spirited immigrants to build their own country.

When he calculated the costs and benefits for the British Empire to hold onto the American colonies, Adam Smith concluded that a free America would benefit the empire. Ludwig von Mises (1881–1973) offered his economic estimation of war: "Wars of aggression are popular nowadays with those nations convinced that only victory and conquest could improve their material well-being....[But] economically considered, war and revolution are always bad business."

As holding onto the American colonies became increasingly costly, the British Empire began to be ruined within, so that independence was socially and economically determined. Immigrants had been equipped with the seeds and fruits of the European Enlightenment. Structurally, it is only a matter of time until they became strong enough to break away.

A civilized society is characterized by whether society obeys the rule and the rule functions effectively. Japan and Germany are obvious examples. They are now respected as they are diligent, obey their rulers, and have an orderly society. China's top leader can simply change the Constitution to fit unknown needs, which gives the measure of the degree of civilization in China as a contemporary nation.

The Declaration of Independence is often extended to international affairs by Americans to justify or even teach other people their concept of freedom. Yet the Declaration was written by a slaveholder. At the time of the War for Independence, slavery was legal in all thirteen colonies.

"The object of war is not to die for your country but to make the other bastard die for his." (George S. Patton, 1885–1945). The American social consensus is built on a perception of freedom and equality as the essence of justice, as reflected in The Declaration of Independence. Written in 1776, it reads: "We hold these truths to be self-evident, that all men are created equal, that they are endowed by their Creator with certain unalienable Rights, that among these are Life, Liberty and the pursuit of Happiness. That to secure these rights, Governments are instituted among Men, deriving their just powers from the consent of the governed. That whenever any form of Government becomes destructive of these ends, it is the Right of the People to alter or to abolish it, and to institute new Government, laying its foundation on such principles and organizing its powers in such form, as to them shall seem most likely to effect their Safety and Happiness."

That begs a question that was not well examined at the time: whose freedom and whose right? This unexamined question remains the key for America to have a harmonious and orderly society once it loses its superpower position in many fields.

"All men are created equal" does not imply that human beings are equal in all respects. It means, fundamentally, political equality. The dominant opinion of the United States was articulated by John Adams, the first vice president and second president: "That all men have one common nature, is a principle that will now universally prevail, and equal rights and equal duties will in a just sense, I hope, be inferred from it. But equal ranks and equal property can never be inferred from it, any more than equal understanding, agility, vigor or beauty. Equal laws are all that can ever be derived from human equality." (McClosky and Zaller, 1984:80). All human beings possess inherent worth and dignity.

The principle of sovereignty of the people distinguished America from the Old World. The Founding Fathers cogitated to form political parties as factions pursuing their own narrow private interests rather than the people's interests overall; but they also devised a constitutional system to guarantee that no party would gain overwhelming power. The American Constitution, signed by the Continental Congress on September 17, 1787, established a divided form of government with power allocated between the presidency, two houses of Congress, and a federal high court. The separate and staggered elections required for Senators, Representatives, and the President keep many electoral interests divided.

The Constitution of the United States, which is the oldest written and codified national constitution still in effect, came into force in 1789 and has been amended 27 times. It is the country's supreme law, framing the national government. Its first three articles give the principle of the separation of powers. The federal government consists of the legislative branch (with the bicameral Congress), the executive (with the president and subordinate officers), and the judicial (with the Supreme Court and other federal courts). It also defines American federalism with the rights and responsibilities of state governments and the relationship of the states to the federal government. It now grants specific protections of individual liberty and justice. The United States Senate describes Constitution Day on its website, pointing out that: "The Constitution's first three words — We the People — affirm that the government of the United States exists to serve its citizens. For over two centuries the Constitution has remained in force because its framers wisely separated and balanced governmental powers to safeguard the interests of majority rule and minority rights, of liberty and equality, and of the federal and state governments."

The government hires over 99% of executive branch workers through competitive examinations, as required by the Civil Service Act. The President is entitled to nominate the highest officials in the executive branch; but the Senate must approve these appointments. The President is commander-in-chief of the armed services, but only Congress has the power to declare war. In this system, a person can only serve one branch at a time. This implies that the President, the heads of the executive departments, and federal judges are prohibited from holding seats in Congress. The separation of the branches prevents the concentration of power in any one and encourages competition and cooperation among the branches through a system of checks and balances. According to the Constitution, the principle of federalism is fundamental to the US government: The ultimate power should be shared between the national government and the states. The powers of each are limited by the reservation or delegation of some powers to the other level of government. The people have the right to limit the powers of both.

The Constitution accentuates political stability and the protection of property; the Declaration advocates the ideal of equality. The Constitution lays the foundation for a system of government appropriate to economic freedom. The purpose of the Constitution is printed in its Preamble: "We the People of the United States in Order to form a more perfect Union, establish Justice, insure domestic Tranquility, provide for the common defense, promote the general Welfare, and secure the Blessings of Liberty to ourselves and our Posterity, do ordain and establish the Constitution for the United States of America." The Constitution is the supreme law of the United States and the Judges in every State should be bound thereby. The Constitution furnishes a framework for the acquisition, use, and transfer of private property and numerous defenses of property against tampering by any level of government. The framers of the Constitution linked liberty to property, not to democracy (Hofstadter, 1972, McClosky and Zaller, 1984:73).

The Constitution has a profound impact on American society. Its exclusion of "others" as "insiders" of the system has significant impact even today. The Constitution initially did not mention eligibility to vote. Each state determined who was eligible. Most states allowed only white male adult property owners to vote. The US political system was based on the Greek ideal of democracy, and naturally it treated slaves as distinct from full members of the same society. Smith (1997) shows that throughout most of US history, lawmakers have structured citizenship in terms of illiberal and undemocratic racial, ethnic, and gender hierarchies for political reasons.

After the Civil War (1861–1865), amendments were made between 1865–1870 that transformed the country from "half slave and half free" — defined by Lincoln — to one in which the entire populace, including the former slaves and their descendants, constitutionally enjoyed the "blessings of liberty." Slavery was abolished. Former slaves were eligible for citizenship and voting rights.

Nevertheless, discrimination on the basis of sex was not forbidden, and it was only in 1920 that the Constitution was amended to prohibit the denial of voting rights to any citizen on the basis of sex.

1.6 Anti-British and Slave-Owning Founding Fathers

> To be able to judge of others by what is right in ourselves — this may be called the art of virtue.
>
> Look at the means which a man employs, consider his motives, observe his pleasures. A man simply cannot conceal himself.
>
> Confucius (551–479 BC)

Confucius (13:18) illustrated misconduct in the following manner: "The duke of She informed Confucius, saying, 'Among us here there are those who may be styled upright in their conduct. If their fathers have stolen a sheep, they will bear witness to the fact.' Confucius said, 'Among us, in our part of the country, those who are upright are different from this. The father conceals the misconduct of the son, and the son conceals the misconduct of the father; Uprightness is to be found in this." Epictetus confirms: "We tell lies, yet it is easy to show that lying is immoral." This is the written history of mankind. Man does not know much about history but makes unlimited lies about history to glorify himself.

Russian writer Fyodor Dostoyevsky (1821–1881) asserted the honesty of man cultivated in the wild: "Above all, don't lie to yourself. The man who lies to himself and listens to his own lie comes to a point that he cannot distinguish the truth within him, or around him, and so loses all respect for himself and for others. And having no respect he ceases to love." Napoleon Bonaparte (1769–1821) noted: "The great proof of madness is the disproportion of one's designs to one's means." He proffers an example from the art of military strategy: "You must not fight too often with one enemy, or you will teach him all your art of war."

This is useful in playing power games. President Trump displayed his strategies a few times to China, and China stopped caring much about America's games just a few months into his presidency. American democratic leaders now lie publicly on TV across the world; this is the necessary evil that they must do to be elected in a large population with a high portion of uneducated and uncultivated voters.

The difference between the first American president George Washington and President Trump illustrates the dynamics of American politics. "Anything that has real and lasting value is always a gift from within." (Franz Kafka). "The health of a democratic society may be measured by the quality of functions performed by private citizens," as Alexis de Tocqueville posited. People will naturally look for the profits available within certain environments. Successful businessmen and entrepreneurs are not so rarely talented as they appear in a highly profitable but risky environment.

As far as rule of game is concerned, three men explain much the cultural features of the three greatest economies in the world. Their likenesses are seen more frequently throughout the world than any superstar in sports and the arts. Benjamin Franklin, Fukuzawa Yukichi, Mao Zedong are honored in their countries by having their photos on the bills with the highest values of their currencies, 100 USD, 10,000 JPY, and 100 CNY, respectively (Photo 1.2). Understanding these three men is basic to approaching the three greatest economic powers and the human qualities of men who are officially and publicly appreciated in their societies.

Fukuzawa's ideas largely formed Japan's modernization.

Mao's best-known saying in mainland China is: "Political power grows out of the barrel of a gun."

As head of the colony of Pennsylvania, Ben Franklin promoted the public banking system which supports the real, wealth-producing economy.

Fukuzawa on a 10,000 Japanese Yen note

Franklin on a USD 100 bill

Mao on a 100 Chinese Yuan bill

Photo 1.1 Symbols of American, Japanese and Mainland Chinese Cultures

It is vital to understand the most influential persons who founded the nation. Wittgenstein (Wright 1998: 12) illustrated the point: "It might be said that civilization can only have its epic poet in advance. Just as one can only foresee one's own death and describe it as something lying in the future, not report it as it happens. So it might be said: If you want to see the epic of a whole culture written you will have to seek it in the works of its greatest figures and hence see it at a time when the end of this culture can only be *foreseen*, for later there is no one there any more to describe it."

The seven founding fathers, who were all once British subjects, drafted the Declaration of Independence and advocated ratification of the Constitution. They united 13 disparate colonies. They fought for independence from Britain (their motherland). "Patriots always talk of dying for their country and never of killing for their country." (Bertrand Russell, 1872–1970). Four of them served as presidents of the newly formed nation. The other three were also immortalized because of their great contributions to nation building. They were wealthy plantation owners and businessmen. They drafted many influential documents that have steered the United States until till today. Many of the founding fathers were influenced not only by the Enlightenment thinkers but also instructed by the classical Greeks and Romans.

George Washington (1732–1799)

Washington, referred as the father of America for his numerous leadership roles, was a prosperous Virginia farmer and owned hundreds of slaves. Practical, useful men do not start life from as Franz Kafka suggested: "Start with what is right rather than what is acceptable." Washington's great-grandfather immigrated in 1656 from England to the English colony of Virginia. He inherited from his father Ferry Farm and ten slaves. He did not have a formal education and had no child his own. He first fought for the British, but he was upset by the taxes and restrictions imposed on the colonies by the Crown. When the War for Independence started in 1775, he led the Continental Army. His army and his French allies expelled the British by 1783. He presided at the Constitutional Convention of 1787, in which the U.S. Constitution and a federal government were created. He served as the first president of the United States (1789–1797). There are debates on whether he was a Christian or a theistic rationalist. He believed in a wise, inscrutable, and irresistible Creator God who was active in the universe.

Alexander Hamilton (1755?–1804)

Hamilton was the illegitimate son of a married woman in the British West Indies, and his mother died when he was an adolescent. He was crafty enough to gain an apprenticeship and impressed his employers so much that they sent him to New York to be educated. He became an American statesmen, politician, lawyer, banker, military commander, and scholar in law and economics. He entered King's College (now Columbia) in New York City in 1773 as a private student. He became prominent during the Revolutionary War. He was an impassioned supporter of a strong central government. He wrote the majority of the Federalist Papers, which justified the Constitution. He was the first U.S. treasury secretary. He was immortalized on the $10 bill. He fought for a strong central government led by a vigorous executive branch, government-controlled banks, and a strong commercial economy and strong military. His ideas laid the foundation for American government and finance. He was killed in an 1804 duel with the vice president of the United States.

Benjamin Franklin (1706–1790)

Franklin received formal education until he was 10 years old. He was the most Renaissance man of early America. He was an American polymath, a politician, diplomat, writer, printer, political philosopher, scientist, inventor, humorist, statesman, and civil activist. He was an important figure in the history of physics for his discoveries and theories regarding electricity. He was against religious and political authoritarianism. He advocated for the scientific and tolerant values of the Enlightenment. In the initial stages of the war, he was a member of the five-member committee that drafted the Declaration of Independence.

John Adams (1735–1826)

John Adams was a well-known Massachusetts lawyer and an early proponent of the revolutionary cause. His great-great-grandfather had immigrated to Massachusetts from England. He was brought up in a family of Puritans. He once recalled his happy childhood as he enjoyed "perhaps the greatest of blessings that can be bestowed upon men — that of a mother who was anxious and capable to form the characters of her children." He received a formal education, and at age sixteen he entered Harvard College. He obtained an A.B. degree in 1755. He was a statesman, attorney, diplomat, keen scholar, and writer. He, too, was a member of the committee that drafted the Declaration of Independence. He was a leader of the fight for independence from Great Britain. He drafted the Massachusetts Constitution which is still in use. He served as vice president under Washington from 1788. He never owned a slave and was principally against using slave labor. He was elected president and served the position from 1779 to 1801. He and Thomas Jefferson both died on July 4, 1826, the 50th anniversary of the Declaration of Independence.

Samuel Adams (1722–1803)

Adams, the second cousin of John Adams, was born in Boston and brought up in a religious family. He was proud of his Puritan heritage and accentuated Puritan values and virtues. He was a graduate of Harvard College, statesman and political philosopher. He was against British policies in Boston and a leader in the American Revolution. He was one of the architects of the principles of American republicanism. He was anti-slavery. He signed the Declaration of Independence. There are many controversial issues about his views on the merits and demerits in American history.

Thomas Jefferson (1743–1826)

Jefferson was well educated and prosperous. He was a Virginia lawyer diplomat, statesman, philosopher, and a lifelong slaveholder. He held that the British Parliament had no authority over the 13 colonies. In 1776, he joined in writing the Declaration of Independence, coining such famous phrases as "all men are created equal," "they are endowed by their creator with certain unalienable rights," "life, liberty and the pursuit of happiness" (excluding African-Americans). He championed the ideas, values, and teachings of the Enlightenment. He was secretary of state under Washington, vice president to John Adams between 1798 and 1802, and president between 1801 and 1809. After retiring from public office, he founded the University of Virginia. He advocated religious freedom and tolerance in Virginia.

James Madison (1751–1836)

Madison grew up on a Virginia plantation. He entered the College of New Jersey (now Princeton University) where he studied the works of the Enlightenment. He was a statesman, diplomat, philosopher, and expansionist. At the 1787 Constitutional Convention, he developed a plan to divide the federal government into three branches — legislative, executive, and judicial — in order to keep a check on the power of any one branch. He is thus named as "Father of the Constitution." He also co-authored the Federalist Papers. He served as secretary of state under Jefferson from 1801 to 1809. He served as the fourth president of the United States from 1809 to 1817.

"American culture is not about experiencing our shame, it's about denying it. It's been that way our whole history" (Christ Jordan, 1963–). National history is made up for the benefit of the dominant group and brainwashing of the masses. The survival of slavery justified in European civilization reflects the founding fathers' sense of justice, concept of freedom, and cultural continuation of immigrants. The enlightened British empire needed slavery to accumulate vast wealth and build its great empire.

It is a puzzle to imagine or re-make how American history would look if there had been neither slavery nor racial discrimination. Man is born into historical flows and he can easily beautify his past paths. His vision and concepts about life are much determined by the environment and the knowledge available. Great men, if their historical conditions and opportunity are fully known, might not appear so great as unlimited stories, private letters, autographs, and the like divulge. Man is a great animal at making up history, not so great at making it. Modern technologies have not only enabled people to produce more fake news but also enabled people to detect falsifications. Technologies also imply possible unknown combinations of national relations. For instance, under current technologies and global institutions no country can economically benefit from colonization and slaves. No rationally civilized country will be interested in diffusing its beliefs or values to the world, as no country can rationally prove the universal validity of its belief system for human societies with certainty. It is understandable that men fought for communism or capitalism about hundred years ago (as mankind was then in an early stage of rational and scientific global civilization), in a similar spirit that monkeys fight for their territories. Emerson (1803–1882) says: "No change of circumstances can repair a defect of character."

One century ago, there were only two simplified rationalized value systems based on scientific knowledge available to mankind. There is little economic benefit, only some spiritual benefits, for those who are interested in brainwashing others — for a nation to diffuse its obviously invalid ideas in this digitalized world. Moreover, in a village-like world, a Chinese proverb says, "Before preparing to improve the world, first look around your own home three times." No country can easily pretend to be self-righteous or decent today, not to say in the future (as any ordinary robot can quickly highlight national as well as personal stupidities).

1.7 The Civil War and Abolishing Slavery

> The sage and the common people are the same in kind.
> Mencius (372–289 BC, 11:7)

With the *General Economic Theory* (Zhang, 2020), it is not recondite to mathematically prove that as American industrialization was deepened, it was more economical for the white race in North to free people of color but collectively discriminate against them than to keep them as slaves. The economic structural changes economically required the abolishment of slavery and re-construction of separation and discrimination.

The structure laid the basis for abolishing slavery. Without the structural change caused by technological advances, slavery would have continued, just as it seemed to be printed in the Greek cultural gene. As America enters the knowledge-based economy, it should weaken discrimination and maintain equality in creative working environments in research labs and international companies. This is a way to maximize profits by enhancing productivity and establishing team spirit.

By the way, freedom in sex is not difficult to collectively actualize, as its impact and energies are locally consumed and have little effect on a large scale (except in the very long term through knotty interactions with the other sectors of a society). Freedom in power and wealth is more perplexing as their implications are abstruse. Most societies failed in practicing freedom in wealth and power but have been quite successful at freedom of sex. Nevertheless, the introduction of freedom in sex and associated sexuality into civilized societies has led to diminishing population of the dominant race, in association with advance of modern higher education among women. Long-term sustainability and short-term pleasure and efficiency do not necessarily work in harmony. There is nothing meaningful or useful to learn from history in long-term sustainability as many factors are unpredictably concomitant in a free social organ.

What the key cause of the civil war was is still under debate. But once war starts, no one can control how it will be brought to an end, as human emotions tend to be unpredictable and chaotic, especially during war. There are unlimited rational explanations of the American civil war. What matters is who won the fight and what were its consequences.

Benjamin Franklin did not strongly advocate abolishing the slave trade because of his vision on balancing wealth and power. He was fully aware of the injustice of slavery. But he also knew other values of slavery. The founding fathers were mostly practical men with a sense of money, not only with a capacity for valuing justice and knowledge. Franklin "calculated the cost of American slave labor in terms of original investment, risk, lack of increase on capital, and maintenance, and discovered that it was far more expensive than free labor in England.... Then why did Americans continue to buy Negroes? There was, Franklin conceded, a shortage of white labor, and hired workers soon left their jobs to acquire land of their own." Davis (1988: 427) endorses this view in his well-known *The Problem of Slavery in Western Culture* first published in 1966.

Western writers gave many reasons to "justify" the tolerance and continuation of the slave system in America. An intellectually challenging question is what would have happened in Greek democratic civilization or American democratic civilization if there were no slave system. Like many important human affairs, in American history it seems that economic calculations is more important than the principles of freedom and liberty. Trump's "America first" banner echoes this spirit. How would America have evolved if not for slavery? In the study of history, there is no such thing as "if," since real history is constantly confronted with multiple possible paths in each period, and history goes down only one such path, perhaps by chance.

Nevertheless, study of the social structure is important as it enables one to list the possibilities in various periods. For instance, what might America look like today if the founding fathers had abolished slavery? Greek thinkers conceived their logically consistent state with slavery assumed. One might further ask whether Greek philosophers could have dreamed about a sustainable democratic state without slavery. There is a logical consistency between the co-existence of heterogeneous peoples with miscellaneous national and domestic conditions. For instance, if some states in Ancient China had developed a democratic format, the people of the state might have been slaughtered long before they could have selected a leader, as China's neighbors were nomads with strong bodies, high IQs, skilled in killing, capable of speedy long-distance travel with little fatigue, and a spirit of establishing or extending teams calculated to gain wealth and to kill with short-term cost-benefit calculations.

The nature, spirit, formation of the game, humanity, and knowledge are combined in varying proportion, and no one knows yet which is the best for collective survival. Democracy leads to human dignity, "fair" play, and prosperity in one cultural and geographical environment; while the same democracy results in poverty, chaos, lack of order and law, a polluted environment and needless waste in another cultural environment, as evidenced around the world. There are many beautiful things or "subjective worlds," but it is lucky for a man even to get one and able to keep it for a lifetime without feeling bored with it. A dream lasts and can be repeatedly sought and even achieved over a thousand years, but the satisfaction leads to boredom and final ending of the dream.

In *The Half Has Never Been Told — Slavery and the Making of American Capitalism*, Baptist (2016) follows the expansion of slavery in the first eighty years after American independence. During the period, America evinced economic evolution and modernization. The South had developed from its narrow strip of worn-out tobacco plantations into a continental cotton empire with slavery. Different from traditional arguments for white virtue, diligence, and cultural advances, based on meticulous, extensive and comprehensive data and narrative records Baptist proves how American capitalism was sustained by products and wealth created by the forced labor of Africans and African-Americans. Slavery was an integral part of the American story of economic miracles. Baptist reveals that although slavery is often conceived by Americans as a pre-modern institution, the original sin of the nation is deeply printed in the cultural gene in alternative forms of racial discrimination. The book shows how America's economic super-success was built on the backs of slaves. In another book, *Slavery's Capitalism*, edited by Beckert and Rockman (2018), it is demonstrated that slavery played a significant role in the emergence of American capitalism during the period between the Revolution and the Civil War. One would misunderstand America's spectacular pattern of economic dynamics if a consideration of slavery were excluded. The great American capitalism with market mechanisms, private property, and free white people was initiated and strengthened with the unshakable assumption that human beings could be legally owned and compelled to work under threat of violence. The authors allege that American credit markets, the practice of offshore investment, and human capital structures are closely related to the historical path of slavery. Slavery is an integral part of the American institutional structures of capitalism.

Abraham Lincoln (1809–1865) has often been valued as one of the greatest American presidents. His family migrated from England to Massachusetts in 1638. He made great contributions to the ending of slavery in the United States. He was born into poverty and was raised in Indiana. He self-educated and became an American statesman and lawyer. He was an avid reader and had a lifelong interest in learning. He was elected the 16th president (1861–1865). He led the nation through American Civil War. He preserved the Union, preventing the split into two weaker nations. He bolstered the federal government, and sped up economic progress. Lincoln won the 1860 election and advocated halting the expansion of slavery.

In his Lyceum speech in 1837, Abraham Lincoln promoted the social importance of the American Revolution: "The jealousy, envy, avarice incident to our nature, and so common to a state of peace, prosperity, and conscious strength, were for a time in a great measure smothered and rendered inactive, while the deep-rooted principles of hate, and the powerful motive of revenge, instead of being turned against each other, were directed exclusively against the British nation." In his inaugural address delivered to the South on March 1861, he did not display an inclination to end slavery in the Southern states: "I do but quote from one of those speeches when I declare that 'I have no purpose, directly or indirectly, to interfere with the institution of slavery in the States where it exists. I believe I have no lawful right to do so, and I have no inclination to do so.'" He concluded his address to the South: "We are not enemies, but friends.... The mystic chords of memory stretching from every battlefield, and patriot grave, to every living heart and hearthstone, all over this broad land, will yet swell the chorus of the Union, when again touched, as surely they will be, by the better angels of our nature."

By this time, he was warned that the South was preparing for war. Soon slave states broke away to form the Confederacy. On April 12, 1861, a US Army ship moved to seize control of the entrance of Charleston Harbor, crucial to Southern trade. Confederate forces fired on Union troops. Lincoln ordered that the Army protect and recruit former slaves. Between the Union and slavery, the British man chose to preserve the Union (Guelzo, 2004).

In a letter of August 22, 1862, Lincoln (Graebner, 1959) wrote: "My paramount object in this struggle is to save the Union, and is not either to save or to destroy slavery. If I could save the Union without freeing any slave I would do it, and if I could save it by freeing all the slaves I would do it; and if I could save it by freeing some and leaving others alone I would also do that. What I do about slavery, and the colored race, I do because I believe it helps to save the Union; and what I forbear, I forbear because I do not believe it would help to save the Union." But the North needed the manpower, and freed slaves were obviously disposed to join the Northern cause against the South.

The Emancipation Proclamation effective on January 1, 1863, confirmed the freedom of slaves in 10 states not then under Union control. By the end of 1863, Lincoln's army had already recruited 20 regiments of blacks from the Mississippi Valley. Lincoln spoke his most well-known phrase at the dedication of the Gettysburg battlefield cemetery on November 19, 1863: "[G]overnment of the people, by the people, for the people, shall not perish from the earth." One might add, the government of the people, by the rich, and for the rich should be destroyed and replaced by government for the people, as ancient Confucianism holds.

The war between the US Army and the Confederacy led to the effective ending of slavery. Following the Union victory in the Civil War, slavery became illegal in the United States, in December 1865. On April 14, a few days after the war had ended, Lincoln was assassinated.

Slavery in the United States was legal from the nation's foundation 1776 until the passage of the Thirteenth Amendment in 1865. It was also practiced in Britain's other colonies. Under the law, a slave was treated as property and could be bought, sold, or given away. The U.S. Constitution (1789) did not terminate slavery. A federal law dating to 1807 barred importing any new slaves to the country, and in most Northern states from that time forward the majority of slaves gradually died off or were set free. However, even by 1840s there were still enslaved people in the Northern states. By 1850, the cotton-growing South had a few million slaves. The South regarded slavery as a positive good and productive force.

The governments of seven of the 34 US states declared to secede from the country in February 1861. They were all from South and slave holding. The Confederate States of America was established in opposition to the United States and drafted its own constitution. The Confederacy later added more territories to its control. The Confederate states were never recognized as a joint entity by the U.S. government or any foreign country.

The states remaining loyal to the U.S. government were known as the Union. The Union and the Confederacy conscripted their own armies and fought, mostly in the South, for four years, with the Southern states standing on a certain view of states' rights as discussed in great depth when during the founding of the nation. They were opposed to strong federal control, in political/economic matters, which they particularly considered to include each state's right to decide whether to permit slaveholding. The Northern economy was more focused on finance and international trade through its seaports, whereas the South was principally agricultural.

It has been estimated that between 0.62 million and 0.75 million soldiers lost their lives in the war. The fighting ended in April 1865 when the Confederate General Robert E. Lee surrendered to the Union General Ulysses S. Grant. The North had always had a superior railway network, and the war destroyed much of the South's infrastructure. Slavery was terminated and four million black people gained their freedom.

Lipset (1996) singularized the American creed by liberty, egalitarianism, individualism, populism, and laissez-faire. Redenius (1981) pointed out that the ideal of equality in America differs from that in Europe in at least three important respects. First, America's equality is expected to be achieved by individuals moving up rather than everyone being leveled down. America encourages the aspirations of ambitious individuals and open opportunities for everyone. American equality refers to individualism rather than collectivism. The abundance of land, the opportunities for advancement, and the absence of long-established classes explain why Americans dislike a collectivist definition of equality.

American equality implies a moral sense that all people are of the same worth and have identical rights. Martin Luther King, Jr. (1929–1968) eloquently expressed the American dream for equality in the widely quoted the *I Have a Dream* speech delivered before the Lincoln Memorial on August 28, 1963 (King, 1992:104-5): "So I say to you, my friends, that even though we must face the difficulties of today and tomorrow, I still have a dream. It is a dream deeply rooted in the American dream that one day this nation will rise up and live out the true meaning of its creed — we hold these truths to be self-evident, that all men are created equal... I have a dream my four little children will one day live in a nation where they will not be judged by the color of their skin but by the content of their character."

1.8 Pondering America Through the Lens of Ancient Confucianism

The highest civilizations the human race has achieved ... are in Europe and China.

Gottfried Wilhelm Leibniz (1647–1716)

Photo 1.1 Moses, Confucius (left), and Solon at the U.S. Supreme Court

High civilization is fabricated with thought and religion. Just as in animal worlds, human societies have dances, songs, ways of communication, and architecture. The construction of higher civilization requires a higher abstract thought system or sophisticated religious systems to meet the basic needs of individuals and society measured in terms of wealth, power, and sex. Civilizations have evolved with such complex networking that one can hardly follow the creation, distribution, and utilization of wealth, power, and sex.

Western social sciences and philosophies deal with these basic issues of individuals and societies in one way or another, but these knowledge systems fail to provide a whole picture that allows us to understand how modern civilizations function, as each of them is focused on certain aspects but neglects many other aspects of the social organism. There are few meaningful connections between these thought systems. Life is closely connected, but theories are mutually isolated (perhaps owing to the principle of evolution or the principle of survival of those intellectual concepts most fit for being passed on, like genes). Some parts of a given theory, if neglected, might destroy societies, and the most romantic or dignified parts can become detrimental parasites on the social organism.

Modern developed economies mostly sprouted from a background of poverty and low levels of education. In the Western world, consider the United States, Australia, and Canada; in East Asia, Japan, South Korea, Taiwan, Hong Kong, and Singapore. When China started its surge of rapid growth in the modern era, the monthly wage of a young worker in Shanghai or Beijing was less than USD 10 (1978). Today's developed economies are built of similar cultural blocks, either Western European cultures or Confucian (or rice-paddy-based) cultures. Although the Confucian nations have played a role as "servants" in modern global political and economic development, their development is deeply rooted in a culture that highly values knowledge and respects education, and practices a strategy of tolerance with a "talented slavish mentality."

Human nature is invariant and is incarnated in infinite forms of personal lives — each with its own characteristics, just as a few basic colors give rise to an inexhaustible variety of paintings due to human creativity. Societies may follow an incalculable number of patterns. But the basic socioeconomic principles steering societies are limited — at least, sustainable ones are.

The American civilization with which we are familiar, as the greatest power, is structurally unsustainable due to its free lifestyles, emphasis on consumption, and global positions. Structural changes will be seen sooner or later. A social pattern formed with an unsustainable combination of principles can only be transitory.

We still know little about the sustainability of human societies, except forcedly stabilized or religion-dominated social structures. Confucianism, which has been applied in East Asia for over a thousand years, led to the evolution of a type of civilization different from American civilization. The German thinker, scientist, and mathematician Leibniz (1647–1716) was interested in the deep reasons for things, especially intellectual things, and was an avid Sinophile, especially as regards Chinese intellectual things (e.g., Mungello, 1977; Leibniz, 1994). Leibniz said long ago: The highest civilizations the human race has achieved ... are in Europe and China." This is incomprehensible even to many contemporary Chinese professors sprinkled randomly throughout top universities in the world, because they have less knowledge of traditional Chinese thought on man and society than Leibniz. A modern reader can reasonably doubt whether his visionary conclusions — derived from his ruminations over Chinese philosophy, political institutions, and socioeconomic structures — could possibly be valid, having any implication for the future. In fact, Leibniz was never in China and knew China mainly through a few classical Confucian books (as most other important Chinese books were not translated into Western languages in his lifetime). It is through the thought represented in these books that he perceived what might occur in China. But surprisingly enough, looking around the world, one sees that the economic powerhouses are indeed European- and Chinese-based cultures. America is an extension of European civilization, and traditionally, Japan and the four little tigers were essentially Chinese in nature before the West penetrated East Asia.

Neither the American nor the East-Asian economic miracle is in the center of the two civilizations but they are built on the cultural bases noted by Leibniz. The last Chinese dynasty perished owing to its resistance to change in association with Western civilization. Japan survived due to its quick adaptation to Western civilization and the application of ancient Confucianism. European civilization fell to the ground as its internal conflicts led to self-destruction and the bifurcation of the center of the world between capitalist America and socialist Russia. America came out on top after joining WWII late and without having had a single battle fought on its own territory. Russia — who contributed far more and suffered far more in subduing Germany — was unable to bankroll the socialist bloc and support its rise as a center of civilization. However, the Russian system has been extraordinarily important to global peace and humanity as it maintained a competitive playing field, in every sphere from military might to ideologies and culture. It is owing to the competition for survival between different variations, rather than giving up our minds to one single ideology, that we have become more human.

American socioeconomic thought is largely formed on the ideas of British economist Adam Smith (1723–1790). He visualized the world through the lens of Newtonian theories on man and society. When Adam Smith began to think of social and economic issues, what Confucianism could offer to Western civilization was absorbed into the thought of great Western thinkers and Chinese thought ended its role in broadening Western views. The great German Leibniz himself was little known to the American civilization. China had been seen as a laughing stock not only in the West but even in its small island neighbor, modern Japan, long since. It is only in recent years that mainland China has started, slowly but steadily, to study anew Chinese thought accumulated since ancient times. Chinese people scattered throughout the world know little about the more elevated parts of China's civilization.

Speaking in terms of vision, an ideology so far created by man is a rule of human game. A society tends to be addicted to one ideology or another, and does not question its foundation, meanings, and vast implications. A man who seriously questions the foundation of the value system is usually laughed at, marginalized and excoriated in his lifetime, or simply killed by those in power. A free society does not publicly and officially listen to penetrating critics who challenge accepted values or assumptions. Value builders are usually created in a value-chaotic environment, like ancient Greece and ancient China about 2500 years ago, and the European Enlightenment.

America did not create any major ideology. Intellectual inquiry about basic issues of man and society are hardly characteristic of American culture. That is the reason why East Asian intellectuals love American academic life so much. Discrimination that is only skin-deep or based on some external symbol or tool such as money might not hurt a talented, slavish people.

Love of freedom is not a human creation. No love is so naturally born as love of freedom. The Ancient Greeks created many gods; they set up a democracy within a slave-based society; and they practiced logic; while the ancient Chinese established many thought systems (such as Confucianism, Taoism, Moism, Legalism, and so on). America does not produce value builders, but applies, perhaps most rationally, heterogeneous values that have been brought in largely by poor and uneducated, or poorly educated, immigrants. As in sports, a society's games are judged largely in accordance with its ideology and value systems. A society's rule should be durable as changes in the main rule (system) causes changes in everything in life. The superpower model implies that in international games, the rule maker, the ruler, and the judge are on the same team (currently called the United States of America). The team players share high spirits, opportunities to train, and profitable games. As long as America holds the power in its own hands, the nation can play a skillful game by absorbing talented players from elsewhere in the world. But once the domestic game is played without an outsider as the competitor/enemy, it becomes challenging for America to produce conformity and continue to maintain its national team spirit.

There is no such simple judgement on final righteousness with regard to the national value system. Ancient societies had their own rules, mostly based on religions. The European Enlightenment introduced more rational rules into their civilization. Western rationality after the Enlightenment has basically created two value systems, communism and capitalism.

Nations were basically separated by the two systems after WWII. Soldiers killed each other over the two ideologies. For instance, the poverty-stricken and little-educated Vietnamese were slaughtered in conflicts between the two Western ideologies — which they had little idea about in any sophisticated sense. In his "Conversations with History" in March 2002, the 40th anniversary of the public announcement by the Kennedy administration that US pilots were to be sent to bomb South Vietnam, Noam Chomsky (2002) explained: "That was the initiation of the chemical warfare to destroy food crops, driving huge numbers of people into concentration camps.... I know [now] that the West was actually supporting fascism, supporting Franco, supporting Mussolini and so on, and even Hitler. I didn't know that at the time."

Wars based on religious differences are a main feature of human games, as man is an animal capable of making dreams and taking the dream-based values for granted. A great game called the Cold War has been played on the human race. The ending of the world war (as a "shooting war") meant the end of the two simplified rules for humans. Mankind needs an alternative value system now, to survive together as the world is becoming a global-ized village. The globalized reality is owing to the success of the ascendant America after WWII and the ubiquitous failures of socialism in further enriching people's lives. China has been making the greatest economic prog-ress, and has its largest national population in history, due to trading in communist ideology for market mechanisms.

The self-destructive mechanisms of civilization also imply the possible loss of American superiority. American values might need to be updated to survive well in the new world. The traditional American values and practices will not make America look glorious and great in the near future. America's domestic mechanisms of evolution do not advance America in the new global game. The average IQ of its population, the high proportion of aged whites with low birth rates in tandem with increasing inflows of large-family immi-grants from diverse backgrounds and generally with lower levels of educa-tion will not contribute to maintaining a happy society while the economy shrinks.

Ideology in society can be exemplified as assumptions in science, axioms in mathematics, rules in sports. Natural sciences and technologies have made rapid progress in the last century. Innovative assumptions and axioms are mixed to create new (invisible) worlds for people to manipulate, control, and use. One example often cited is Albert Einstein, who made his original assumptions and applied unusual axioms in mathematics to substantiate a world unknown and invisible to mankind. Nevertheless, social sciences and economics have shown little revolutionary change, as the values and assumptions in social sciences were basically dreamt up and adopted long ago.

The initially stunning declaration, "God is dead," was diffused long ago in the West, but no substitute has been created yet. The Cultural Revolution in China attempted to thoroughly destroy traditional Chinese values. Ruination can be completed quickly (in physical terms, America is now capable of destroying most man-made parts of the earth in a few hours); but meaningful construction takes generations.

Mankind is at turning point of creating an alternative value set to foster harmonious co-existence. Many cunning, uncultivated, and uneducated politicians without any sense of shame or spirit of global co-operation can take to the TV news and lead the world from one disaster to another. If we could gather all the important politicians on the earth and test them on some basic issues related to what it means to be human, on justice, and economic principles, the test results would collectively make a laughingstock of mankind rather than providing any meaningful insights into the complexity of human society.

The world has perhaps been led by uneducated monkeys rather than gentleman-scholars, as Confucius and ancient Greek philosophers envisioned. Still, mankind did not vanish altogether at the end of WWII. The world has luckily co-existed somehow, in a relatively peaceful state, despite the miscellaneous ideologies guiding the major players who are equipped with nuclear power. Global peace will be maintained, with a high probability, because the alternative would bring immediate global destruction. Human history shows that man has no limit when it comes to inflicting cruelty on others. No other animal can be so consciously and systematically cruel towards its own kind. This human characteristic may not be changeable through human efforts in the long term, as this cruelty is perhaps determined at the genetic level. But there is a chance for mankind to learn to act more "humanely" with others, as human have mutated into a unique species that can overcome or cheat his own genes.

Andre Weil (1906–1998) expresses the *yin-yang* world in the following way: "God exists since mathematics is consistent, and the Devil exists since we cannot prove it." Following this great mathematician, we may mathematically say that if mathematics was created by God, then man was certainly created by the Devil. Historically, one might read many positive attitudes towards Confucianism in the West. I mentioned Leibniz in the preface. Voltaire (1694–1778) recognized the rationalism in Confucius: "I admire Confucius. He was the first man who did not receive a divine inspiration." He also praised the Confucian system (in comparison to the religious Europe): "The constitution of their [Chinese] empire is in truth the best that there is in the world." François Quesnay (1694–1774) was another Western giant who appreciated Confucius. Confucianism, which does not promote hereditary aristocracy, was advocated as a weapon to attack hereditary privilege in France and in England. Quesnay greatly adored the education system in China which helped the state to select talented people for public service through a rigorous program of study and a competitive examination system. The Chinese idea of government through merit, knowledge, and formal education rather than through heredity was greatly attractive to him. In his lifetime Quesnay was called "the Confucius of Europe." Max Weber (1864–1920, 1951), after some years of studying Chinese thought, concluded: "In the absence of all metaphysics and almost all residues of religious anchorage, Confucianism is rationalist to such a far-going extent that it stands at the extreme boundary of what one might possibly call a 'religious' ethic. At the same time, Confucianism is more rationalist and sober, in the sense of the absence and the rejection of all non-utilitarian yardsticks, than any other ethical system, with the possible exception of J. Bentham's."

I systematically compare the basic ideas related to, for instance, virtue and non-government intervention between Confucius and Adam Smith (Zhang, 2000). This study is another attempt to make some contribution to cultural comparison by quoting extensively from ancient Confucian sayings.

2. Wealth with Capitalism

> How can man form a society? I say it is due to the division of society into classes. How can social divisions be transformed into behavior? I say it is because of humans' sense of morality and justice. Thus, if the sense of morality and justice is used to divide society into classes, concord will result.
>
> Xun Zi (298–238 BC, 9:19)

Jane Austen (1775–1817) forthrightly unmasks one simple source of happiness for common people: "A large income is the best recipe for happiness I ever heard of." And she pairs it with a common behavior pattern: "It is very difficult for the prosperous to be humble."

"The deepest definition of youth is life yet untouched by tragedy," says Alfred North Whitehead. The hit 2018 US movie, *Crazy Asian Rich*, is about the plain pleasure and happiness of wealthy Asian families. Younger generations of rich Asian Chinese remind one of wealthy American white families in the 1960s and rags-to-riches Japanese in the 1980s. Current American youth consumer behaviors are called conservative and out of fashion in Shanghai, where all kinds of varieties of life and fashion are tried, as they were among American youth in the 1960s. If East Asians have never behaved "crazily" in America, it is because they have been collectively repressed in the environment.

The contemporary romantic comedy directed by Joh Chu verifies what Friedrich von Schiller (1759–1805) sustains: "The world's history is constant, like the laws of nature, and simple, like the souls of men. The same conditions continually produce the same results." Real phenomena are chaotic and are never identically repeated. But the social and economic structures of societies have a limited number of patterns.

2.1 Adam Smith, Keynes, and America's Market Economy

> If your Majesty will indeed . . . be sparing in the use of punish-
> ments and fines, and making the taxes and levies light, so causing
> that the fields shall be ploughed deep, and the weeding of them be
> carefully attended to, and that the strong-bodied, during their days
> of leisure, shall cultivate their filial piety, fraternal respectfulness,
> sincerity and trustfulness, serving thereby, at home, their fathers
> and elder brothers, and, abroad, their elders and superiors — you
> will then have a people who can be employed.

Mencius (372–289 BC, 1:5)

Japanese-American theoretical physicist Michio Kaku (1947–), who was
a member of a discriminated minority yet joined the United States Army
during the Vietnam War to fight against East Asians, said this in describing
the current state of capitalism: "We are headed toward 'perfect capitalism,'
when the laws of supply and demand become exact, because everyone
knows everything about a product, service or customer. We will know
precisely where the supply curve meets the demand curve, which will make
the marketplace vastly more efficient." The theoretical physicist refers to
technological change and (often fake) information availability. It is perhaps
the Chinese market economy with socialist characteristics, rather than
capitalist economies, which are most effectively exploring economic efficiency in association with advanced technologies, through widely diffused
internets and free competition. When Adam Smith was building up his
economic dynamics with Newtonian vision, modern chaos theory and the
internet were not available. The historical conditions limited what Adam
Smith could imagine. But Adam Smith's thought is America's grand paradigm of economics. This explains why his simple theory, which has little
to do with modern advanced economies, is proper for America's society. In
modern economies, a few families within an economy are able to collect an
astounding percentage of the national wealth by exploiting the economies of
scale and of scope, monopolistic power in an imperfect market with mostly
manipulated and biased information, that Smith could hardly imagine and
that America (at least the rich and the elite) takes pains to hide.

Wealth, power, and sex are the main, objectively measurable goals for
man to seek externally. The dynamics of economic profits and wealth are
key factors for understanding multi-cultural America. American economists
(especially certain famous Jewish economists) applied Newton's physics
to explain and predict phenomena which should be explored by contemporary chaos theory. American political economists have over the years
talked about American economies, and especially international economies,

with Newtonian economics. In America economic knowledge has not been so useful as medical knowledge. An important difference between the two fields is that (political) economic decisions are made in the end through politicians whose personal interests and ignorance might deviate considerably from objective economic decisions, but medical experts can directly apply their knowledge — one hopes — without political and other arbitrary interferences. An unavoidable tragedy of economics is that it is not designed for special interest group(s), but its applications are often made by non-economists with personal interests.

Adam Smith (1776) used the example of a pin factory to illustrate the division of labor and human capital accumulation by producing. As his skill increases, the worker will concentrate on one specific task and thus further increase his skill. The division of labor has an interdependent relationship with growth. As production is increased and the market expands, machinery and the division of labor need to be correspondingly shifted. The division of labor enhances the efficiency of workers, and society collectively produces more. Economic progress (in association with technological change, as later added by Schumpeter) causes further division of labor. Interactions are continued till the system achieves an equilibrium point. Adam Smith's world view did not include multiple equilibria, chaos, bifurcations, and catastrophes as he was living in the Newtonian world. He was convinced that the world would come to an equilibrium along a single path of economic change. This is how traditional scientists perceived the world.

Smith conceived important insights into economic mechanisms and forces of development. But he could not imagine the modern scale and scope of economies and rapid speeds of transactions entailing goods, people, and information, not to mention contemporary science and technology. His conclusions on the role of government are based on the British Empire's practice and Newton's physics, which have respectively limited relevance to modern economic reality and physics. He assumed the existence of a unique long-run stable economic equilibrium without any rigorous mathematical proof. His theory is suitable for explaining the economy of the Chinese countryside some decades ago, but it has little to do with New York stock markets and the behavior of high-tech industrial sectors.

The search for a unique, stable equilibrium in a competitive economy was the main concern of theoretical equilibrium economists at least during the 1960s and the 1980s. In this kind of imagined systems, government intervention plays no essential role as small changes only result in small consequences and the market can do a perfect job in improving social welfare.

To the contrary, chaos theory demonstrates that in a structurally unstable system, a small change can lead to catastrophic changes (as China has already seen, with Marx's idea on using a market economy for economic growth within an initially industrializing system). This has important implications for political economics. It makes traditional political and economic thought invalid as general theory or ideology. The mainstream of economics insisted on a false model of the world, but thousands of professional economists still live there.

The Wealth of Nations has played the essential role in capitalism over the world. The theory is still the main content in introductory economics textbooks. The important message from Smith is that a society can be developed economically, with social order, purely on the basis of self-interest. Public spirit, sympathy, religions, and other emotions or nonconcrete aspects are important but not necessary for an orderly society with free markets and law. Religion might be spread, but it is not necessary in a rational economy operating under laws, as self-interest and freedom to pursue one's own benefits are sufficient to promote an orderly society. This implies freedom of religions, because religions would not be harmful so far as people with distinct religions pursue their own material interests under a common set of laws. The American economic system has been fundamentally operating according to Adam Smith's thought, even though his theory was "reformed" by Keynes (1936), who justified government intervention in free market economy on a large scale.

Investment in public goods, resistance to technological change, big business, big government, barriers to entrepreneurship, racism and sexism can be widely witnessed in American-style societies. In American capitalism, government intervention has played an increasing role in the economy. Numerous laws now cover such matters as minimum wages and pension programs, industrial and banking systems, labor relations, employment of minorities, the safety of manufactured products, and protection against environmental damage. The laissez-faire economy has been replaced by a more regulated economy.

American economic doctrine is now Keynesian. Keynes was not interested in pure capitalism as he was certain that capitalism would die, sooner or later. He did not trust planned economies, either. He advocated an active role for the government in reducing the severity of business cycles through proper management of money supply and proper social policy. He was convinced that neither socialism nor capitalism would benefit mankind as whole. His justification for government intervention was influenced by this broad vision. He promoted a theoretical model of an economy with a strong government sector. His theory replaces Adam Smith's *laissez-faire* philosophy. After WWII, American economic paradigms have oscillated between Adam Smith and Keynes as the dominant doctrine.

Keynes' theory has had a revolutionary impact on our understanding of how economic systems should operate. His argument for the role savings would play in national economic development has been influential. In an earlier stage of capitalism, he justified the unequal distribution of wealth. As economic conditions of the 19th century required a large sum of savings to support fast economic expansion, the unequal distribution of wealth could encourage social savings as capitalists, having a more than sufficient income, had a higher propensity to save. Higher savings would supply more capital to the economic system.

But changes in economic conditions would make high savings rates slow down the expansion of capitalist economies. His argument is that employment is determined by effective demand, and great differences in wealth and income among people reduce demand. The rich hold too much to spend, and the poor have too little income to consume much. By redistributing money from the rich to the poor through taxation, demand for consumer goods will be increased.

But Keynes' ideas are now misleading when the times have changed. Mencius (13:26) points out why neither capitalism nor socialism, nor Keynesianism for that matter, can enable a society to experience prosperity without shifting economic policies:

> The principle of the philosopher Yang was — 'Each one for himself.' Though he might have benefited the whole empire by plucking out a single hair, he would not have done it. The philosopher Mo loves all equally. If by rubbing smooth his whole body from the crown to the heel, he would have benefited the empire, he would have done it. Zimo holds a middle ground between these. By holding that middle, he is nearer to being right. But by holding it without leaving room for the exigency of circumstances, it becomes like their holding to their one point. The reason why I abhor that holding to one point is the injury it does to the way of right principle. It takes up one point and disregards a hundred others.

In modern economics, it simply means that the scale and scope of government intervention should be situation dependent. The best policy for an economy cannot be pre-determined. It oscillates between the extremes — pure capitalism and pure socialism. Personal wisdom — not to mention wisely-balanced national development policy — is not pre-determined or given by a set of equations. When the nation needs wise and skillful politicians whose hearts are for the welfare of the people, the society most often ends up with cunningly selfish players. Once it enters this kind of political trap, a society is faced with possible destruction. China has repeatedly failed in putting the right people in the right place, over more than two thousand years, irrespective of its excellent ancient doctrines in national management.

2.2 Economic Growth and Improved Living Conditions

> Let the people be employed in the way which is tended to secure their ease, and though they be toiled, they will not murmur.
>
> Mencius (372–289 BC, 13:13)

Mencius's above saying relates why the American Dream is vital for making America great again, even though few now are likely to actualize their dreams. Yet millions of mainland Chinese have made great achievements in various fields even before they had the time and the ability to have any big dreams.

"The civilized man is a more experienced and wiser savage," observed American philosopher Thoreau (1910:83). He sensed the direction toward which man would advance. He was living in the epoch when Americans were rapidly becoming more civilized. America as a nation has succeeded in building the greatest country. It has attracted many millions of immigrants to the dream land. The founders of the United States advocated individual liberty in all fields. America trusted Adam Smith, who confirmed that resources would be efficiently allocated if citizens pursued their own self-interest and profit-making activities. Wealth is a significant social symbol for success in American society and is seen as the protector of one's future.

Tocqueville (1835:149) scrutinized the fundamental feature of American society: "The Present-day American republic ... [is] like companies of merchants formed to exploit the empty lands of the New World, and prosperous commerce is their occupation." He also envisaged that wealth accumulation was the fundamental motivation of American behavior. He admitted that he had seen no other country that devoted such a deep love to money and exhibited such a strong scorn for the idea of equality of property.

Human behavior is not pre-determined. It is largely patterned by the environment in which they are born, brought up and survived. American freedom is manifested in several forms of liberty such as political, religious, moral, and economic freedom. Economic freedoms, such as freedom of competition, freedom of exchange between producers and consumers, buyers and sellers, free choice of one's vocation, free acquisition of rewards for one's efforts, and free accumulation of wealth, are the key elements in this liberty matrix.

The US appreciates freedom not only as a virtue but also as a source of creativity, efficiency, and entrepreneurship. The economy has enjoyed sustained progress since WWII, as plotted in Figure 2.1. (The almost linear expansion that started before WWII in terms of per capita income has already been given in Figure 1.1.)

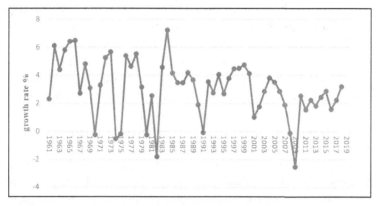

Figure 2.1 U.S. GDP Growth Rate, 1961–2019, in 2010 U.S.

The sustained development owes much to the synergetic effects of innovation, free competition, market forces, immigration, the global environment, and monopolistic power. America is now the world's second-largest manufacturer, although the manufacturing sector has undergone substantial job losses in recent years. Its main industries include automobiles, steel, petroleum, construction machinery, aerospace, agricultural machinery, consumer goods, lumber, telecommunications, chemicals, electronics, food processing, and mining. It leads the world in airplane manufacturing, producing most of the world's civilian and military aircraft in factories across the country. Agricultural products include vegetables, fruits, cotton, wheat, corn, other grains, pork, beef, poultry, dairy products, forest products, and fish. Road transport plays a significant role in American economy. Personal transportation is dominated by automobiles, which operate on a network of 4 million miles of public roads, including one of the world's longest highway systems at 57,000 miles. It has the world's second largest automobile market and highest rate of per capita vehicle ownership in the world. Per 1000 Americans have 765 vehicles. Mass transit accounts for 9% of total U.S. work trips. Transport of goods by rail is extensive. The United States is the second-largest trading nation in the world. U.S. dollars are circulating all around the planet. As of this writing, about of 60% of funds in international trade are U.S. dollars. The dollar is the standard unit of currency in international markets for goods, resources, and services. Since 1976, America has had merchandise trade deficits. Since 1982, it has sustained current account deficits. America has maintained a long-standing surplus in its trade in services.

The United States is rich in natural resources. Its size and natural resources are important reasons for its rapid economic expansion since the 19th century. Protestant religions, the pioneer spirit of early settlers, and few restrictions on business ventures plus laissez-faire economic principles were also basic determinants for the economic advance. Hughes and Cain (1998:521) identify a few principal elements that sustained the United States' economic expansion. The combination of available arable land and other resources, and an able population, gave America a history of unprecedented overall economic expansion. Those favorable conditions created a built-in optimism about the future. Americans were confident that with diligence, they could build a good life. American optimism was maintained by social mobility. It inherited no identifiable system of class barriers and no class of nobility. People born into poverty dreamed about getting rich through their own efforts, and society encouraged them to make these dreams come true.

Early Americans were restless and enterprising immigrants largely from the poorer classes in Europe, both rural and urban. They were pragmatic and open-minded. Their minds were not limited by scarcity of resources or fixed ideas. Modern East Asian economic history indicates that other, non-Western societies, with similar pre-conditions (even without natural resources — but, rather, hope) can establish similar values that move a society toward profit and free competition.

"American economic individualism, American traditional laissez-faire policy," Kallen (1970:80) expounds, "is largely the effect of environment; where nature offers more than enough potential wealth to go round, there is no immediate need for regulating distribution. What poverty and unemployment exist in the United States is the result of unskilled and wasteful social housekeeping, not of any actual natural barrenness. And until the disparity between the economic resources and the population of the United States become equalized, so that the country will attain an approximate economic equilibrium, this is likely to continue to be the case." American optimism was formed in association with the plenitude of natural resources, individualism, and other frontier virtues.

Americans have believed in self-reliance and independence. Social services, for instance, were largely seen as personal matters and the responsibility of the family or individual, rather than of state or federal institutions. Americans are sympathetic toward the poor; but the American public did not much like welfare and did not want social policy to be wasteful. American society easily accepts new ideas and new practices. It is part of American life to consume new products and to enjoy new services. America has secure property rights and traditional respect for contract law. They are the essential instruments for economic progress of a market economy. It also has a stable legal framework under which people can feel confident in making private estimates of future values; this trust adds motivation to all contractual agreements designed to yield a future return. Irrespective of its short-run chaos and unpredictability, American popular democracy has bestowed long-term order and stability on American politics.

2.3 The U.S. Stock Exchange

> When good government prevails in a state, to be thinking only of one's salary; and, when bad government prevails, to be thinking, in the same way, only of one's salary, this is shameful.

Confucius (551-479 BC, 14:1)

Modern technologies and institutions provide many new ways to earn money. Bill Gates is an interesting model; think how easily he could have accumulated even more money on his "rights" on innovations perhaps made by low-paid Indian or Chinese employees if he were also making money on spam: "Like almost everyone who uses e-mail, I receive a ton of spam every day. Much of it offers to help me get out of debt or get rich quick. It would be funny if it weren't so exciting."

In an observation valid for traditional European and East Asian societies, Honoré de Balzac (1799–1850) said: "I do not regard a broker as a member of the human race." The attitude changed long ago; and the financial market has played an especially significant and special role in modern America. Greenspan (1996, 2013; see also Greenspan and Wooldridge, 2018) uses the term "irrational exuberance" to warn about the behavior of stock market investors.

America's stock exchange history started in 1790, with the Philadelphia Stock Exchange established. In the last decade of the 18th century, the New York Stock Exchange (NYSE), which had been called the Security Exchange Office till 1863, was formed. Today the NYSE is the largest exchange in America. The NASDAQ, the world's first electric market, was founded in the early 1970s. It has since partnered with a Swedish exchange called OMX and purchased the Philadelphia Stock Exchange. The NASDAQ is today the largest electronic trading market in the world. It is the second trading market in America.

America has not forgotten its painful economic past during the Great Depression, a worldwide depression. It is commonly said that the depression started after a major fall in stock prices around September 4, 1929, in the U.S. and lasted until the late 1930s. Then the stock market crashed on October 29, 1929, "Black Tuesday." This was certainly not the first depression in the U.S., but it was the longest, deepest, and most widespread depression of the 20th century and it was the worst financial crisis in America. Unemployment in the US rose to 23%. U.S. stock markets lost over 85% of their total value. Internationally, the impact lasted globally until the beginning of WWII. Between 1929 and 1932, the global GDP fell by 15%.

America, as well as the rest of the world, learned a few things about the destructive forces of financial markets and began to implement countermeasures and regulations to prevent such economic disasters. Some economists say the crash caused the global depression. Motley traditional economic theories were applied to explain the phenomenon but they came to no convincing conclusion. With regard to so-called "leave-it-alone liquidationism," Milton Friedman (Lawrence, 2008) wrote: "I think the Austrian business-cycle theory has done the world a great deal of harm. If you go back to the 1930s, which is a key point, here you had the Austrians sitting in London, Hayek and Lionel Robbins, and saying you just have to let the bottom drop out of the world. You've just got to let it cure itself. You can't do anything about it. You will only make it worse.... I think by encouraging that kind of do-nothing policy both in Britain and in the United States, they did harm."

The financial industry has evolved in tandem with promoting business and providing liquidity that firms and individuals require to prosper. It has moved far from its traditionally supported role in economic progress. Banks profit greatly now but their loans to business and consumers have shrunk. The "casino" part of the banking business has recently continued to be significant. As discussed earlier, America's dominant economic reasoning is that of Adam Smith, whose vision was limited to a static economy with small firms and slowly evolving financial markets. America's financial economy is now characterized by special interests, fast and huge transactions, and monopolies. The market mechanism is not functioning within Adam Smith's theoretical framework.

Modern economic theory has little meaningful insight into the impact of financial markets on economic development and wealth distribution. Henry Ford (1863–1947), an American industrialist and business magnate, founder of the Ford Motor Company, points out the spirit of traditional American freedom: "If money is your hope for independence you will never have it. The only real security that a man will have in this world is a reserve of knowledge, experience, and ability." Ford was also a chief developer of the assembly line technique of mass production: the most basic and solid method to make America great. If gamblers have become most influential persons in a country, it needs a proof in the sustainability of decency of a human society.

In her popular *Makers and Takers*, Foroohar (2017) points out that Wall Street does not create jobs for the middle and working classes of America, and the financialization of America is threatening the American Dream. "The financialization of America," according to Foroohar (2017, 5-6), "includes everything from the growth in size and scope of finance and financial activity in our economy to the rise of debt-fueled speculation over productive lending to the ascendancy of shareholder value as a model for corporate government, to the proliferation of risky, selfish thinking in both our private and public sectors, to the increasing political power of financiers and the CEOs they enrich, to the way in which a 'market knows best' ideology remains the status quo, even after it caused the worst financial crisis in seventy-five years."

American businesses have come to favor balance-sheet engineering over the actual kind, short-term profits over a passion and respect for working, and greed over real growth. There are cozy relationships between Wall Street and Washington which make American business and politics intricately connected to each other. Even taxation is designed to benefit wealthy individuals and corporations. The Spanish poet Federico Garcia Lorca (1898–1936) portrays the American financial center: "The terrible, cold, cruel part is Wall Street. Rivers of gold flow there from all over the earth, and death comes with it. There, as nowhere else, you feel a total absence of the spirit: herds of men who cannot count past three, herds more who cannot get past six, scorn for pure science and demoniacal respect for the present. And the terrible thing is that the crowd that fills the street believes that the world will always be the same and that it is their duty to keep that huge machine running, day and night, forever."

Emotional description has often little to do with the economic efficiency of labyrinthine finance on the national economy. A soldier exists for the sake of killing enemies. A gambler exists for the sake of gambling. Professionalism is the basis for an effective division of labor. Compared to soldiers, pure gamblers have a higher probability of making the national system weaker if they perform better. Many of world's smartest gamblers are now connected to Wall Street in one way or another. If they were only skillful at collecting American commoners' money, the long-term consequence might be disastrous for the country. But fortunately for America, these smart players seem to be able to get extra profit from all across the earth, mainly based on America's status as a superpower.

A free financial market, even if it is subject to many regulations, is only one of the unstable subsystems in the organic system. Instability is self-destructive in societies in the long term.

The given direction for an unstable system can be sustained by using extraordinary methods, such as bringing in immigrants on a large scale to be exploited for a while, and printing money, and borrowing money to satisfy the desires of gamblers and parasites. Catastrophes are often associated with unstable systems. Catastrophes may appear somewhere, in unknown places for unknown reasons, as creative humans produce conditions for disasters with their never-ending innovations and socioeconomic structural changes. It is a natural law of market economies deepening self-destructiveness brings with it catastrophes.

2.4 Household Income and Wealth Inequalities

> Extravagance leads to insubordination, and parsimony to meanness. It is better to be mean than to be insubordinate.
>
> Confucius (551–479 BC, 7:36)

A recent book, *Capital in the Twenty-First Century*, by the French economist Thomas Piketty (2017) has attracted great attention. Its popularity is perhaps not so much due to the author's intelligence and deep insights but rather to the fact that the book addresses one of the most important issues in capitalism in an intellectually accessible manner for non-economists. Issues related to income and wealth inequality have been largely neglected in economic academics in capitalist economies. That is a result of rational behavior on the part of economists. Deep insights into these issues tend to lead readers to dismal, critical and destructive conclusions about capitalist systems. The book documents the growing inequality between the poor and the small number of the super-rich. The Frenchman points out that capitalist economies are dominated by "patrimonial capitalism," in which inherited wealth from birth makes more difference than effort and talent. This opinion has little relevance to the second largest capitalist economy, China, so far, as the first generation of the rich has just begun to die and many are still very energetically active. Piketty empirically substantiates that the American system was rigged to facilitate the rapid enrichment of the privileged elites and even to make hardworking Americans suffer from deteriorating living standards. A small group of wealthy rentiers live lavish lifestyles secured by inherited wealth while the rest struggle to live to pay parasites of human society. Even a monkey society does not have this style of justice, under rule of group survival.

America believes in the worth of every human being with equal justice and equal political rights. Social and economic inequalities do not conflict with this value. Differences in wealth and status are commonly attributed to individual distinction, character, and achievement, rather than inequality per se. Mainstream American political economists fantasize about democracy and fair competition and they assume that the present arrangement will cause no serious social disaster owing to income and wealth inequality.

In his journey to America in 1831–1832, Tocqueville discerned that the men in America were indeed more equal in wealth and mental endowments than in any other country of the world in recorded history. However, Tocqueville (1835:101) argued that democratic institutions would cultivate sentiments of envy among masses, awakening and strengthening the desire for equality without being able to satisfy them entirely. His conclusion was drawn when America was still a farmer-dominated economy. He had little idea how today's American economy would operate, with almost half the population consisting of non-European immigrants. In democratic America, people are taught they will be able to rise to the level of everybody else. People are motivated to keep trying, but they are often upset by repeated failures.

American capitalism is primarily concerned with maximizing profit and one's own utility. The democratic principles advocate for maximizing freedom, equality, and the public good. While capitalism increases the income inequality between people, the democratic system may not tolerate enlarged income and wealth gaps. By the 1970s, Hofstadter (1972: xxxviii) affirmed that "American traditions also show a strong bias in favor of egalitarian democracy, but it has been a democracy in cupidity, rather than a democracy in fraternity."

Williamson and Lindert (1980) demonstrate that income and wealth gap was enlarged with the beginning of America's modern economic growth in the early 19th century. Inequality was then reduced with the advent of mature capitalist development in the 20th century. In the interim, the US economy saw extensive inequality for seven decades. The wage structure around 1816 was quite narrow. Then, the difference in the nominal pay for common labor and skilled workers such as engineers, teachers, carpenters, and mechanics rose rapidly between 1816 and 1856. A slight decline in later 19th-century pay ratios was followed by another abrupt increase in difference between the 1890s and 1914. The advantages gained by the skilled groups were maintained and even reinforced through 1916.

America saw the longest period of shared prosperity in history from the 1940s into the 1970s. During this period, a worker with limited formal education could earn a middle-class income. Since the energy price shocks of the 1970s, the American economy evinced slower expansion in productivity and output. It also saw the rise of long-term joblessness. The income gap between the poor and the rich was widened in association with the slowdown in economic expansion. According to Okun (1975:1): "Such is the double standard of a capitalist democracy, professing and pursuing an egalitarian political and social system and simultaneously generating gaping disparities in economic well-being." In 1997, *Forbes* magazine counted 170 billionaires. Microsoft's Bill Gates had $40 billion, the investor Warren Buffet, $21 billion, the Dupont family $14 billion, the Rockefeller family $7 billion. At the same time, in 1995 the average American family was worth $45,600. Real wage rates for most Americans did not increase much during the 1990s–2000s.

Household income varies substantially based on diverse determinants such as the age of the head of household, education, ethnic background, and gender. For instance, the median household income rises as the head of household ages, until retirement age, and falls afterwards. Here, by household income we mean the total of the income of every resident over the age of 15, including pre-tax wages and salaries, any pre-tax personal business, investment, or other recurring sources of income, and any kind of governmental entitlement such as unemployment insurance payments, social security, disability payments or child support payments received. In the calculation of the household income, which is a widely accepted measure of income in America, the residents of the household do not have to be related to the head of the household.

As plotted in Figure 2.2, during the period of 1968 to 2018 the share of the national total income held by the highest-earning 20% of American households steadily increased. By 2018, households in the top 20% brought in 52% of all US income, while in 1968 that number was only 43%. The top 5% of households had 23% of all US income, while that number was only 16% in 1968.

Wage stagnation for the lower-income classes is caused by many factors. Unskilled and skilled labor might lose jobs due to wider utilization of modern machines and computers. In many jobs involving administrative tasks, manufacturing, and farming, humans have been largely replaced by computers. The decline of labor unions has also reduced unskilled workers' wage bargaining power. Globalization implies that many unskilled jobs are directly shifted abroad, while at home global labor competition reduces the pay that American unskilled workers can expect. Many foreign-born workers enter American labor markets and reduce low- and middle-income workers' wages. Especially in recent decades, many immigrants have arrived in the U.S. already equipped with a higher education; meanwhile, cheap foreign goods produced by skilled labor flow into the America market, which appears to benefit consumers but reduces job availability. There is no consensus as to the net effect of each of these factors, as they all have negative as well positive influences on the nation's wage rates.

The highest-earning 20% of families made more than half of all U.S. income in 2018

Share of U.S. aggregate household income, by income quintile

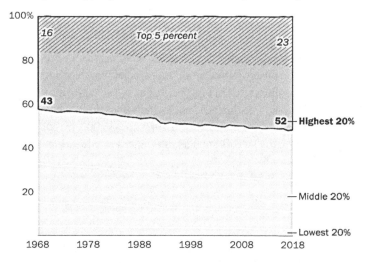

Note: Figures may not add to 100% due to rounding.
Source: U.S. Census Bureau, Income and Poverty in the U.S.: 2018, Table A-4.

PEW RESEARCH CENTER

Figure 2.2 Dynamics of American Income Distribution from 1968 to 2018

Education is deemed to be the main requirement for socioeconomic upward mobility in modern economies, and America now has the best university system in the world, catering to its citizens as well as to international students. Most of the 100 top universities ranked are American. Household income and per capita income are positively related, to a significant degree, to educational attainment, as shown in Figure 2.3. Data from the same source as the figure says that in 2005, graduates with an MBA were expected to earn a base salary of $88,626 with an average possible bonus of $17,428. Persons with doctorates had an average income of $81,400. High school dropouts earned $18,900, high school graduates $25,900, and college graduates $45,400. There are gender differences.

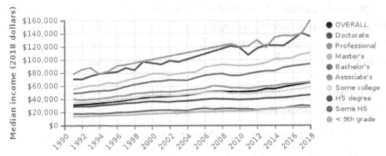

Figure 2.3 Household Income Distribution due to Education Degree

Another important aspect of the American economy is the ethnic income distribution. Inequalities between diverse social and economic groups persist over time as illustrated in Figure 2.4. The black/white income gap has persisted over history. The difference in median household income between the two has increased from $23,800 in 1970 to $33,000 in 2018 (in 2018 dollars) owing to many factors such as differences in education and single-parent households.

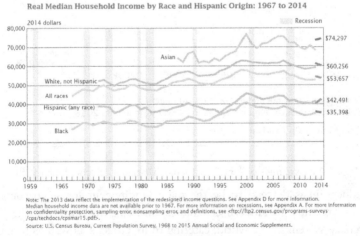

Figure 2.4 Ethnicity-Based Household Income Distribution

Wealth inequality in contemporary America and its multiple determinants are scrutinized in multifarious academic fields. A well-addressed phenomenon is the fact that most wealth is owned by a small portion of the population. It is generally agreed that the over-concentration is a natural consequence of American values and America's high use of advanced technologies. Encouraged selfishness plus free market mechanisms and an effective legal system will naturally lead to the concentration of wealth in a few hands under modern technologies.

The heritage of political power is put to an end in rational societies. Wealth heritage is a more convenient way to enjoy power and other benefits, as the wealthy do not even have a duty to maintain proper behavior and manners when applying their power. A wealthy person, like a barbarian smart recent immigrant — uneducated and ill-mannered as he might be — can employ decent American citizens under American laws which he does not respect.

Household wealth is the value of assets, such as a home and a savings account, owned by a family, minus outstanding debt such as mortgages or student loans. In 1989, the richest 5% of families (at the median $2.3 million) had 114 times in the second quintile (one tier above the lowest, at the median $23,300). By 2016, the top 5% held 248 times in the second quintile.

The richest families were the only ones whose wealth increased after the start of the Great Recession. From 2007 to 2016, the median net worth of the top 20% rose 13% to $1.2 million. For the top 5%, it rose 4% to $4.8 million. During the same period, the median net worth of all families decreased by 20%.

Similar to the pattern of household income distribution, Figure 2.5 (Leiserson, et al., 2019) plots the dynamics of wealth distribution during the period of 1989–2016. The wealth distribution also confirms that the top 1%'s share has increased rapidly in recent decades.

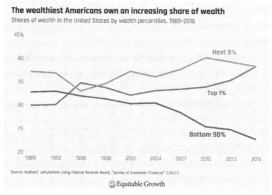

Figure 2.5. The Dynamics of Wealth in American Economy, 1989–2016

The OECD uses the Gini coefficient to measure and compare income inequality across countries. The number ranges from extreme inequality (« 1) to perfect equality (=1). The Gini ranges from 0.25 to 0.6 for the selected countries in the world. In 2017, the U.S. had a Gini coefficient of 0.434, the highest among the G7 nations as plotted in Figure 2.6 (PEW Research Center, 2020).

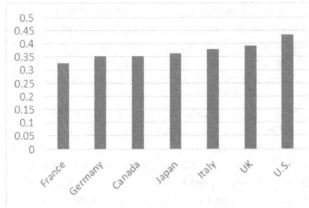

Figure 2.6 U.S. Has Highest Level of Inequality Among G7 Countries

Figure 2.7 (Alvaredo *et al.* 2015) measures the dynamic shares of aggregated income earned by the top 1% in G7 countries during the period of 1975–2014. The data exclude capital gains. All the countries underwent a trend of rising inequality during the period. From 1975 to 1985, the top 1% garnered a similar share of the income in America as in the other G7 countries. Since then, the share of the top 1% in the U.S. has vastly exceeded that in the other countries.

According to *Forbes*, the net worth for America's top 5 richest persons in 2020, using stock prices and exchange rates from March 18, 2020, is as follows:

No.1: Jeff Bezos $113 billion (source of wealth: Amazon)
No.2: Bill Gates $98 billion (Microsoft)
No.3: Warren Buffett $67.5 billion (Berkshire Hathaway)
No.4: Larry Ellison $59 billion (Oracle ORCL)
No.5: Mark Zuckerberg $54.7 billion (Facebook)

On January 6, 2021, the top person was Elon Musk with a net worth of $188 billion.

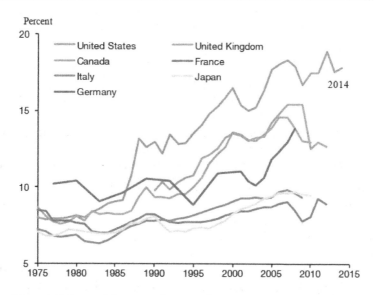

Figure 2.7 Shares of Aggregated Income by Top 1% in G7 Countries

Due to their abilities, talents, and luck, these individuals accumulated wealth which could feed their families over a hundred generations without work. The top man could theoretically have employed all the mainland Chinese for one year in 1978 (at either the current or the 1978 exchange rate). A similar phenomenon occurs in many parts of the world so long as there is a secure social and economic environment for making money and for keeping one's wealth. This is determined by technology and the market. Luck is a factor and timing is important. Someone will make/take those huge sums of money. It is often a socially given fortuity for risk-taking men without any special talents to become hugely rich. Modern technologies can enable just a dozen people to collect most of their countries' wealth using free-market institutions (plus, perhaps, biased information and fortunes). But such rich people interfere with the national media, citizens' freedom, the sex market, power market, and wealth market. Sustainability of the system becomes challenging in any nation with free markets and modern technologies.

2.5 Dynamics of the Productivity and Wage Gaps

When a country is on the verge of a great florescence, it is certain to prize its teachers and give great importance to breadth of learning. If it does this, then laws and standards will be preserved. When a country is on the verge of decay, then it is sure to show contempt for teachers and slight masters. If it does this, then its people will be smug. If the people are smugly self-satisfied, then laws and standards will be allowed to go to ruin.

Xun Zi (298–238 BC, 27: 97)

A rising tide lifts all boats — as long as they are floating nearby, in the same ocean. In a globalized world with no trade barriers and low transaction costs, a rise in the wage rate in producing one transportable commodity or service in America may possibly lead to increases in the rest of the world. If countries come together on the global ocean, it is reasonable that some higher-wage jobs in specific economies are taken away by economies with lower wage rates, if capital inputs, know-how, and knowledge are freely mobile among the economies. As America places its trust in free trade, it is to be expected that wages for jobs which can be done much more cheaply abroad should be reduced due to free trade. Some jobs which are not faced with international rivalry and enjoy special privileges might be paid far higher.

Figure 2.7 plots growth rates (%) of productivity and worker's hourly compensation for America's economy. The data are for compensation (wages and benefits) of production (and nonsupervisory) workers in the private sector and net productivity — the rise of output of goods and services less depreciation per hour worked — of the total economy.

From the late 1940s to the early 1980s, the pay of typical workers rose in tandem with the increase in national productivity. This implies that as the national economy comes to be more efficient, the typical worker is paid more. But after the 1980s, America's national productivity has continued to increase rapidly, while the speed at which wages rise has fallen far behind. This implies that although American workers might have worked more productively, their contribution to the economy has not been fully shared with them but part of the increase has accrued to those at the top, in other words, corporate profits.

The gap between productivity and workers' compensation deviates from the 1980s when computers and other new technologies were widely applied, and developing countries like China started to be opened to the American economy. The income, wages, and wealth generated in recent years did not trickle down to common workers and middle- and low-income households. American policy, which has been strongly manipulated by the rich and the powerful, has exacerbated inequality. Rising inequality tends to further prevent potential pay increases for most workers. Wage stagnation has been a main feature of the American labor market. America needs institutional change to connect actual pay and productivity. Otherwise, the globalization of technological innovations may lead to further reductions in workers' wages.

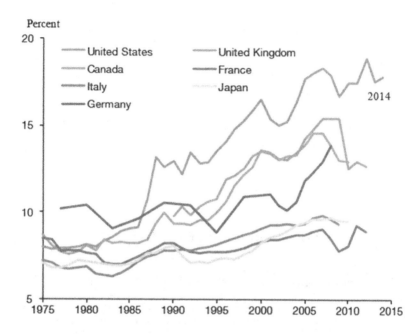

Figure 2.7 Growth Rates (%) of Productivity and Worker's Hourly Compensation

"American culture is CEO obsessed. We celebrate the hard-charging heroes and mythologize the iconoclastic visionaries" (Marcus Buckingham, 1966–). Figure 2.8 plots the aggregated CEO-to-worker compensation ratio for the 350 largest public-owned companies in the United States from 1965 to 2019.

By 2019 the ratio reached 320. On average, CEOs received about 320 times the annual salary of production and nonsupervisory workers in the key industry of their firm. American CEOs collect large paychecks, stock options, bonuses, luxury gifts and other unseen benefits. They are among the "luckiest" of groups from the standpoint of the American ideals of free market mechanisms and an ideology of selfism.

One day of a CEO's work is equal to the worker's whole year of labor. Some CEOs take home a huge income without any sense of duty, when much of the income is due to the contributions made by those who are losing their jobs.

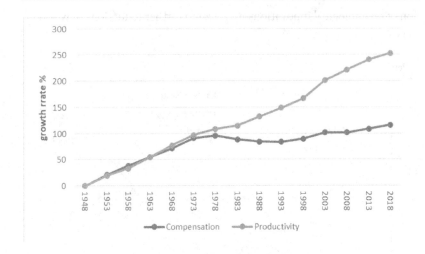

Figure 2.8 The Compensation Ratio of CEO and Worker, 1965–2019

2.6 Poverty and Distribution of Social Welfare

> Who says of Weisheng Gao that he is right? Someone begged
> some vinegar of him, and he begged it of a neighbor and gave it to
> him.
>
> Confucius (551-479 BC)

A nation built by immigrants has its own problems of morality, loyalty, and the concept of justice. Throughout history, Chinese society has been cyclically Confucian and anti-Confucian; the Chinese is cyclically "slave" and master. In its historical cycle, America is so young that it is just sinking slowly and steadily from its greatness, as it has no strong enemy to quickly exhaust its energy. No one can easily stop historical flows. To recognize the main flow and live with it is the way to success and glory, as a Chinese proverb says.

In 1977, China was at a bifurcation point so that Deng "easily" changed the path of China's modernization and enabled hundreds of millions of people to escape poverty in just a few decades. Deng, who received almost no formal education and was famous for having no interest in reading books, knew perhaps little about modern societies (although he did live in France for five years before WWII, where he formed a vision of the society that would be right for China later on).

America, by contrast, is structurally stable as its internal relations, rules, and interests among groups are so closely interconnected that it is difficult to analyze even each sub-system, not to say the entire organ. The traditional solution of free markets has worked relatively successfully for China in the last few decades but would not work for the current American economy, dominated as it is by monopolies, oligopolies, manipulated information (fake news at all levels of society and even within the family), and powerful state governments and national government. "My fellow Americans, we are and always will be a nation of immigrants. We were strangers once, too." (Barack Obama, 1961–). People from miscellaneous races may live as strangers to each other over centuries in the same society. America has never offered a social environment for assimilation.

America is founded on the principle "[that] all men are created equal, that they are endowed by their Creator with certain unalienable Rights, that among these are Life, Liberty and the pursuit of Happiness." New people, for instance the Chinese, were permitted to enter but had no right to become citizens owing to the Greece-based mentality, till America wanted a friend in East Asia. One might wonder about how one enjoys the right to pursue happiness in a society where discrimination on the basis of skin color is widespread for the economic benefit of the dominant group.

When the world was largely separated, physically and mentally and spiritually isolated from each other, people outside perceived America as a land where one could realize beautiful dreams. As the world has been rapidly connected due to (largely) American innovations and power, and people of motley cultures immigrated in the last several decades, people around the globe know more about what has been happening within America. Modern economic theory proves that free competition with profit maximization may either enlarge or reduce gaps in income and wealth among distinct groups under a variety of conditions.

American political equality implies that all people are equal as persons before the law. Everyone is politically a first-class citizen. Nevertheless, this does not betoken that people are socially and economically equal. On the contrary, economic conditions and social status have become further divided in recent years. This occurs especially with technological change and rich-biased institutions. In America, wealth ownership brings more than economic benefits. Ownership of wealth confers direct or indirect political influence, for instance, through lobbying, private funding of research and policy institutes, and campaign financing.

Marilyn Monroe (1926–1961) perceived the economic priorities of females more correctly than modern economists who are good at manipulating statistical data. She said, "When you don't have any money, the problem is food. When you have money, it's sex. When you have both, it's health." The economist has little idea about sex, but the actress knew that human preference is dependent on economic conditions. Economists traditionally treat preferences as invariant irrespective of whether one's life is full of great variety or not.

Monroe did not include power in her concept of the necessities of life as she did not need to explicitly know it. She got it, as Lao Zi says, by standing quietly somewhere. For a male scholar, beauty is truth and vice versa; for a successful businessman, beauty is money and vice versa. For people who have children and work at low-paying jobs, higher education costs for children are unbearably high.

Desires for sex can be satisfied within a system emphasizing individualism and market mechanisms, due to the principles of consumption and supply. Without a sex partner, life may not be so intolerable for many modern people in metropolitan areas. But food is necessary for everyone. Health is expensive and health care can cost dearly. Great America has major problems solving issues related to food, health care, and education — basic human rights in any decent human society — for poor families.

It is imperative to see the dynamics of a nation's rise and differences in living conditions and wealth between heterogeneous groups of people. Issues related to economic growth and distribution are the main concerns of classical economists such as Ricardo and Marx. But there are only a few rigorous theories about the interdependence between endogenous savings and income and wealth distribution. Socialists maintain that governments should act to secure equal distribution of income and wealth. But aspirations for socialist equality result in ubiquitous poverty. The leading socialist economies did reduce income inequality dramatically and provide a universal right to education and health care, but in the end they had to carry out economic reforms by applying market mechanisms. There could be income egalitarianism which requires equal incomes among individuals; welfare egalitarianism which demands equal welfare levels; classical utilitarianism which looks for equal utility for all; and pure libertarianism which asks for equality with respect to an entire class of rights and liberties. It is known that Malthus (who was concerned with the dynamics of a supply-driven economy) held that redistribution from the rich to the poor may neither benefit the poor nor make the rich richer. By redistributing income from the rich to the poor, the savings rate of the economy tends to decrease, thus reducing capital accumulation.

In contrast to Malthus (1798), Keynes (who was concerned with a demand-driven economy) was of the opinion that redistributive policies would benefit the poor and would not harm the rich. By redistributing income, the savings rate of the economy tends to be decreased, thus raising the level of aggregate demand in the economy. The economic performance of the system will be improved. Hayek (1991) brought another perspective: "But the abolition of absolute poverty is not helped by the endeavour to achieve 'social justice'; in fact, in many of the countries in which absolute poverty is still an acute pain, the concern with 'social justice' has become one of the greatest obstacles to the elimination of poverty."

There are many other studies on the relationships between redistribution and development in economic literature. My general economic theory gives a more comprehensive approach to the issue than any traditional theory (Zhang, 2020). The concept of equality is multifaceted and often ambiguous. It can take diverse forms and apply to legal, political, moral, and economic domains. A society has strongly egalitarian attitudes toward some matters and inegalitarian attitudes towards others. It is reasonable to expect, at least from the mathematical equations of civilizations built upon the invariant human nature, the problems of inequality that America have accumulated and have not yet solved have become, steadily and gradually, more deeply rooted in the system.

Household income is an important indicator of social class in American society. Another important indicator is education. The two variables do not always reflect perceived class. Class involves multiple determents. Social classes overlap because of blurred boundaries. According to Gilbert (2002), American social structure is grouped into 6 classes. Capitalist class (1%) consists of typically top-level executives, high-rung politicians, heirs, and Ivy League education common. Upper middle class (15%) consists of highly-educated, most commonly salaried, professionals and middle management with large work autonomy. Lower middle class (30%) consists of semi-professionals and craftsmen with a roughly average standard of living. Most are white-collar and have some college education. Working class (30%) are typically clerical and most blue-collar workers engaged in highly routinized work. They received high school education. Working poor class (13%) work in service sector or are low-rung clerical and some blue-collar workers. They have some high school education. They have high economic insecurity and risk of poverty. The underclass (12%) has limited or no participation in the labor force. They are strongly reliant on government transfers. There are other classifications of social structure. The proportions vary nationally and inter-regionally over time.

Since the 1980s relative poverty rates in America have been higher than those of other wealthy economies. Extreme poverty, which is defined in the U.S. as a household living on less than $2 per day before government benefits, reached 1.5 million households with 2.8 million children in 2011, doubling the level in 1996. As of 2015, 44% of children in America lived with low-income families. The number-in-poverty rate during the period of 1959 to 2016 is given in Figure 2.9. It is reported that the poverty rate in 2019 was 10.5%, down 1.3% from 11.8 in 2018. Immigrant America tends to have stress on economic and social successes through one's own action. As data demonstrate, those without the means to win out legitimately tend to violate the rule of the game. Citizens know the right to participate equally in the choice of elected representatives, but they have also gradually recognized that they have little opportunity to move upwards, either socially or economically.

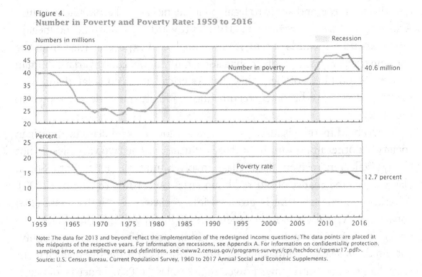

Figure 4.
Number in Poverty and Poverty Rate: 1959 to 2016

Note: The data for 2013 and beyond reflect the implementation of the redesigned income questions. The data points are placed at the midpoints of the respective years. For information on recessions, see Appendix A. For information on confidentiality protection, sampling error, nonsampling error, and definitions, see <www2.census.gov/programs-surveys/cps/techdocs/cpsmar17.pdf>.
Source: U.S. Census Bureau, Current Population Survey, 1960 to 2017 Annual Social and Economic Supplements.

Figure 2.9 Poverty and Poverty Rate of America, 1959–2016

2.7 Growth, Consumption, and Saving

> When I look at what the world does and where people nowadays believe they can find happiness, I am not sure that that is true happiness. The happiness of these ordinary people seems to consist in slavishly imitating the majority, as if this were their only choice.
>
> Zhuangzi (369–295 BC)

Emerson (1803–1882) warns: "A man in debt is so far a slave." A man in a large debt may be great masters of many in modern world. A nation in big debt may earn some comparative advantage in international relations.

America has so large debts to nations that they often worry about bankruptcy of the government of the greatest economy on the earth.

America is well known as a happy country in the sense as exposed by Hermann Hesse (1877–1962): "To be able to throw one's self away for the sake of a moment, to be able to sacrifice years for a woman's smile — that is happiness." The new culture of heterogeneous populations with great power and wealth has no opportunity to be melancholy. It just kicks off its "usual process" (as a great power in the middle of a cyclical process) of learning how to express its decline owing to other's unfair and improper behavior.

In *Essays in Persuasion*, Keynes applied economic principles to foresee the future: "for the first time since his creation man will be faced with his ... permanent problem — how to use his freedom from pressing economic cares, how to occupy the leisure, which science and compound interest will have won for him, to live wisely and agreeably and well." (Galbraith, 1972:339). Reilly (1974) foresaw the current status of America: "It is paradoxical that when man through scientific knowledge has become too efficient in securing with little effort his basic necessities of life, he becomes deadly serious and looks nostalgically at the creative centuries of the past when he still had time and detachment for play and creativity."

Alexis de Tocqueville made a well-known analysis of the relationship between character and society in America in the 1830s in *Democracy in America*. He envisaged that some aspects of American individualism would tend to isolate Americans one from another. A citizen might withdraw himself from the mass of his fellows, believing that destiny is in one's own hands. This aspect of individualism would undermine public virtue. But American history does not show that individualist isolation is a serious American dilemma. Americans hail individualism as a desirable social principle. They had faith that individualism would liberate men from the Old World. McClosky and Zaller (1984:107) sketched the traditional American character: "'At the heart of the doctrine ... of the Protestant ethic ... are two normative injunctions: one should work zealously, dutifully, and methodically in order to avoid sin and demonstrate one's worth; and one should acquire good habits such as frugality, sobriety, humility, and simplicity in conduct in order to demonstrate one's capacity for self-restraint, self-denial, and devotion to one's calling and one's God. As Weber observes, the Protestant ethic lent, in effect, the rationale by which acquisitiveness could be reconciled with restraint."

Competitive acquisition to attain social status manifests strongly in America. Immigrants are proud to demonstrate their new housing conditions, luxury cars, resorts visited, particular designer labels, the beauty of their wives, the successes of their husbands, the amount and quality of their children's education, the prices of wines, the breeds of pets, and the like. This is the American way to present themselves to society. In *The Theory of the Leisure Class*, Veblen (1899) coined the phrase "conspicuous consumption" to sketch the phenomenon. Mainland China is having the same fever as a reasonable stage of social and economic evolution. According to Veblen, in affluent societies, people establish social position through spending. Men display their incomes to the outside world through the conspicuous display of wealth and leisure, and even wives. The rich use conspicuous consumption to secure a place in the social hierarchy. The mass prosperity resulted in convergence among consumers' acquisition and purchasing patterns (Schor, 1998). Americans are often said to express their individuality, their desire to prevail over their fellows and to better their lives through conspicuous consumption. The individualistic energy of liberal society, which was manifested in entrepreneurship, has been directed into the prodigious consumption of goods and services.

While the average American's buying patterns become more ostentatious (Stanley and Danko, 1996), most millionaires are inclined to be less showy and more frugal. The rich have no need to display, which the poor are eager to demonstrate even by purchasing. Brogan (1941:116-7) elucidates: "It is only an apparent contradiction in terms to assert that the fundamental democratic and egalitarian character of American life is demonstrated by the ingenuity and persistence shown in inventing marks of difference and symbols of superiority.

In a truly class-conscious and caste-dominated society, the marks of difference are universally recognized even if resented. In America, they must be stressed or they might easily be forgotten, and they must be added to, as the old standards of distinction cease to serve their purpose. Apart from the simple economic criterion of conspicuous display, there are no generally accepted marks of social difference in America." Blaise Pascal (1623–1662) commented on how men may feel: "All men's miseries derive from not being able to sit in a quiet room alone.... All human evil comes from a single cause, man's inability to sit still in a room."

Mauk and Oakland (1997) distinguished the American civilization by three major cultures, which may conflict with each other and operate on levels of idealism or pragmatism. The ethnic culture is built on Native-American civilization, Black slavery, and immigration, which express human diversity. The political culture unites the people under American ideals such as egalitarianism, morality, and patriotism. The economic and consumer culture is driven by corporate and individual competition and encourages the consumption of goods and services. American capitalism rewards individuals with imagination, talent, and industriousness and encourages accumulation of material wealth.

Even since colonial times, American civil self-identification has been characterized by the dignity of work and of personal achievement, and the contempt for aristocratic idleness (Shklar, 1995). Americans had faith in that social right includes the right to have the opportunity to work and to be paid properly for one's work. This value distinguishes the United States from the European past. After the end of its involvement in WWII, in August 1945, the United States emerged as the economic colossus of the entire world. Its superiority in industry, science, and affluence made its people to feel living in the American century.

From WWII until the 1960s, the American economy went through rapid structural transformation. The Korean War (25 June 1950—27 July 1953) lent the occasion for a renewed surge of US economic expansion. The economic expansion lasted until 1960. By then, the GNP had more than doubled, and real GNP had risen nearly two thirds over the 1945 level (Hughes and Cain, 1998:521).

It can be expected that in a country of multi-racial immigrants without any official religion, wealth and conspicuous consumption symbolize social status. Manson (1981:80) points out: "Wealth and privilege have never been greatly resented in the United States but have often stimulated those less fortunate to emulate the successful. Wealthy families have in consequence enjoyed a considerable status and prestige which has often been absent in other societies. Paradoxically, the very great emphasis placed on equality as a fundamental of American society may have produced a great respect for money and for wealth which can still be observed today. Precisely as a result of the stress laid on the need for equality of treatment and of opportunity, Americans were (and are) often more status conscious than those who lived in the more aristocratic societies of Europe."

Paul Samuelson (1915–2009) reminisced: "American society was economically ill-run in the 1980s. Our society has been on a consumption binge. If the American people had a town meeting and said, 'What do we care about posterity?' Posterity hasn't done anything for us; we're going to whoop it up now,' that is a rational judgment. But nobody ever did that." In each rational economy, after a short period of prosperity with a secure future, quite a high proportion of people feel like they can spend like there is no tomorrow. It is not typically American. Many consumers in Japan's 1980s, Singapore's

2000s, and contemporary mainland China devoted all available income to spending.

Consumer expenditures together with government encouragements, and scale and scope economies, like Keynesianism teaches, buttress virtuous cycles of economic development: consumption encourages production and enhances productivity, people get more income, and processes are continued infinitely. This linear vision of economic change is reflected in conscious or unconscious decisions regarding spending.

American consumers have never disappointed the expectations of the national economy since the end of WWII.

Figure 2.10 plots the Gross National Savings Rates of GDP of the U.S., Japan, and China for the period of 1980 to 2019. The savings rate is the ratio of gross national savings in current local currency and GDP in current local currency. Gross national savings is gross disposable income less final consumption expenditure after making adjustment for pension funds.

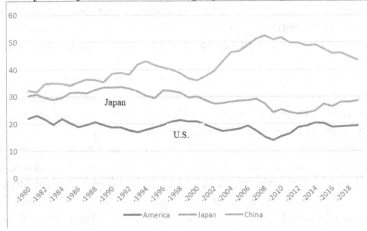

Figure 2.10 Gross National Saving Rates of U.S., Japan, and China, 1980–2018

Household saving behavior is reflected in personal saving rate. Figure 2.11 exhibits dynamics of personal saving rate — the ratio saved by individuals or families to the disposable income — of the United States, 1960—2019. In recent years, American households save more out of their disposable income. Except some determinants for this tendency, an important factor is often mentioned. As income and wealth distribution is enlarged, the poor has nothing to save and the rich has too much to be consumed. For instance, in 2018 over 10% of American adults would be unable to cover $400 emergency expense. The rich have taken a greater share of national income, implying increases in the national average saving rate. Moreover, American households are very uncertain about the future. Domestic rapid automation, global rivalry, and trade wars worry Americans.

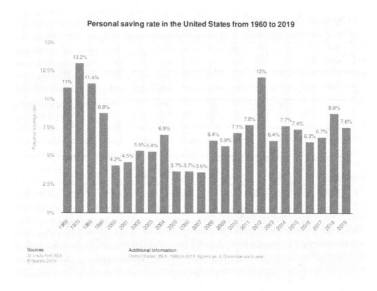

Figure 2.11 Dynamics of Personal Saving Behavior in America, 1960–2019

Conspicuous consumption speeds up economic growth by encouraging consumption and enhancing human capital, makes people feel happy and pleasant, forgetting potential future woes and brandishing their "meanings of life". But like anything valuable and pleasant, the positive impact of conspicuous consumption can be felt, but how long it lasts is determined by assorted combinations of conditions, as demonstrated in my general economic theory.

2.8 Education and Its Role in Enriching and Empowering People

There being instruction, there will be no distinction of classes. (15:39)

In antiquity men undertook learning for the sake of self-improvement; today people undertake learning for the sake of others.

Xun Zi (298–238 BC, 1:10)

"Common sense is judgement without reflection, shared by an entire class, an entire nation, or entire human race." Giambattista Vico (1668–1744). The American dream has been one such global signal accepted without reflection and examination. Its attractiveness has seldom been doubted. Nevertheless, the term has meant different things over time (Mills, 1951; Johnson, 2006; Ludwig, 2020; Mayfield, 2020). The principles of the American dream were proliferated from the earliest British settlers. The term was coined by the early 1930s. It essentially refers to equal opportunity for one to achieve one's aspirations, regardless of background. It also implies that the American social system functions as a meritocracy and highly values the powers and capabilities of the individual. Social mobility is understood to be largely determined by personal achievement. In *Facing Up to the American Dream*, Hochschild (1995) summed up the dream as a set of deeply held beliefs. The beliefs justify social status and influence the social and economic structure.

It is often warned that intergenerational wealth inequalities have a tendency to break the American dream. People born rich have many advantages not available for those starting life in poverty (Putnam, 2016). Children born into miserable conditions have few opportunities to achieve upward social mobility. A main feature of the American dream — that talent and diligence lead to success — is no longer true.

Americans have trusted that education would be the leveler, leading the way to democratic equality. Thomas Jefferson (1743–1826) stated: "No people can be both ignorant and free." But after so many years of expansion many Americans have remained confidently ignorant. It did not matter so much, until now, as most Americans could have shared the enlarging pie, even not equally proportionally among them. The Founding Fathers held that universal public education is essential to producing an informed citizenry on which a democracy depends. Schooling would facilitate people to discover natural merit in citizens and create an elite to defend the republic from tyranny. By the time of the Civil War (1861–1865), every state had tax-supported, free elementary schools, even though most teachers were not well trained, and most children went to school only sporadically if at all. Most parents still needed their children's work or wages to sustain family. By 1819, the Supreme Court differentiated public and private colleges and freed private institutions of higher learning from state control. During the Civil War, the Land Grant College Act started the federal government's involvement in public higher education, giving each state huge land areas to be used for the benefit of higher education. The Act promoted the higher education of larger numbers of students and called for college-level courses in agriculture, technical and industrial subjects. African Americans and women were first admitted to (certain) colleges before the Civil War.

Tocqueville (1835:158) noted: "Anyone trying to find out how enlightened the Anglo-Americans are is liable to see the same phenomenon from two distinct angles. If his attention is concentrated on the learned, he will be astonished how few they are; but if he looks at the uneducated, he will think the Americans the most enlightened people in the world." He asserted (1835:25) that the American people pursue the study of science in the same spirit as trade, and they only treasure matters of immediate and recognized practical applications. There was little spirit of pursuing knowledge for the sake of knowledge. They learn for the sake of some specified and profitable objectives.

Tocqueville contemplated the cultural formation as a consequence of the fact that there were few rich families in America, and everyone had to work at an early age. Before WWII, Americans could afford to indulge in general education only in the earliest years, and then, by the time curiosity began to meet with intellectual maturity, they had to start to work. When one had a taste for study, one had no means for the pursuit; when one had means and time for study, the taste had disappeared. Tocqueville (1835:25) concluded: "So there is no class in America in which a taste for intellectual pleasures is transmitted with hereditary wealth and leisure and which holds the labors of the mind in esteem."

In fields of economics, America has collected the most Nobel prizes. Most of these Nobel prize winners are communicative, talky, and well-off. They share similar main characters and make efforts in distinguishing themselves in refined matters like modern Seoul and Shanghai girls who make great efforts to build the mainstream body and face and distinguish themselves by expensive plastic surgeries in a catch-as-catch-can fashion. There is neither lasting name in economics nor lasting beauty in the long term.

"Man is born similar, but practice makes them divergent," Confucius believed. If the social environment is similar, the society will produce similar men. One is born into the historical flow of time. As the Chinese curse says: "May you live in interesting times." China is a civilization where social mobility has been largely determined by education for many centuries.

The traditional Confucian perspective of social life is illustrated by Confucius (16:9): "Those who are born with the possession of knowledge are the highest class of men. Those who learn, and so readily get possession of knowledge, are the next. Those who learn after they meet with difficulties are another class next to these. As to those who meet with difficulties and yet do not learn — they are the lowest of the people." When he went to Wei,

Confucius observed, "How numerous are the people!" His disciple asked him what more should be done for the people. He said: "Enrich them." And what then? "Teach them." The history of American economic development experienced similar pattern: first growth with little education and then more education. Purposes and contents of education vary in different societies.

In *The Power Elite*, Mills (1956) catechizes the dominant view that America had become a relatively classless and pluralistic society and that power was relatively equally shared by the people through their political parties and public opinion. He scrutinized the social backgrounds and career paths of the people in the highest positions in the corporations, the executive branch of the federal government, and the military. He pinpointed out that almost all the members of this "power elite" were white Christian males, most coming from the upper third of the income and occupational pyramids. Zweigenhaft and Domhoff (1991:140) pointed out that being White and poor had more positive consequences than being Black and poor. Nevertheless, within the middle ranges of corporations and government, a good education had a greater short-term payoff for a Black than for a White person. Lind (1996:1941) argued that the contemporary American White class benefits more than middle-class Black and Hispanic Americans from adopting the racial preference policies of multicultural America. Zweigenhaft and Domhoff (1998) analyzed how the power elite has been distributed among gender, ethnicity, race, sexual orientation, and social class. They researched the social, educational, and occupational backgrounds of the leaders of the three major institutional hierarchies in postwar America — the corporations, the executive branch of the federal government, and the military. They identified some general characteristics of the power elite: (1) It had considerable diversity with white Christian males as the core group; (2) The top position tended to be obtained by those with high social origins; (3) Newcomers were willing to show their loyalty to the prevailing values structure; (4) Boards of large mingled with multiple races, even though women, Blacks, Latinos, and Asian Americans were all underrepresented.

Like in the rest of American society, discrimination is conducted in American higher education (e.g., Wechsler, 1984; Thelin, 2019). For instance, Jews were once rationed in number in permission to be recruited into colleges. This is similar for other people of color in different periods of American history. America's higher education was initiated with Harvard College in 1636, focusing on training young men for the ministry. It was named after an early benefactor. Most of early colleges were established mainly for training ministers. They followed the styles of Oxford and Cambridge Universities as well as Scottish universities. Yale College was founded in 1701, with the initial purpose to train orthodox ministers. Early universities were small and limited to undergraduate curriculum. Students learned Greek, Latin, geometry, ancient history, logic, ethics, and rhetoric. Like any other countries' education, exact repetition was evaluated, and originality and creativity were neglected. But tuition was low, and scholarships were rarely available. Students were mostly sons of clergymen. Most of them became ministers, lawyers, or teachers. From the 1820s, Greek and Latin were started to be gradually replaced by modern languages. From the 19th century colleges were upgraded towards modern universities. Higher education played a significant role in economic structural change and occupational shifts. During the 19th century elite colleges were exclusive and made little contribution to upward social mobility. They focused on educating children of wealthy families, ministers, and a few others. Soon after WWII, the American system of higher education has dominated higher education in the world, with great money, talent, scholarly esteem, and academic performances. Figure 2.12 plots the dynamics of number of higher education students in America.

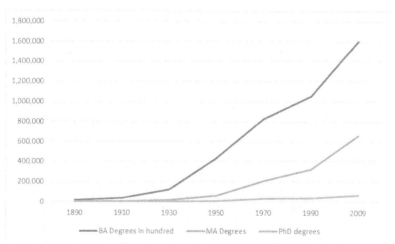

Figure 2.12 College Degrees Awarded in US, 1987–2009

The United States attained its superpower position by its ability to turn knowledge into markets and military advantages. From the 1870s, the Americans established a series of institutions to compete Europe's economic, scientific, and technological leadership. These new institutions include research universities such as Johns Hopkins University (founded in 1876) and the University of Chicago (1892), colleges and agricultural stations, specialized institutions of technology, and corporate laboratories. American higher education was dramatically spread after WWII. In 1944, Congress passed the Servicemen's Readjustment Act to ease the return of war veterans to civil life. Under the Act, the federal government paid tuition and living costs for veterans enrolled in programs of higher education and directly funded the expansion of study programs for the first time. Within two years, half the people in college were veterans. By 1971 when the program was completed, nearly 2.5 million veterans had obtained higher education. By then, a high proportion of the population had received higher education. The federal government also widened its role in public education. The National Defense Education Act in 1958 encouraged research and university programs in science and technology. The federal government handed over money to research institutions and universities and loans to college students. In 1954, the Supreme Court ended the principle of separate-but-equal educational facilities for Blacks and Whites. In 1955 the Court required that public school districts all over the nation had to present plans for achieving racial balances in their schools. At the beginning of the 20th century, very low proportion of American youth attended college. The United States had only 25,000 faculty and staff and 9,300 graduate students. There were fewer than a thousand colleges and universities; and only 38 institutions offered doctoral degrees. By the early 1990s, the number of students attending college had grown more than 40-fold; the faculty was 35 times as large; the number of institutions was multiplied by four; number of graduates was as many as 160 times in the beginning of the 20th century.

John Dewey (1859–1952), the American philosopher and educator, popularized philosophical pragmatism which is the main characteristic of American education. He encourages a broad-based system of practical experience. His acclaimed book *Democracy and Education* argues for education as a necessity of life and for maintaining America's continuous existence. In a stabilized society, education is conducted for the purpose of continuing established customs, traditions, and behavior. Young people were taught to accurately follow predetermined roles and habits. In a progressive democratic society like America, Dewey argued, the society has not and should not follow predetermined roles and habits. To be progressive is to search what is good for the society and no one can determine what is good for the society beforehand. Education should be aimed at making progresses. It is the process, not only the achieved state that matter in education. Education to render the student capacity of further improvement. Students should be cultivated with spirit of freedom and be taught about how to develop active qualities of initiative, independence, and resourcefulness. Dewey did not believe that human improvement was the unfolding of latent powers from within and the formation of such powers from without. Education is thus a reconstruction of experience, which adds to the meaning of experience and increases one's ability to direct the course of subsequent experience. Experience is referred to the interaction of the self with its environment. Dewey deemed growth as using the scientific method to solve questions.

Kallen (1970:237–238) related early American education in 1924: "aims not at truth, but at conformity. In the grade schools it is a regimentation of the mind; in the institutions of the higher learning it is directly a servant of the interests.... 'America has a body and no soul,' therefore many professors and no scholars." That kind of education product is what America needed, even though free education and modern ideals of education were already available in Europe. American universities supplied what American societies needed, like in Japan and China.

"He migrates," Kallen (1970:236) pointed out in 1924, "to escape the oppression of the landlord at home only to come under the oppression of the industrialist abroad. He performs the hard and 'dirty' work of the country in mine and mill under impossible conditions. When he seeks to improve these conditions he is hounded and denounced. The phase 'likely to become a public charge' is held over his head and is used to compel his acquiescence in a condition no better than peonage, without right even to an opinion unacceptable to authority." He was of the opinion that if the immigrant had become domiciled in the United States, he was fortunate if he was not categorized as a racial minority like the Oriental. If he was Oriental and exhibited any sign of power or competency in rivalry with the racial majority, he would be subjected to racial discrimination. The law had not been designed to correct racial prejudice.

The academic sector was a training factory. As America was entering a fast industrializing stage, universities needed to supply creative and highly disciplined types of people. Creativity is needed in society and intellectually discipline is required for modern workers. "This is the difference between slavery and freedom. The slave must do what his superior orders him to do, but the free citizen — and this is what freedom means — is in a position to choose his own way of life." (Ludwig von Mises, 1881–1973).

A non-depressed environment is necessary for bringing up effective workers. It is expected that American universities would conduct education as fair as possible as this is way for the society to train and pick up the talented from the human capital reservoir of miscellaneous races. Nevertheless, as almost all national wealth is controlled by a few rich families and highly paid jobs by a few giant companies in present America, most American people might not benefit much from receiving higher education as education fees are high. Moreover, many students in the best America universities are foreign-born, national factories of human capital are facing with new global rivalry. American universities have "equipped" Chinese societies as many of smart and productive types of America-educated Chinese tend to find jobs in Chinese-dominated societies.

2.9 Science and Technology in National Development

> Learning without thought is labor lost; thought without learning is perilous.
>
> Confucius (551–479 BC)

Stephen Hawking (1942–2018) found "far greater enthusiasm for science in America than here in Britain. There is more enthusiasm for everything in America." America's technological achievements have dominated the world almost one hundred years, even though America were not so successful in producing grand thinkers and highly creative scientists reputed for high creativity and broad knowledge. Many of influential American intellectuals are born outside America. They got basic training, basic vision, basic values, and creative ideas before they became American citizen. America has been a grand field for academic game. The American academic world has flourished with detailed division of academic disciplines, professionalism, and profit-oriented motivations. The vitality of a modern society is reflected in the manifestation of the values and attitudes of its leaders, public officials, entrepreneurs, engineers, and workers. In *An Enquiry Concerning Human Understanding*, the David Hume (1711–1776) defined a chief aim of the science of man is "to discover the constant and universal principles of human nature, by showing men in all varieties of circumstances and situations, and furnishing us with materials, from which we may form our observations, and become acquainted with the regular springs of human action and behavior." The United States has a plenty of academic institutions that can boast of more than a century of scientific discovery and innovation. Vast campuses, the finest and most convenient libraries in the world, and highest pays have attracted the best brains on the earth to sustain the American superiority in higher education and research. Laboratories and research centers from which scientists born in various parts and cultures of the world have won the most Nobel Prizes in science. The United States is a global center of education and research. Best students and researchers from the world come to the United States to enjoy the most favorable conditions for education and research. Like processes in socioeconomic changes, there may be decreasing returns to scale after early stage of increasing stages.

Innovations for improving productivities are encouraged in America's free markets. The founding father Franklin is well known for his scientific knowledge and innovative activities. Oscar Wilde (1854–1900) pored over the difference between England and America: "In England, an inventor is regarded almost as a crazy man, and in too many instances, invention ends in disappointment and poverty. In America, an inventor is honored, help is forthcoming, and exercise of ingenuity, the application of science to the work of man, is there the shortest road to wealth." Early white immigrants mostly belonged to low classes and did not receive proper education in Europe. There was not much science in early America as new arrivals were busy with farming and had little leisure for abstract intellectual training and thinking.

Before the middle 19th century, American scholars mainly followed the breakthroughs and thought of Europe. There are great American innovations, such as the Franklin stove, Whitney's cotton gin, Fulton's steamship, Edison's electric light, and the Bell telephone, which have shaped the world. American great achievements in science and technology are uncountable.

Europeans started innovations as a source of profit. America has applied the practice extensively. In recent decades East Asians have valued originality and started innovative activities for growth and survival in global markets. Once social order is maintained and profits from innovation are secured, societies are innovative because man is born both profit-oriented and capable of innovation. European immigrants inherited European tradition in science and technology. American people are creative in almost all fields in science, technology, mathematics, medicine, art, literature, and fashion with rich natural resources and great profits. America has emerged as the superpower after WWII not only due to its abundance of natural resources and flood of new immigrants, but largely owing to its successes in science and technology. Dominant positions in various fields of technology have kept the country as the leading producer as well as the most confident consumer. Young Americans have a higher probability of getting a higher education than those of any other nation.

America made innovations in areas of cars, aircrafts, computers, and antibiotics that are globally used today. These technological advances are closely related to social change (e.g., Harrington, 2008; Ede, 2019; Stein, 2019). Cowan and Hersch (2017) study interdependence between technological change, American society, and American geography. America excelled in applied sciences and technologies. The great Edison had more than a thousand inventions created to his name. His inventions equipped millions of homes with electric lighting. The well-known Wright brothers successfully flied the first heavier-than-air, mechanically propelled airplane, on December 17, 1903. An invention called transistor in Bell Laboratories in 1947 would usher in the information age. The transistor and the integrated circuit invented 10 years later made it possible for scientists to package enormous amounts of electronics into tiny containers. This made a book-sized computer to outperform huge computers of the 1960s. America is known for its capacity of attracting talented scientists. Bell came to America from Scotland in 1872, developed and patented the telephone and other inventions. Steinmetz from Germany in 1889 created alternating-current electric systems at General Electric Company. There are other great scientists who came to America in the 19ᵗʰ century and made influential innovations, such as Vladimir Zworykin from Russia, the Serbian Nikola Tesla. By the early 1890s, the global center of science research had been Europe. From the 1920s onwards, America started to receive scientific immigration in large number. Many of these were Jewish, especially from Germany and Italy. America got the best physical talents from Europe, including Albert Einstein in 1933, Enrico Fermi from Italy in 1938, and Niels Bohr, Victor Weisskopf, and Eugene Wigner. Those "giant immigrants" made scientific and technological breakthroughs. They helped America to build an unrivaled scientific juggernaut during WWII. When WWII ended, America capitalized Nazi research. After WWII, America was left an incontestable position as global scientific leadership. The cold war made the American government to signify pure research, especially theoretical physics. Science and technology helped a rapid expansion of American industry. Fast economic progress laid economic foundation for investment in science and technology. The US government soon became the largest supporter of basic and applied scientific research. American scientists were well equipped with best research facilities in the world. It gained many talented people in all fields from countries where people could move to America during the Cold War. These immigrant and American scientists first succeeded in nuclear fission. From 1901 to 1950, American scientists won the Nobel Prize in science less than Europe (even one country Germany got more). But since 1950, Americans have won almost half of the Nobel Prizes in science. Many of these American winners were born outside America. Even in recent years, all the American Nobel Prize winners were not born in America in some years. Its super money in research funds even attracted talented Japanese to do research in America. It is the greatest country to do natural sciences with high spirits of playfulness. But there are not many intellectually interesting things, except popular books and technical/mathematical modelling, occur in fields of philosophy, social sciences, and economics, which are not profitable and not so playful for talented American immigrants. China is also making great progresses in similar fields with playfulness and profitability (and political certainty).

American inventions have transformed how people live, work, study, communicate, and do research not only in America, but also in every part of the earth. Before WWII, the federal government was not deeply involved with promoting science and technology. During the war, the government built a close relation with science. After the war, the government decided to strongly support science and technology. America soon established the most advanced science and technology system, playing the leading role in the world. The preeminence has been supported by the huge investment and immigrants of the highly talented. America has made progresses in an endless list of invention and innovation after WWII. Figure 2.13 plots the shifts of the government budget for R&D in the United States during the period of 1953 to 2013. During the period, the government allocated 4 to 5% of the federal budget for all R&D activities and about 2% for non-defense R&D. From the figure one sees why America has been the most advanced medical research systems. Nevertheless, the best medical care system, like many good things, is inaccessible to many of American people as demonstrated during the COVID-19 pandemic.

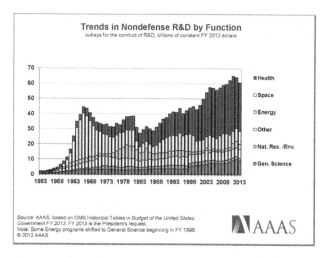

Figure 2.13 The Government Budget for R&D in the United States, 1953–2013

R&D is financed both by government and the private sector. Firms carry out R&D to go ahead in their products and win against their domestic and international competitors. Government R&D conducts general research and "crowds in" private firms as knowledge and research results can be transferred through multifarious channels. Government's R&D can enhance productivities of the whole society. Figure 2.14 plots the expenditures of the two greatest economies on R&D. The figure explains why China is catching up both in firms-based technologies and nation-level projects in space and infrastructures. As the two countries' GDP are approaching and expenditure structures are similar, rivalry between the two should evolve severe in many fields, especially because China has many talented people (many of them received higher education in America) and workers are energetic and lowly (with regards to America) paid. Europe has been already fully recovered from WWII and is competitive with America in all fields. Japan and the four tigers are technologically advanced in multifarious fields. Many other countries are advancing in different fields in miscellaneous areas, with America as the main target to serve or even to compete with. All these economies make America strong as well as weaken the American superpower position in one way or another.

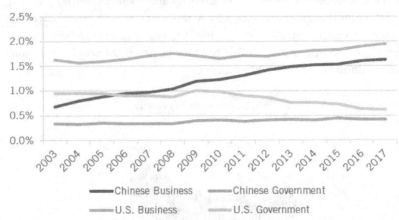

Figure 2.14 Convergences of R&D Structure Between America and China
https://itif.org/publications/2019/08/12/federal-support-rd-continues-its-ignominious-slide

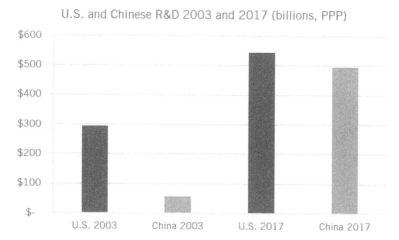

Figure 2.15 China is Catching up America in Total R&D Expenditures
https://itif.org/publications/2019/08/12/federal-support-rd-continues-its-
ignominious-slide

China is catching up America in total R&D expenditures as illustrated
in Figure 2.15. In 2020, China already surpassed America in R&D spending.

3. Power with Democracy

> When the multitude hates a man, it is necessary to examine the case. When the multitude likes a man, it is necessary to examine the case.
>
> Confucius (551–479 BC, 15:28)

> Those who are right do not argue. Those who argue are not right.
>
> Lao Zi (6th –4th BC?)

Friedrich Nietzsche (1844–1900) described common pattern of human behavior: "Many are stubborn in pursuit of the path they have chosen, few in pursuit of the goal." To persistently pursue a rationally solid goal of "high life" does not lead to material awards and is not profitable. It is often not profitable, and even "suicidal" to be deeply and genuinely concerned with man's nature and collective behavior of human societies as man, by nature, is a self-deceptive social animal. Mankind's history is characterized by murdering, torturing, and neglecting original and talented thinkers on man and human societies. Society is a game field kept together with rule of game. An original and talented thinker may reveal meaninglessness of the game and point out more effective directions for improvement. The dominant players (such as the dictator, the Party, the rich, the elite, or the most powerful) tend to forbid free thinkers to survive with freedom as new thought might endanger his power and devaluate his falsified meaningfulness of life.

Wealth, power, and sex are the key observable connectors of human networks. To further the national glory, or to make America great again, would be a matter of combining the three variables in such a way that the nation was both rich and enjoyed a tolerable, if not fair, distribution of wealth. America nominally creates, distributes, and utilizes the three variables under market mechanisms (when it comes to wealth), a democratic structure (when it comes to power), and romanticism and freedom (for sexual relations). The three variables are mutually entangled. For instance, political power, one of many kinds of power, is not always easy to trace because there are many hidden powerful persons and untold motivations and mechanisms within the political system. Democracy has no clear link to morality and justice. It is a game of creating, distributing, and applying political power. As a rule, it is neither universal nor lasting.

In America all adult citizens, including the very high percentage who have no interest in politics at all and/or have little knowledge of history and society, can participate in the vote for President. This is akin to allowing the public to appoint cancer experts, on the basis of each candidate's self-promotion, fake information, telegenic appearance, and professional market analysis, test polls, campaign strategists and most of all the backing by wealthy sponsors who make possible all the fore-going. Among the 100 candidates, one is chosen. The man and the woman on the street have no way of knowing what is real.

This is the history of the American presidency. President Trump has changed America's image in the world owing to global digitalization. In the contemporary world, the American president is no longer a political idol or respectable symbol, at least for the properly cultivated, as he was a few decades ago when the world was so minimally educated, so ill-informed, and so biased.

New technologies imply both the possible introduction and the abolishment of institutions which are more rational, fairer, and more effective. It is necessary to re-examine what are more suitable and useful political institutions in well-connected and well-informed societies. Perhaps there is no need for politicians at all in a future with robots. This is an intellectually challenging task for future generations, if there are still humans in the contemporary sense, in the remote future. A super robot might design a much better management system for the creation, distribution, and consumption of wealth, power, and sex. Currently, American elections are wasteful, futile, and outdated in the light of available technologies and knowledge stock. American presidential election processes would soon be converted into a source of global humor if there is no essential change in the system and if America is still getting the greatest attention as the greatest power.

Man's capacity and efficiency are largely determined by technology. America's technological innovations bring about changes in every aspect of life domestically as well as internationally.

Human beings are different, in shape, size, sex, genetic endowments, abilities, sense of humor, ear for music, intelligence, social sensitivity, health, longevity, strength, athletic prowess, and so on. Jane Austen expresses: "Every savage can dance." The bee builds great architectures. The monkey climbs tree gaily and plays joyfully. The bird has a great variety of sex and sexual relations. The tiger, the lion, the rat, the chicken, the dog, and the cat all have their own ways of coping with the complexity of interdependence between wealth, sex, and power. And human society can theoretically encompass far more varieties than any of these species.

American democracy assumes that political leaders are determined through democratic procedures. Social, economic, and political structures have been constructed for the sake of democracy. In *Politics* (Book V), Aristotle asked: "Now justice is recognized universally as some sort of equality. Justice involves as assignment of things to persons. Equals are entitled to equal things. But here we are met by the important question: equal and unequal in what?" Tocqueville (1835: 238) deems the desire for equality as a motivation for well-being: "A passion for well-being is . . . the most lively of all the emotions aroused or inflamed by equality, and it is a passion shared by all. So this taste for well-being is the most striking and unalterable characteristic of democratic ages." Nevertheless, modern economies with democratic institutions have resulted in great inequalities in wealth and income (and thus access to sexuality and power). Thoreau (1817–1862, 1910:31) stressed: "It is a mistake to suppose that, in a country where the usual evidences of civilisation exist, the condition of a very large body of the inhabitants may not be as degraded as that of savages. I refer to the degraded poor, not now to the degraded rich."

Social evolution is a dynamic interaction of assorted parts. One ideology or a religion may function well in one organic system, but dysfunction in another. A typical example is that democracy works well in Western economies, while it does not work well, at least economically, in India or certain other democratic societies (but India develops a qualified labor force for the West).

In modern times, no country has succeeded in achieving take-off with genuine democracy. The first wave of industrialized economies was associated with colonization and slavery. Japan and the four little tigers developed after World War II under America's protection. China is making progress with socialism with servitude (under the single party). The bureaucratic system is more important than politicians in East Asia's economic systems. A happy and healthy life is a subtle combination of playfulness and rationality. Only lucky country, like lucky person, can maintain a healthy, happy, and long-lived system. A society can seldom keep everyone healthy, happy, and long-lived as human nature implies, even though dream-builders would never stop making up such societies. A great portion of humans support a tiny portion to live healthy, happy, and long-lived lives. It is a common sense for modern educated mind that an absolute equality in income and wealth (without spread education and new technologies) across the globe leads to possible suicide of mankind with unchecked population, used-up resources, and pollution. American greatness has also been bolstered by socialist countries, underdeveloped economies, and democratic underdeveloped economies. Russia played a role of enemy for America's national order and harmony. China dealt with America's garbage and supplied cheap goods for sustaining American low-income peoples' American dreams and helped the rich to be wealthier. India supplied many talented people to U.S. Politically weak economies, like Japan and the four little tigers, bought weapons from and supplied low-cost industrial goods to America. Developing economies smile politically to the superpower without understanding benefits of their own countries.

3.1 The Political Game Between the Democratic and the Republican Party

> Chase after money and security and your heart will never unclench.
> Care about people's approval and you will be their prisoner.
>
> Lao Zi (6th –4th BC?)
>
> Having not and yet affecting to have, empty and yet affecting to be full, straitened and yet affecting to be at ease — it is difficult with such characteristics to have constancy.
>
> Confucius (551–479 BC, 7:26)

The determination of the top power in human societies variegates greatly over history. Even today there are vast discrepant ways in selecting top leaders in the system and leaders in different levels of the system. Monkey, wolf, and lion societies are far fairer than some human societies with regards to this matter (of course, depending on the definition of fairness). Survival of a monkey (lion, ants, bees, or some other community-based animals) community needs a strong leader for the group survival. In history of China, the emperors were numerously killed either by foreign invaders or domestic emulators, while the Japanese monarchy is said to be the oldest continuous hereditary monarchy in the world. The Chinese emperors had absolute power and had to make decisions on many matters, while the Japanese emperors did not have absolute power during most of the hereditary monarchy period. The geography of China implies discontinuation of dynasties. This is similarly true in Europe.

Athenian democracy was developed around the 6th century BC in the Greek city state. This is a basic way of selecting the national leader in Western civilization. The selected leader governed a very small number of people. Since the city size was relatively small and information among the leisure-walking citizens were relatively well fed and salves and women had no right to be involved in democracy, the selected leader by a small number of citizens could deal with social complexity. In Chinese civilization since the first emperor in 221 BC, it is through wars and killing that the top position is earned. Today China has one party instead a single family to govern the country. This is already a great progress within Chinese culture. "The power is out of a barrel of gun" by Chairman Mao is still a slogan in the Chinese Communist Party. For Chinese people, the Party has a "natural right" to do in whatever way the party wants according to its will. This is the main practice of Chinese since the first emperor of Chinese history got the top power in 221 BC.

Deng Xiaoping (1904–1997) epitomized the American political practice: "The United States brags about its political system, but the President says one thing during the election, something else when he takes office, something else at midterm and something else when he leaves." The president could serve the country maximum 8 years. A president might love to spend public money as much as to establish his own reputation. America borrows from the world without even thinking carefully of how to pay it. "People demand freedom of speech as a compensation for the freedom of thought which they seldom use," Søren Kierkegaard (1813–1855) describes the behavior of common people. The American institutional structure essentially guarantees that a president elected by the general public, the "masses," can hardly have a strong character and solid principles. Bernays (1928) saw the process of how public ideas are formed in America: "It may seem an exaggeration to say that the American public gets most of its ideas in this wholesale fashion. The mechanism by which ideas are disseminated on a large scale is propaganda, in the broad sense of an organized effort to spread a particular belief or doctrine." Americans speak freely, but one might wonder where the deep and original thinkers are, in the social and political sciences. Professors in fields directly related to human thought and social behavior are deep to the level to maximize number of admirers and citations under constraint of a secure academic position. Groucho Marx (1905–1976) vividly scoffed at American democracy: "Politics is the art of looking for trouble, finding it everywhere, diagnosing it incorrectly and applying the wrong remedies."

This is not very fair as politicians elected by the common people are normal humans and they do whatever rationally and profitably they can for themselves, under the institutional constraints.

The concept of democracy as a form of government was created by the Greek philosophers. Modern democracy is referred to a political system in which free and fair elections with participation by all social groups are regularly held with basic civil and political liberties being respected. Democracy is manifested in many forms. Within North America and northern Europe, "One finds presidential, parliamentary, and semipresidential systems of government; federal states and unitary states; monarchies and republic; unicameral legislatures and bicameral legislatures; plurality, majority, and all manner of proportional electoral systems; common law and statutory law; and states with written constitutions and states without." (Lipset, 1998:xiii). The United States became genuinely democratic only in recent years. Its modern journey was started in Western society by the end of the 18th century. There were dynamic forces for democratic changes from the beginning of colonial America. Democracy as the form of government remains unchallenged on American soil. Democracy was first rejected on the grounds that the poorly educated, the non-English immigrants, and the lower classes were not worthy and would not be able to fulfill the inherent responsibilities. After democracy was accepted, there was a tension between individual and representative democracy. Gradually, individual democratic rights based on suffrage and majority became the mainstream and communitarian democratic ideas were less acceptable (Lipset, 1998:199).

The United States, according to Commager (1951:109), is "the oldest republic, the oldest democracy, the oldest federal system; it has the oldest written constitution and boasts the oldest of genuine political parties." America was founded on European civilization. Its "grand" ideas are mostly imported from Europe: "In the United States, the majority undertakes to supply a multitude of ready-made opinions for the use of individuals, who are thus relieved from the necessity of forming opinions of their own," Alexis de Tocqueville pointed out. This is also applicable to another technologically advanced economy, Japan. In the West technology has been advanced by America and in East Asia by Japan. They concentrated their energies on economic development and innovation with social stability and economic security.

Unity tied by love is often evanescent; unity fettered by hate tends to endure. This monkey-grouping principle is continued as it fits for growth and expansion of genes. A dictator succeeds in encouraging nationalism as the motive unites people to protect the group and kill the outsider. One generation after another generation, thinkers live on by selling love, while politicians solidify their power by manipulating hates. "Men are so simple and so much inclined to obey immediate needs that a deceiver will never lack victims for his deceptions," Niccolò Machiavelli (1469-1527) penetrated the mind of humans. The American political culture was typified by Alexis de Tocqueville (1805-1859): "There are many men of principle in both parties in America, but there is no party of principle." As it is not principle-based and the practical way to get power is to maximize number of (mostly uneducated before WWII) voters, game theory tells that two parties have similar opinions and tend to avoid sensitive issues which confuse masses in long-term repeated learning and games. The two parties might, perhaps occasionally, agree upon policies of dealing with other countries in the name of national interest. "The Democrats are the party that says government will make you smarter, taller, richer, and remove the crabgrass on your lawn. The Republicans are the party that says government doesn't work and then they get elected and prove it," P.J. O'Rourke (1947-) taunted. The dynamic balance of varied factors during the election process betokens unpredictability of result. The last day of the American election is very exciting as the rational expectational result made by best professions of the two sides is 50% to 50%.

There are two major political parties, the Democratic Party (1830-) and the Republican Party (1854-), in America. "The superior man is catholic and not partisan. The mean man is a partisan and not catholic," Confucius (2:14) classified men. The Democratic Party is the oldest voter-based political party in the world. It was institutionally formed in the 1830s and 1840s with its earlier years from the 1790s in the name of Thomas Jefferson and James Madison's Democratic-Republican Party. The party, also known as the party of the common man, propped individual rights and state sovereignty, and battled against high tariffs in its early history. From 1932 to 1968, the party was dominant, starting from the 32nd (1933-1945) President Franklin D. Roosevelt. During the Wall Street Crash of 1929 and the Great Depression in the 1930s the party supported progressive liberal policies to deal with financial crises. Recent presidents from the party were Bill Clinton (1993-2001), Barack Obama (2009-2017), and Joe Biden (2021-).

Republican Party — also referred to as Grand Old Party (GOP) — is the second extant political party in America. It was initiated in 1854 to resist the Kansan–Nebraska Act and the expansion of slavery into American territories. In early years it consisted of northern Protestants, workers, farmers, black slaves, and many others. The party had little support from white Southerners. It was successful in Northern America in early years. The first Republican president, Abraham Lincoln, was elected in 1860. The party played a significant role in the American Civil War (1861-1865) and abolition of slavery (1865). It dominated the national politics from 1860 to 1932, while the Democratic Party from 1932 through 1964. The Republican Party won five of the six presidential elections from 1968 to 1988. President Ronald Reagan (1911–2004) who was in office from 1981 to 1989, supported reduction of government spending and regulation, low taxes, and an anti-Soviet Union policy. The party now supports free market capitalism, lower taxes, a strong nation defense, capital punishment, gun rights, and limitations on labor unions. Recent presidents from the party were Ronald Reagan (1981–1989), George H.W. Bush (1989–1993), George W. Bush (2001–2009), and Donald Trump (2017–2021).

3.2 Converging Political Ideas Between the Parties

> He who acts from a love of the law is a scholar. He who embodies it with a firm sense of purpose is a gentleman. He who has an understanding of it that is acute without limit is a sage. If a man lacks the law, he acts with rash and aimless confusion. If he possesses the law, but has no recognition of what is congruent with it, he nervously looks about, anxiously wondering what to do. Only after he has come to rely on the law and then gone on to penetrate deeply into its application through analogical extension to other categories and types of things does he act with gentle warmth and calm confidence.
>
> Xun Zi (298–238 BC, 2:10)

Plato expounds the force of democracy to satisfy man's basic desires for equality: "Democracy ...is a charming form of government, full of variety and disorder; and dispensing a sort of equality to equals and unequals alike." Tocqueville (1835:183) denounced the hypocrisy of early America: "By abolishing the principle of servitude, the Americans do not make the slaves free." In *Capitalism, Socialism, and Democracy*, Schumpeter (1942) argued that the "classical theory of democracy" — democracy defined in terms of "the will of the people" and "the common good" — is deficient. Instead, he defines: "The democratic method is that institutional arrangement for arriving at political decisions in which individuals acquire the power to decide by means of a competitive struggle for the people's vote." Democracy is a system in which the people chose leaders through competitive elections. The original European settlers brought with them rigid hierarchies of power and the most undemocratic of institutions: slavery and indentured servitude. In 1700 there were only 20,000 Blacks in America, but by the time of the Declaration of Independence that population had been increased to half a million. The proportion of Blacks in the total population was one fifth in 1776. The ratio remained almost unchanged until after the Civil War when slavery was officially nullified (1861—5). For another hundred years after 1865, black people largely served as a lower-castle group. They work under explicit or implicit "Jim Crow" policies. They had little opportunity to receive educational and financial resources. Advances made after the war (voting rights, congressional representation) quickly evaporated. A society which had slavery institution and has conducted discrimination as a matter of fact should not be very serious in principles of humanity, liberty, and human freedom. Only since the 1960s Blacks have obtained a legally secured access to political equality and economic opportunity. The idea "all men are created equal" took a long time to be realized.

"Politics has no relation to morals," Niccolò Machiavelli (1469-1527) told honestly. Mark Twain saw the continuation of American politics: "We have the best government that money can buy". American political game has been played largely between the two parties. Game theory and psychology of masses mathematically verify that no party should have a solid, rational principle to abide by. One might consider a party as a firm in market economy. Its strategies are political ideas and promises about benefits and its award (power) is the number of votes. Masses' emotions are in flow without a fixed principle. Collective emotions and weak rationality (and shallow knowledge) determine who win the game. Thoughtless mass hearts are collectively manipulated by media and the public elite which are largely controlled by the rich and the powerful in American society. Politicians can easily do their jobs when America is progressing all the way and the national pie is augmented. The share of the pie among the society causes some conflicts but bearable for masses as their welfare levels are enhanced. Flows of immigrants also imply that low-class people-born in America might also perk up when seeing hard life of new immigrants. Although discrimination against born-in-America people of color, new immigrants stabilize the American society in many subtle ways. How to live on large inflows of immigrants with justice and social order is a theoretical question that few people know anything about when no social class or group is verifiably dominant and respectable. America knows little yet hearts of people of color as many of the minorities have been obedient, silent, and servile.

American assimilation is gathering of miscellaneous peoples — some are aware of conducting (but might never be aware of) discrimination and some never forget the experiences of being discriminated. Eighteenth-century Americans tolerated slavery; 19th-century Americans tolerated violence and discrimination against immigrants and ethnic minorities; and early 20th-century Americans tolerated the concept of inferiority of women to men. The United States still has dilemmas in the treatment of ethnic minorities, and women, but efforts are constantly made to achieve more equitable arrangements. America is a culture of the crowd organized mainly with material benefits. The two political parties direct the crowds according to their duopolistic style of game. Le Bon (1876) identified three key processes that create the psychology of the political crowd. The first process is called anonymity which lends individuals a feeling of individualism and the loss of personal responsibility. The process manipulates individuals to become primitive, unreasoning, and emotional. Individuals will lose self-restraints and yield to instincts. They accept the instinctual drives of their political party's "unconscious". The crowd inverts Darwin's law of evolution, which theoretically or mathematically implies that the two parties should have accumulated so many lies over years and no one knows what they stand for now. The second process is called contagion through which particular behaviors are spread in the crowd. In this process individuals sacrifice their personal interest for the collective interest. With regards to the American two-party system, lies are accumulated and a stock of lies is built. The stocks of lies spread and are further accumulated in the crowd of party members who would sacrifice their personal interest for the collective survival. The third process is called suggestibility through which the contagion is achieved. The crowd coalesces into a singular mind, listening to ideas suggested by strong voices in the crowd. The crowd's behavior is thus homogeneously guided by its strongest members with little patience to any scientific suggestions which are not in conformity with the crowd. Le Bon (1876) confirms that "The leaders we speak of are usually men of action rather than of words. They are not gifted with keen foresight.... They are especially recruited from the ranks of those morbidly nervous excitable half-deranged persons who are bordering on madness."

Madness is often a necessity of collective strength and power. America loves parties. Each president election campaign is nationwide lighthearted and frivolous, financially supported by the rich, the interested, the powerful, the celebrated, and the partisans. It is also a time of excitement for those who have no genuine interest in improving themselves through diligence, frugality, and learning, as an opportunity of satisfying playfulness. The expensive rapture has not memorable result, but the process is hectic and jubilant. Confucius (551–479 BC, 2:19) says: "Advance the upright and set aside the crooked, then the people will submit. Advance the crooked, and set aside the upright, then the people will not submit." Success of democracy is often associated with already militarily powerful and rich societies, a state in which the society is orderly maintained by "routine" political decisions and strategies. When a society is in decline or in poverty trap, an elected president tends to make national situations much worse. The collective stupidity is unfathomable as human history recodes. It is paltry to appear wise when things have already been unmistakably parable or occurred. The leader's greatness is his ability to deal with crisis, not so much to read and carry out what has been prepared by experts.

"I know of no country in which there is so little independence of mind and real freedom of discussion as in America," observed Alexis de Tocqueville so long time. One can still feel about the continuation of American culture in TV debates. It makes people, who are not yet accustomed to American culture, feel that American people debate in way that maximum number of words can be regurgitated from their months. "The modern conservative is engaged in one of man's oldest exercises in moral philosophy; that is, the search for a superior moral justification for selfishness" (Galbraith, 1908–2006). Modern technology makes the two-party system less effective as entire world is simultaneously watching American political behavior and America loses its capacity to create crowds of global masses to follow its accumulated lies. The stocks of lies accumulated over American history would be no longer effective for leading globalizing world with multiple self-organized crowds rationally as well as randomly dispersed on the earth. The global leader needs a global way to benefit the global village as well as the local nation. America has successfully been a global superpower and even a global "moral" leader during the epoch when there were no communications among quasi-isolated nations. The global leadership is increasingly demanding in internet-connected world as global stock and style of political lies are not yet established. Even within the Western cultures shared with similar political stocks young generations who receive more education and have more cultural experiences have little trust in the stock of traditional political lies.

3.3 Law and Social Justice

In hearing litigations, I am like any other body. What is necessary is to cause the people to have no litigations.

Confucius (Great Learning)

Nature makes only dumb animals. We owe the fools to society,

Honoré de Balzac (1799–1850).

Balzac's aphorism above might be germane in describing the leaders of some societies. For instance, nobody has damaged American respectability in East Asia as much as the greatest American president (as he himself bragged). No man has made mainland Chinese people appreciate the Chinese Communist Party more than this wheeler-dealer. A democratic leader, as Plato mentions, has the right to lie. But even Plato might have had difficulty imagining how much the president in a contemporary democratic system can lie.

The national game is composed of unlimited sub-games. Americans enjoy various lifestyles with few social and moral constraints, changing even the meaning of marriage. Some typical American traits are restlessness, dislike of restraints, an urge for change, action, mobility, the quest for new experiences, self-improvement, a belief in progress, and a belief in law.

The United States has a hierarchy of law. The federal Constitution is the supreme legal authority to which all other laws must conform. States' laws must conform to the state constitutions, and the state legal structures must not contravene the US Constitution. The federal Supreme Court plays the role of final interpreter of the US Constitution. It hands down decisions on what government activity is permissible on any level, under the Constitution. Kallen (1970:51) points out: "The United States . . . has a peculiar anonymity . . . which . . . is formulated in the phrase that the American government is a government of laws, not men."

In America, some people follow the rules while others do not. Law and morality are often in conflict as life has an unlimited number of possibilities and law can cover only limited situations. Hermann Hesse (1877–1962) illustrated the point: "It is possible for one never to transgress a single law and still be a bastard."

There are other rules, such as customs and rituals, in social games. There is a reverential regard for the legal order among the American people. Americans have long been proud of their wide civil liberties, the equality of all persons before the law, and the availability of judicial remedies in case of any abuse in the administration of justice. Justice implies equal opportunities for every individual to pursue whatever he desires under law. Equal opportunities are protected by fair and democratic procedures and enforced by equal educational opportunity. In his 1838 address to the Young Men's Lyceum, Abraham Lincoln (1809–1865), the 16th President (1861–1865), advocated, "Let reverence for the laws, be breathed by every American mother, to the lisping babe that prattles on her lap — let it be taught in schools, in seminaries, and in colleges; — let it be written in Primers, spelling books, and Almanacs; — let it be preached from the pulpit, proclaimed in legislative halls, and enforced in courts of justice. And in short, let it become the political religion of the nation."

Historically, it took a long time for the law to function in the United States. Kallen (1970:237) related: "The life of pioneer, the psychology of the immigrant, the interest of big business all serve to invest the United States with the temper of lawlessness. This lawlessness is enhanced by the fact that American law is antiquated and thus irrelevant to American life." In Confucianism, how to balance between written law and unwritten rule is in debates over centuries. For instance, if one follows the rule of a special party (either republic or democratic) in lifetime, one might become a man without any sense of shame except habitually following the party line. Even if one, like a financial professional in the Wall Street, is a successful one, one might be a shameless man. If its important positions are mostly occupied by shameless men, the society, how glory it looks, is rotten within.

Western humanity, since the time of ancient Greek, is constructed with the separation of humanity. Western thinkers have no systematical theory — but a lot of unconnected theories — about how a human society with democratic institutions can function with efficiency and justice. Efficiency with law is the basic mechanism of human coexistence in modern Western civilization. Historically, the East Asian immobile rice-paddy farmer was ruled by custom and habit rather than law, while the Western mobile conqueror (and industrialist) was ruled by law. After its golden period of economic expansion, America is now increasingly bewildered with how to deal with issues related to law and justice in association with rapidly increasing gaps between the rich and the poor and phenomena scrupulously related to income distribution. Internationally, as global competition and cooperation have increasingly become knotty and America's status as a superpower is steadily weakening, the international relationships formed after WWII are becoming fickle.

Instead of the crowd culture of free grouping, Confucius argued for the correspondence between language and reality for the Chinese farmer: "If language be not in accordance with the truth of things, affairs cannot be carried on to success. When affairs cannot be carried on to success, proprieties, and music will not flourish. When proprieties and music do not flourish, punishments will not be properly awarded. When punishments are not properly awarded, the people do not know how to move hand or foot. Therefore, a superior man considers it necessary that the names he uses may be spoken appropriately, and also that what he speaks may be carried out appropriately." Trust in institutions of all sorts has been in decline in the United States (Fukuyama, 1999: 49). Jane Austen (1775–1817) spotted: "There are people, who the more you do for them, the less they will do for themselves." American society has created many wealthy people but failed to give opportunities to more needy people. Albert Einstein evaluated American culture: "Too many of us look upon Americans as dollar chasers. This is a cruel libel, even if it is reiterated thoughtlessly by the Americans themselves." Xun Zi (19:1) rationalized the existence of the rule: "I say that men are born with desires which, if not satisfied, cannot but lead men to seek to satisfy them. If in seeking to satisfy their desires men observe no measure and apportion things without limits, then it would be impossible for them not to contend over the means to satisfy their desires. Such contention leads to disorder. Disorder leads to poverty. The Ancient Kings abhorred such disorder; so they established the regulations contained within ritual and moral principles in order to apportion things, to nurture the desires of men, and to supply the means for their satisfaction. They so fashioned their regulations that desires should not want for the things which satisfy them and goods would not be exhausted by the desires. In this way the two of them, desires and goods, sustained each other over the course of time. This is the origin of ritual principles."

By "human rights" one might refer to many things, such as freedom of thought and expression, freedom from arbitrary arrest and torture, freedom of movement and peaceful assembly, the right to work and receive fair wages, to protect the family, to adequate standards of living, to education, to health care, to self-determination regarding political status and economic, social, and cultural development, and to ethnic and religious minorities' enjoyment of their own culture, language, and religion (Twiss, 1998:28). Freedom in creation, consumption, and consumption of wealth, power, and sex is basic implications of American freedom. Freedom does not have the same meaning over time in American society. Schlesinger (1998:44-5) followed evolution of implications of freedom: "White settlers had systematically pushed the American Indians back, killed their braves, seized their lands, and sequestered their tribes. They had brought Africans to America to work their plantations and Chinese to build their railroads. They had enunciated glittering generalities of freedom and withheld them from people of color. Their Constitution protected slavery, and their laws made distinctions based on race. Though they eventually emancipated the slaves, they conspired in the reduction of the freedmen to third-class citizenship. Their Chinese Exclusion acts culminated in the total prohibition of Asian immigration in the Immigration Act of 1924." After WWII, especially through the civil rights revolution of the 1960s, America has emerged more prosperous, egalitarian, and democratic, even though it fails to deliver benefits to a large proportion to members of the society, especially born in America, in the bottom.

3.4 Political Power

Those who know virtue are few.

Those whose courses are different cannot lay plans for one another.

Without feelings of respect, what is there to distinguish men from beast?

Confucius (551–479 BC)

Galirndo (2018: 1-2) delineated the frustrating paradox that the founding fathers left in the government system designed in the 18th century: "to reconcile the sweeping promises they articulate in the founding documents with the reality of wide spread and brutal inequality that characterized the nation at that time.... American democracy is at once vibrant because of their vision and imperfect because of their blind spots." This is true also for China' fast economic expansion in the last four decades — vision for growth with unlimited blind spots. Japan is also faced with social issues caused by many blind spots after the fast growth. The founding fathers designed the system much on basis of European ideas. America has had the vision for wealth with blind spots hidden within its greatness and global superpower. Any human-maintained greatness has hidden dark spots in long-term perspectives. A healthy civilization is its capacity to evolve towards to the higher with self-correcting mechanisms (rather than increasing abilities to blame others for one's own faults).

Except wisdom, almost all aspects of a late-50s men enter stages of degenerating as time passes. According to Kant (1724–1804) lying is always morally wrong and is never right. The opposite point of view by Benjamin Constant (1767–1830) is that man has a right to lie. The utilitarian belief is that to lie or to tell the truth must be judged by a calculation between advantages and disadvantages. One should lie if the lie maximizes the benefits of a situation. In a free society dominated by the utilitarian belief like the United States, lying is justified and politicians would never be ashamed if they can find a way to justify the group's benefits. Theoretically, a sheer liar, who has no sense of morality and is good at learning, can survive better politically than a man, who strictly follows Kant's moral principles, in a democratic society. "The majority never has right on its side. Never, I say! That is one of these social lies against which an independent, intelligent men must wage war. Who is it that constitute the majority of the population in a country? Is it the clever folk, or the stupid? I don't imagine you will dispute the fact that at present the stupid people are in an absolutely overwhelming majority all the world over." (Henrik, Ibsen, 1828–1906). Noam Chomsky (1928–)

described the obvious in the American culture: "In the US, there is basically one party — the business party. It has two factions, called Democrats and Republicans, which are somewhat different but carry out variations on the same policies." American democracy leads to power concentration and American market mechanism leads to wealth concentration. President Trump is a capable and honest German-American businessman. He straightforwardly informed the world that in a mature democratic society an immature politician can only indulge the truth to the people electing him in the sense that when he is making a white lie, the American people understand the truth. As the president, he was perhaps confident in whatever he was doing was right. He did seem to be sure about that politics is a business in which the victory is won through lying and manipulating news. He did politics by following his belief. Plato justifies his behavior:

The rulers of the state are the only persons who ought to have the privilege of lying, either at home or abroad; they may be allowed to lie for the good of the state.

In a recent book "*Lying in State: Why Presidents Lie — And Why Trump is Worse,*" Alterman (2020) estimates how many glaring lies President Trump made and illustrates many types of lies, such as necessary lies, white lies, pathetic lies, and consequential lies. Trump barefacedly made many abnormal or non-professional lies. As the German-American man came from property markets and fashion world and had perused American political culture as the outsider, he might think of lying as a natural matter of politics. He might think of doing politics as in business. An honest man might morally value lying as much as telling truth if he is engaged in a business where gains are judged disregarding means under law. Alterman shows how American standards for trustfulness have eroded. The key idea is the cumulative effective of deception and lying in American political culture. What a president successfully lies about "permits" the American society to accept this kind of lying and the media's complicity in diffusing misinformation. Subsequent presidents benefit from the lying strategy and innovate ways of lying. The public has thus gotten custom to miscellaneous types of lying and the media have more alternatives to spread misinformation. Alterman assessed that the persistent expansion of power and hegemony was conducted on the basis of presidential lies. To become more civilized is not only to increase the collective ability, knowledge, and capacity to effectively spread truth, but also a process to accumulate cultural and political scums. When a civilization is at its greatest point, its accumulated scums are perhaps also at its greatest stock, mostly reflected in the state of mind and accumulated habits. America has evolved into a culturally and political mature and sophisticated stage. It is no longer composed of penniless and uneducated passionate immigrants. A higher stage of civilization often stands upon lost truthfulness and is pervaded with cunning lies beneficial to the powerful groups. It is human, not exceptionally American.

Pearl S. Buck (1892–1973, 1949:119–120), a Nobel Prize laureate, reflected on why she considered America was the world's hope: "All the world's peoples — not the politicians and militarists and the big money-makers, but the peoples — were looking to the United States. They . . . were looking for a statement for humanity. . . . Our Constitution and the Bill of Rights were known around the world. Men hidden in caves and villages in countries ridden by tyrants memorized these documents in order to strengthen their own spirits." This imparts to the world about how attractive the public image of America has been as a land of spirit and freedom. Albert Einstein stated: "Weak people revenge. Strong people forgive. Intelligent people ignore." White Americans made the genuine Americans factually homeless. Real racial hatred cannot occur in America as the natives are too weak to get back what belong to them, except those apologies done by generations for things they did not do. Nicolas Cage (1964–) sincerely reflected: "I always see America as really belonging to the Native Americans. Even though I'm American, I still feel like a visitor in my own country." Wallerstein (2001:250) saw the Western way of arrogance: "Human arrogance has been humanity's greatest self-imposed limitation. This, it seems to me, is the message of the story of Adam in the Garden of Eden. We were arrogant in claiming to have received and understood the revelation of God, to know the intent of the gods. We were even more arrogant in asserting that we were capable of arriving at eternal truth through the use of human reason, so fallible a tool. And we have been continuously arrogant in seeking to impose on each other, and with such violence and cruelty, our subjective images of the perfect society."

"It's heartbreaking that so many hundreds of millions of people around the world are desperate for the right to vote, but here in America people stay home on election day." (Moby, 1965–). By the mid-20 century voting rights had been extended to all citizens aged 18 or older. Voter turnout rate in United States presidential elections was low, especially among young generation in recent decades. As illustrated in Figure 3.1, the turnout rate in the US president elections oscillated between 50% and 60%. The low turnout rate implies that the people have no trust American democracy and the power of the people, even though the American government makes efforts to establish the image of democracy in global affairs. The 2020 election had the highest turnout rate. Trump aroused America's spirits. It is said that America is never so deeply divided as now.

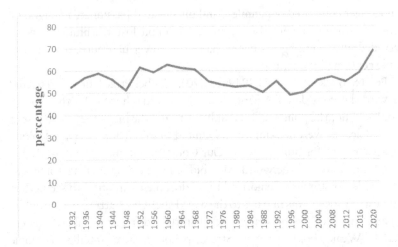

Figure 3.1 The Eligible Voter Turnout Rate in the US Presidential Elections

Education complicates tastes and tastes separate and divide people. People with little education and taste for comfortable life could be easily united with the material profit (plus religious spirits or nationalism). But there is no converging assimilation among cultured and affluent peoples. With regards to America's cultural development, Levine (2009) described: "If there is a tragedy in this development, it is not only that millions of Americans were now separated from exposure to such creators as Shakespeare, Beethoven, and Verdi, whom they had enjoyed in various formats for much of the nineteenth century, but also that the rigid cultural categories, once they were in place, made it so difficult for so long for so many to understand the value and importance of the popular art forms that were all around them. Too many of those who considered themselves educated and cultured lost for a significant period — and many have still not regained — their ability to discriminate independently, to sort things out for themselves and understand that simply because a form of expressive culture was widely accessible and highly popular it was not therefore necessarily devoid of any redeeming value of artistic merit." As authenticated by Shapiro (2020), a growing number of Americans do not want to continue the (mainstreams of) shared history, ideals, and culture. America is further divided due to vanishing traditional areas of civil agreement. American people see their country from varied histories, philosophies, religions, and cultures as natural consequences of spread education, prosperity, freedom of speech, culturally heterogeneous peoples, and stable social welfare system. People see America not only with the same thought and ideas from British and other European traditions, but also through the lens of discriminated groups. They are no longer simple-minded to believe in the perfection of "universal ideology". For some, the American values are perceived as beautiful words pasted over a rotted system. Instead of freedom for individuals, they see a system for reinforcing traditional hierarchies of power and further enriching the few already very rich. People understand by seeing. The powerful, equipped with modern technology and wealth, know and take away almost all he principal opportunities for realizing the American dream. New talented immigrants, who are recruited by big companies to the country in order to sustain their own monopolistic powers, are quick to grasp opportunities. But modern immigrants have no need to adapt to American culture except to acquire fluency in English. Traditional culture is solidified with time and space. Technological innovations change the role of time and space in cultural formation and cultural assimilation. Many new immigrants of color, especially properly educated and cultivated, are bicultural. They might follow neither white culture nor their native cultures.

In America free competition in accumulating wealth leads to concentration of wealth into a few hands. The rich will manipulate the political system to create, secure and increase wealth. "Power corrupts, and absolute power corrupts absolutely". In a matured capitalist democratic society, the rich have great power over the political system. The politicians are elected by the democratic process, but the masses are brain washed by the media controlled by the rich. Politician for society is like medical doctor for man. When a man is young and strong, there is no need for great doctor; one cannot even judge whether a doctor is useful. When America was great, even an artist and professional actor like Regan could be very successful by making people laughing and speaking about traditional American slogan of freedom and democracy without making any sophisticated political decisions. "Luck makes a dastard appear a hero," as ancient Chinese saying tells. For a great country with plenty of resources, full of positive energies, and easy access to knowledge, whether the national leader is capable or mediocre does count much as the society can self-organize itself towards a healthy situation. When America is not so effective in self-organization and global situation becomes increasingly complex, the leader should have professional knowledge and practical experiences and skills in balancing varied forces. But human history repeatedly shows that "The worst evils which mankind has ever had to endure were inflicted by bad governments." (Ludwig von Mises, 1881–1973).

3.5 Trump Elected as the President

> The petty man is eager to make boasts yet desires that others
> should believe in him. He enthusiastically engages in deception yet
> wants others to have affection for him. He conducts himself like an
> animal yet wants others to think well of him. Despite his utter disor-
> derliness, a petty man hates for men to consider him in the wrong;
> despite his utter unworthiness, he desires that men should consider
> him worthy. Though his heart is that of tigers and wolves and his
> behavior like that of wild bears, he nonetheless also despises those
> who are his malefactors. Intimate with flatters and sycophants, he
> is estranged from those who would reprove or admonish him.

> Xun Zi (298–238 BC, 2:1)

"Whoever looks at America will see: the ship is powered by stupidity,
corruption, or prejudice," Johann Most (1846–1946) probed so long ago.
When Most was judging this, America was moving towards constructing
the greatest country in human history. It does not matter so much how
the ship is powered so far it moves speedily towards the target. It is quite
another matter in what direction the ship will move. In the last 40 years,
China's social order has been maintained, and free market has been initiated and continues by the Party. But the nation has achieved great economic
advancement and gender markets have now become free and "effective" with
regards to reduced social and economic costs of divorce and reduction of
the population. Political power is not democratic, but all other markets are
moving towards freedom in China. Similarly, it may not matter so much
whoever is elected as president of the greatest country if America's social
and economic bases are solid. "Stupidity" of the top is even preferred in
some rich society as the character is suitable for keeping society in harmony.
Smart, energetic, and politically "abecedarian" Trump has waltzed America
and the world in the global village. His political style as the president of the
greatest country in the world has enticed more people into political issues in
the world, for better or for worse. The American politician, who has served
as the junior United States senator from Vermont since 2007, Bernie Sanders
(1941–) remarks: "While Donald Trump is busy insulting one group after
another, Hillary Clinton understands that our diversity is one of our greatest
strengths. Yes, we become stronger when black and white, Latino, Asian-
American, Native American — when all of us stand together." It is Trump
who took the national power and Clinton loss American people's support.
Old fox never learns new tricks. But "Our greatest stupidities may be very
wise." (Ludwig Wittgenstein, 1889–1951). Anything could have turned into
possible forces in America partly because America has enjoyed such lucky
combinations of nature and global environment.

Donald John Trump (1946–) began to have his first political job at 70 years old. This tells that American presidency is a mediocre job without high demanding professionalism and trustful certificate. To get a job in university needs a Ph.D and to drive a car requires a driver license. American presidency does not require any solid and trustful id but money and ability to manipulate hearts of masses. The American president is an aggregated number of millions minds whose ability qualifications for making the voting are needless to explain. To have rights and no ability to use the rights is a source of human tragedies in human history. Before rightly performing human rights, one ought to be human first and foremost. Mr. Trump was born and raised in Queens. He took the 45th president of the United States as his first job in government. His father was a German immigrant and real estate developer. His mother was Scottish-born housewife. He was the first president without prior military or government service. His career was mainly in business and television shows before he decided to try his luck in politics. He is described as protectionist and nationalist and is also called racist by some. His many — perhaps non-professional or even "honest" — statements were original to American politics, but attractive to many American people. The readiest way for a trivial man to attain greatness is to vilify worthy and virtuous people. Trump had few obstacles to handle with virtuous ones as there would few virtuous politicians who could have politically hovered over the American public in the complex political cycles.

Trump's victory in the democratic election is the collective measurement of the American mindset state. His "America first" reminds me of "Everyone who wants to do good to the human race always ends in universal bullying." (Aldous Huxley, 1894–1963). As early as in 1992, in his *The End of History and the Last Man*, Fukuyama (1992: 328), a Japanese-American, brain-washed with Greek terminologies, exemplified Donald Trump in such a context: "are there not reservoirs of idealism that cannot be exhausted ... if one becomes a developer like Donald Trump or a mountain climber...? Difficult as it is ... to be these individuals, and for all the recognition they receive,... the causes they serve are not the most serious or the most just. And as long as they are not, the horizon of human possibilities that they define will not be ultimately satisfying for the most thymotic natures." Affairs, chaotic as they appear, are structurally determined. Samuel Johnson (1709–1784) illustrated how a man being luckily put to superpower position might talk about human affairs: "one of the disadvantages of wine is that it makes a man mistake words for thoughts." Plato's following statement gauges the ideal politician in the American political world: "There will be no end to the troubles of states, or of humanity itself, till philosophers become kings in this world, or till those we now call kings and rulers really and truly become philosophers, and political power and philosophy thus come into the same hands." Ancient Chinese Confucianists have the same standard for leaders.

"The trouble with the world is that the stupid are cocksure and the intelligent are full of doubt." (Bertrand Russell, 1872–1970). The president Trump of the United States is exceptionally self-confident. He encouraged the American citizens: "When America is united, America is totally unstoppable." This is not typically American. No country is stoppable when it is united with some simple and well-defined goal, as Mongolian empire already proved, Japan showed with fighting against America, and mainland China showed through the Cultural Revolution and is now doing in economic progress, not to mention the history of the West. Poor and uneducated masses are easily united when profits are obvious for almost everyone. East Asian and Western countries have exhibited that result since the end of WWII. One finds unstoppable periods of miscellaneous races and nations one after another over history. Mongolian empire was built with the united spirit, while it collapsed in association with separation within. Mr. Trump might have "sped up" separating America more than any American president in America's long history. He was elected because he had historically been located at a turning point of America's separation. President Trump might be the most honest American presidents in entire American history, depending on how to see it. He revealed the world the American presidency. Nevertheless, no leader in human history has such a bad luck in that each of his obvious lies has immediately converted into laughingstocks not only for American people who dislike him, but also for some people in every corner of the world. He must have been the greatest seed of humors in hundred languages in human history.

America has been prosperous for a long period. Its recent domestic intensified conflicts are inner dynamic mechanism of socioeconomic evolution. It has not much to do with international conditions. America cannot now deliver its domestic troubles and scums abroad and absorb "cheaply" the best talents from the rest of the world. Mencius (372–289 BC; 7:8) summarizes the ancient history: "A man must first despise himself, and then others will despise him. A family must destroy itself, and then others will destroy it. A kingdom must first smite itself, and then others will smite it." Mencius (372–289 BC; 3:4) also catechized that a leader should heartedly take care of the poor in a national crisis like the current Covid-19: "Benevolence brings glory to a prince, and the opposite of it brings disgrace. For the princes of the present day to hate disgrace and yet live complacently doing what is not benevolent, is like hating moisture and yet living in a low situation. If a prince hates disgrace, the best course for him to pursue is to esteem virtue and honor virtuous scholars, giving the worthiest among them places of dignity, and the able offices of trust. . . . Let him clearly digest the principles of his government with legal sanctions, and then even great kingdoms will be constrained to stand in awe of him."

An amateur in politics had become the most powerful man of a globally declining country itself should be a proof that the country is in deep troubles and losing confidence in its greatness. Young and rich America did not need real great politicians in its golden time. The country which itches for boosting economic development and is losing social harmony needs a leader for miracle of reversing the historical direction. History is not a simply reversible pendulum like Adam Smith taught. History is a great river likes Confucius exemplifies. Hayek, who is quite familiar about how Hitler got the power, befogged: "Perhaps the fact that we have seen millions voting themselves into complete dependence on a tyrant has made our generation understand that to choose one's government is not necessarily secure freedom." Frank Herbert (1920–1986) exhorts the strategy of winning the support of confusing masses: "If you think yourselves as helpless and ineffectual, it is certain that you will create a despotic government to be your master. The wise despot, therefore, maintains among his subjects a popular sense that they are helpless and ineffectual." America was at a state which needs some man like Trump to bring about changes, while Trump had the proper human capital to be likened by many American people. The state of civilization is measured by the state of mind of its people. A great society consists of wise, mediocre, chichi, stupid, virtuous, educated, skillful, sexy, serious, playful, and evil people of varied ages. The 26th president of the United States (1901–1909), Theodore Roosevelt (1858–1919) warned America people: "The things that will destroy America are prosperity-at-any-price, peace-at-any-price, safety-first instead of duty-first, the love of soft living, and the get-rich-quick theory of life." He does not mention possible foreign competition on Great America perhaps because any alternative could not be perceived. Roosevelt was leading America to be greater, while Trump boosted America up being great again. They represent the irreconcilable America spirits. Blaise Pascal (1623–1662) reverts what Confucius says: "The only shame is to have none."

Consequences of American freedom give mankind good lessons about how to create, distribute, and apply freedom in a welfare-enhancing manner. Freedom is the trickiest human game in a populated society, as human nature consciously or habitually curb others' freedom, physically, economically, emotionally, or mentally. If one feels oneself superior over others and one is nothing but a fake human, one should be miserable, at least within. A mathematical equation is described by Fulton J. Sheen (895–1979): "Civilization is always in danger when those who have never learned to obey are given the right to command." This was proved by Hitler in Germany and Mao in China. After the deep destruction, in those two cultures construction, fortunately, followed. America has not yet experienced the possible cycles of civilization because it is still in the middle of the superpower phase.

4. Gender and Racial Relations with Individualism

> If the lord of men desires to be secure, no policy is as good as evenhanded government and love of the people. If he desires glory, none is as good as exalting ritual principles and treating scholars with strict observance of forms of respect. If he desires to establish his fame and meritorious accomplishments, none is as good as advancing the worthy and bringing the capable into one's service.
>
> Xun Zi (298–238 BC, 9:4)

Human society is a bio-system. Its continuation is based on production and reproduction of people. A race which makes a great contribution to mankind may disappear if it fails to reproduce itself. East Asian economic powers, like Japan, might crop up negligible in global economy after less than one hundred years since it fails to reproduce the population with their current gender relations. Malthus gives a dismal picture of mankind due to overpopulation. Malthusian theory is still valid if one looks the world as an organ. Mankind is collectively gliding toward possible suicide with its unstoppable population expansion and deteriorating environment. Even a few decades ago no one could have predicted the capacity and speed that mankind collectively destroys the nature in such scales and scopes. Even if people in India and China live as richly as in America, the earth perhaps cannot support mankind if without alternative energies and more environment-friendly technologies. The mother of mankind is now destroyed by fast population expansion. In the *Yi Ying* system, a balanced relation between gender is a key for family relations as well as national survival. Economics has few sophisticated ideas on the issues related to population dynamics. The topic on population may be dismal for any modern society. Population dynamics can destroy a country, keep an economy in poverty trap forever, and make cultural purity unsustainable.

Among the three key objectively measurable variables — wealth, power, and sex — emphasized in this book, sex and its associated products, such as family, children born outside marriage, and adultery, are seldom integrated with theories of socioeconomic evolution. Sex and sexuality have been studied in isolation without properly integrating its dynamic interdependence with economic, social, and political variables. Among freedom in wealth, power, and sex, freedom in gender relations is mostly desired and "easily" conducted with low social costs in rational societies. Sex with love is mostly evaluated in human relations. Mankind could not have reproduced itself, so far, without direct or indirect sexual relations between man and woman. Desire for physical sex may disappear as baby may be produced by some unknown technologies in future. Nevertheless, endless sexual playfulness even without the motivation for reproduction seems to be uniquely human.

Human genes evolve to optimize various processes to make re-production fruitful. Although philosophers, scientists, artists, poets, and writers are concerned with love and sex in micro levels, many aspects of its role on social evolution on macro level is almost unknown. Rises and falls of races and nations are closely related to gender relations. For instance, mainland China and Northern Korea, as well as Japan, Hong Kong, Taiwan, and North Korea, have higher average IQs than Western countries. Sexually free America's average IQ is low (with regards to its education and income). High IQs do not necessarily imply big successes in life, especially in modern economies with emotions, information, playfulness as important inputs in leisure-oriented and service-based societies. Many superstars with low IQs — most productive creators of sexuality — are significant inputs to creating flows of pleasure and sadness in association with varied emotions. Widely spread modern media enable these kinds of people to earn million dollars overnight in numerous cultures. "Love me tender, love me true, all my dreams fulfill. For my darling, I love you, and I always will." has been frequently heard globally. There is nothing so valuable and constructive in building a valuable life as love and there is nothing so destructive as well. Love, by nature, is fragile as the basis of long-term human relations as its basic motivation is satisfied by enabling the lover to give without conditions. It is a most primary desire in human life. A place claimed to be full of love might be full of deception in adult groupings as human nature implies. The desire for sex and ways to approach and satisfy it explain much about how human society is evolved and constructed. Many of traditional moral codes are reasonably broken initially from America as the superpower has been the leader in producing technological changes, spreading mass consumption culture, and encouraging freedom and individualism. American freedom and abundant natural conditions plus romanticism manufactured in European civilization nurture all possible patterns of sexes and sexuality. The law of evolution and natural selection might deepen self-destructiveness of American society in the future as the basic human institution, family, is broken. Low social and economic costs of divorce, adultery, and irresponsibility make life socially colored and emotionally enriched, especially for the beautiful and the rich. But men still have little knowledge about long-term implications for common people. Without wars, there may be a large proportion of poor men who may be put into unlimited predicament in supporting stable family life (if they could offer to build family). In future mankind might evolve into a gender-less society with further knotty sexual playfulness as there is no convincing theory about what is a collectively effective organizational form of gender relations.

4.1 Individualism and Gender Relations

> Virtue is not left to stand alone. He who practices it will have neighbors.
>
> Confucius (551-479 BC)

"I don't know why we are here, but I'm pretty sure that it is not in order to enjoy ourselves," (Ludwig Wittgenstein, 1889-1951). Man exists not to enjoy himself but to continue the human species. Sex and its associated by-products such as sexuality, human relations, and family based on heterogeneous genders are among the main determinants of social, economic, and political structures. In modern societies, sexual relations and sexuality are no longer singly constructed to produce babies. Sigmund Freud (1856-1939) admitted: "The great question that has never been answered, and which I have not yet been able to answer, despite my thirty years of research into the feminine soul, is 'What does a woman want'." Woman genetically wants man's resources. If he had lived in post-war civilizations, Freud might have little idea about what man wants. It is to too early to judge long-tern repercussions of gender division of labor and consumption as gender relations have evinced great and rapid changes only after WWII. From economist Malthus' population theory warns: "The superior power of population cannot be checked without producing misery or vice."

Gender relations built on love is such a strong (ephemeral) human tie that almost any "highly" civilized culture had made great efforts to control it. Marriage based on romantic love is mainly a modern phenomenon in Western as well as East Asian civilizations. Western societies arrive at the natural state in their gender market with freedom in sex and sexuality.

But deception is a common strategy in gender markets. In prosperous capitalist societies, family is strongly tied perhaps among the rich and the powerful. Among the poor and the middle classes, when love is gone, the motivation to live together is gone for many who fail to solidify the relation with other reasons. Capitalism would not dampen freedom of divorces as the rich and the powerful would not suffer much and could enjoy more freedom and pleasure, for instance, with alternative partners. Poor men's alternatives are quite different. Without wars, poor and single men accumulate more proportionally in the society. For instance, once market mechanism was started in China, freedom in gender markets has never met with strong government intervention like in other markets. Owing to its unstable and non-sustainable character, romantic love does not furnish a solid and lasting foundation for stable family. "Love and live together" without lasting relationship is becoming a popular choice among rational people when separation costs are low even in Chinese society which has enjoyed modern lifestyle only a few decades. America still requires a procedure of divorce to break the family relationship, while some countries may not even need a marriage certification for people to build an officially admitted marriage relation. A cultural area which has highly valued rationality, market mechanism, and freedom of gender are now slowly and steadily faced with declining populations if not by increasing hybrid variation. Sexually free and economically prosperous regions fail to maintain the fertility rate. Freedom of sexuality partly explains why America will soon be populated by a majority of people of color. Except for historical buildings, London is no longer British; Paris stands for anything but being French; and Berlin is not fully characterized by its erstwhile disciplined and austere German culture. Regions like Taiwan, Japan, and Korea, which are economically prosperous but have low attraction or accessibility to foreign immigrants are now faced with decline in the near future as the population is steadily falling. America is a melting pot partly because the West colonized most parts of the world and people from English-based colonized regions feel at home in America and (many parts of) Europe due to the colonization, since Spain and Portugal initiated modern globalization.

Gunnar Myrdal (1897–1987) sketched American culture as of the 1980s: "Compared with members of other nations of Western civilization, the ordinary American is a rationalistic being, and there are close relations between his moralism and his rationalism. Even romanticism, transcendentalism, and mysticism tend to be, in the American culture, rational, pragmatic and optimistic." There was no reason for poor white immigrants equipped with the basic concepts of Western civilization not to be rational, pragmatic and optimistic in comparison with what would have happened to them in their homeland.

Traditional American lifestyle and values are portrayed by Lee Iacocca (1924–2019): "The only rock I know that stays steady, the only institution I know that works, is the family." Contemporary America now sees one divorce in two marriages. Fifty percent of marriages still last a lifetime, to put it positively. Positive thinking is encouraging in many situations but is becoming an effective tool of self-deception in modern civilizations. Love is so tender that nothing can create such a flow of pleasure as American culture highly evaluates, and its biologically meaningful products may be so troublesome that rationalized American romanticism increasingly leads to falling fertility rates among the America-born. No one has proven yet how America can sustain its superpower status with a high proportion of people of color in this global village. White people "earned" international respect through social, political, and economic as well as scientific and technological progress, with its military mighty. What the rest of the world will think of America when more than half its population is made up of people of color is unknown. " 'Face' takes decades to build but can be defamed overnight," is a Chinese saying. As nations are kept less bounded, new identities and original forms of discriminations appear as technologies advance and ideologies and religions experience changes of acceptability among masses. "Skin discrimination," "regional discrimination" or "xxx discrimination" will be seen in changed manners in the globalized world in the future as discrimination is welfare-enhancing for some interest groups.

Man's mindset is formed by society (Bourdieu, 2001). Nevertheless, there were few studies of how men related to the household, domesticity, and family life in any rigorous manner. Except naturally/biologically fixed or slowly changing factors, domestic and global gender markets and miscellaneous economic opportunities also affect manhood. American masculinity (manhood or manliness) — a set of attributes, behaviors, and roles associated with men — changes as a part of American socioeconomic evolution. Bourdieu suggested that masculinity is produced by society and culture and reproduced in daily life. The concept of masculinity is perceived differently across cultures. In the traditional West, manhood is personalized by courage, strength, independence, leadership, and assertiveness, while in traditional East Asia rather than independence and assertiveness, coopera-tiveness, and flexibility or adaptivity are highly rated in manhood. In some cultures, manhood is featured as *machismo* which values power, disregarding consequences, and responsibility, or as virility which highly values energy and sex drive. Australian archeologist McAllister alerted us to the changing gender market: "I have a strong feeling that masculinity is in crisis. Men are really searching for a role in modern society; the things we used to do aren't in much demand anymore." (Rooger, 1994). Labor markets affect manhood and gender relations not only in America, but also in other countries owing to modern lifestyles and other external environments. Technological prog-ress devalues physical strength and enhances exchange values of flexibility, variety, and situation-dependent applications of knowledge. In Chinese *yin-yang* dynamic vision, manhood and womanhood are always in transforma-tion as they are internal parts of socioeconomic dynamics. In a boring and stationary society, like the dark age in Europe, manhood is almost invariant. In a vibrant society with freedom and gender equality like contemporary America, there should be no stabilized manhood and womanhood — man learns more female strategies and woman adopts traditional male strategies in gender and labor markets to maximize their personal welfare.

Tocqueville (1835:236) reasoned: "Equality, while it brings great bene-fits to mankind, opens the door . . . to very dangerous instincts. It tends to isolate men from each other so that each thinks only of himself." Individu-alism and prosperity inherently tend to erode community, to reduce face-to-face interaction, to detach individuals from participation in civil affairs, to accelerate the recursive process of marriage-divorce-re-marriage, to break down rational or religious authority. This self-centered trend has led to some long-term consequences. It had already damaged the social system (Collier, 1991). Collier pointed to many problems of American life in which the heightened selfishness had caused substantial harm. Before WWII, a tradi-tional family consisted of the father as the source of family income and the mother as homemaker. Men's identities were focused on working lives and their contributions to family income. Goffman (1963) lists traits of American masculinity: "In an important sense there is only one complete unblushing male in America: a young, married, white, urban, northern, heterosexual Protestant father of college education, fully employed, of good complexion, weight and height, and a recent record in sports." As woman started to enter labor market and receive education after WWII, man's relative importance in family income tends to fall.

In China's *Yi Jing*, when the *yin* spirit dominates, the *yang* spirit is weak, and vice versa. The movement between strong and weak oscillate between masculinity and femininity. In traditional societies, domination of woman over man implies that man has become socially too weak to protect the country and the society would be dominated by men of other societies. The rise and fall of Chinese dynasties have been characterized by the rise and fall of masculinity.

Modern technologies might transform man and woman's effective relationships in the macro world, even though American history is too short to know the long-term implications of female liberation. "To understand how any society functions you must understand the relationship between the men and the women." (Angela Davis, 1944–). Micro and macro worlds do not always work in mutual beneficial relations. America is characterized by modern technology, individualist freedom (in rationalized manner), information diffusion, free market, and public access to varied forms of sex and sexuality. High divorce rate (some traditional societies had even no concept of marriage) is a result of "effective" exploration and utilization of sexuality. Contemporary capitalist and (especially Chinese) socialist economies are common in freedom of marriage and divorce. Socialist economies "allow" low costs of divorce and freedom in market of sexuality as people would put more attention and energies to creation and stability of gender relationship, have less interest in political lies, and macro-economically spend more money and other resources on gender relations.

There are not many extensive studies on gender relations and dynamics of family in classical economics. Classical political economists had little concern about what would happen when women received education and participated in the labor market. "I predict that technology will enable people to transmit their neuronal, actual feelings over the internet" (Michio Kaku, 1947–). It is politically challenging to predict national fates basing on gender relations for future societies. "Clever and attractive women do not want to vote, they are willing to let men govern as long as they govern men." (George Bernard Shaw, 1856–1950). In contemporary American culture, "It is not women's liberation, it is women's and men's liberation." (Ruth Bader Ginsburg, 1933–2020). After WWII, America valuates gender equality, individualism, and freedom. This is an indictor to hint on the character of the nation: "You can tell the strength of a nation by the women behind its men." (Benjamin Disraeli, 1804–1881). The American man was energetic, confident, and straightforwardly honest. There is another mechanism in gender market. "Women want mediocre men, and men are working to be as mediocre as possible." (Margaret Mead, 1901–1978). This needs to be re-confirmed by modern history. But social experiments are very expensive and often take generations.

A strong and progressive race or nation is readily proud of its greatness and tends to, perhaps gradually, forget possible long-term destructiveness in association with greatness. European countries with long history of civilization evince transitory sides of greatness. It is worthwhile to cite Jung (1930): "The most amazing feature of American life is its boundless publicity. Everyone has to meet everybody else, and they seem to enjoy doing it. To a Central European like myself the lack of distance between people, the absence of hedges and fences round the gardens, the belief in popularity, the gossip columns in the newspapers, the open doors in the houses (from the street one can look right through the sitting room and the adjoining bedroom into the backyard) — all this is more than disgusting; it is directly terrifying. You are immediately swallowed up by a hot and all-engulfing wave of emotional incontinence which knows no restraint. You see it in the eagerness and the hustling of everyday life, in all sorts of enthusiasms such as orgiastic sectarian outbursts, and the violence of collective emotions spreads into everything. It easily goes too far and leads people into situations which individual deliberation would hardly ever have chosen. It has a decidedly flattening influence upon American psychology. You see this particularly in the sex problem as it has developed since the war. There is a marked tendency to promiscuity, which not only shows itself in the frequency of divorce, but more especially still in the younger generation's peculiar freedom from sex prejudices.... As an inevitable consequence, the individual rapport between the sexes will suffer from it. Easy access never calls forth, and therefore never develops, the values of character, because it forestalls any deep mutual understanding. Such an understanding, without which no real love can exist, can only be reached by overcoming all the difficulties that arise from psychological difference between the sexes. Promiscuity paralyzes all these efforts so that individual rapport seems quite superfluous. Thus, the more so-called unprejudiced freedom and easy promiscuity prevail, the more love becomes flat; it degenerates into transitory sex interludes."

Things change in the flow of history. Ideal manhood and womanhood are not invariant. The founding fathers and President Trump might have few common characters as being Man. According to Italian-American Camille Paglia (1947–), "Manhood coerced into sensitivity is not manhood at all.... Pursuit and seduction are the essence of sexuality. It's part of the sizzle." Kimmel (2018: 1-2) specifies: "the sources of the current confusion, defensiveness, and malaise among America men lie deep in our nation's past. Beginning in the early part of the nineteenth century, the idea of testing and proving one's manhood became one of the defining experiences in American men's lives. The long-term causes of the idea of proving one's manhood were structural — change in the work world, the political arena, and the family." This variation has social and psychological consequences on the nation's strength.

Gender relations and economic conditions have important implications on national population growth. Poor countries produce too fast and too many babies, while developed economies cannot replace population declination. Some developed economies take in immigrants to sustain national development, faced with risks of disappearance of its own culture. Other developed economies see population to decline and would not allow many immigrants. They are faced with the risk of vanishing of nations. China is starting to encourage young people to have more babies. America is permitting itself to be flooded with immigrants from non-Western societies. Whether these new immigrants can help America to enhance productivity per capita and boost its already low average IQ population is another challenging question.

4.2 Romantic Playfulness and the Dynamics of Family

> The ancients who wished to illustrate illustrious virtue throughout the empire, first ordered well their own States. Wishing to order well their States, they first regulated their families. Wishing to regulate their families, they first cultivated their persons. Wishing to cultivate their persons, they first rectified their hearts. Wishing to rectify their hearts, they first sought to be sincere in their thoughts. Wishing to be sincere in their thoughts, they first extended to the utmost their knowledge.

Confucius (551–479 BC)

Stephen Hawking (1942–2018) sees the complexity of matters in the universe and life: "Many people find the universe confusing — it's not.... Women. They are a complex mystery." For him, the evolution of the universe is clear, but woman is beyond comprehension. He also blusters about his married life: "My wife and I love each other very much." This is not verifiable. He honestly and correctly gloats over the commercial success of his globally popular book: "I had not expected 'A Brief History of Time' to be a best seller." Many financial gamblers have succeeded in predicting financial markets, while geniuses on the evolution of the universe, such as Einstein and Hawking, failed in playing the romantic market and made mistakes in predicting financial or book markets. Newton and Einstein are famous for losing their monetary fortunes — which they earned from discovering laws of the universe — in the investment and gender markets. Human hearts, tiny as they are, defy prediction more surely than the evolution of the universe. The heart is made to prey on other hearts, not to pamper itself, at least in the biological sense. Somerset Maugham felt love in an alternative way: "Love is only a dirty trick played on us to achieve continuation of the species." Man is unique in that his sexual playfulness can be repeatedly conducted even without expecting the genuine consequence. This character bolsters continuation of the modern economy.

Economic theory has a long way to go before it satisfactorily integrates gender relations into its kingdom. America is the first civilization that has re-defined, if not broken, almost all traditional moral codes and duties on woman and man's relations. Sustainability of American sexuality and gender relations is another question that no theory rigorously addresses. The literature about gender issues is characterized by emotions rather than rational analyses (at least from macroeconomic perspectives). Scientists ask all important questions about evolution of the universe. But implications of American freedom of sex are little examined in an integrative manner. American society might be finally destroyed by freedom of sex, for instance, if the rich produce too many social parasites, the middle class have fewer children, and the poor bear too many to feed their children, not to mention to afford higher education. Unskilled immigrants might be unable to engender America great again in the global village as they would turn out negative contributors to society with penetration of robots into global labor markets and fast development of the rest world.

"Woman is the civilizer of man" is valid, perhaps, in societies with a traditional division of labor and consumption. In contemporary metropolitan areas, cultivated and educated men have neither need nor time to be cultivated by women. They get socially, economically, and sexually cultivated through all channels possibly perceivable and available. Mae West (1907–1980) says women should stick to men who are trained or experienced: "Don't marry a man to reform him — that's what reform schools are for." It is much more convenient to buy almost cooked food in supermarket. What Tyne Daly (1946–) says might make no sense for some of her children: "I think mothers get a raw deal in American culture, so I've been defending them. I have three daughters, and I know that as they became mothers, they got a lot more gentle towards me." One might wonder whether this attitude has any relevance to women born and brought up in America. If they are "allowed" to be freely established in human society, like in the bird world, gender relations would exhibit chaotic patterns.

Chaos camouflages self-destructiveness as well as constructiveness. No one can predict towards which equilibrium, if there is any, a society will evolve owing to unlimited variations of gender relations and relations between power and sex. Mike Pence (1959–) touches on human trust in

American life: "What is real is that adultery destroys tens of thousands of families every year across America. What is real is that adultery scars tens of thousands of children emotionally and psychologically every year. What is real is that adultery is an open wound in a relationship which more often than not overflows into domestic violence or worse." America once adored great scientists such as Einstein. Its fashionable persons are now switched to gamblers in financial markets and CEOs, as well as super stars in sports, arts, and music. Financial gambling and effective creators of flows of pleasure, which are traditionally perceived as potential killers of the national long-term power, are playing an increasing important role in the global image of America.

Jordan Peterson (1962–) expounded: "The masculine spirit is under assault. It's obvious." America has enlarged population base with huge immigrants over its short history. Its domestic population dynamics is determined by marriage decisions, household composition, fertility, child-rearing, and education. A profound change in the history of the America family is the separation of the workplace from the home. Men increasingly spent their wage-earning careers in factories and small industries after 1800 (Smith, 1982). During the 1970s, American society evinced changes in rates of fertility and illegitimacy (Freedman, 1982). There were concerns over marital intercourse, contraceptives, abortion, and meanings of sexuality. Barack Obama (1961–), the 44th president of the United States from 2009 to 2017, states his attitude on gay marriage: "I believe marriage is between a man and a woman. I am not in favor of gay marriage. But when you start playing around with constitutions, just to prohibit somebody who cares about another person, it just seems to me that's not what America's about. Usually, our constitutions expand liberties, they don't contract them."

"Woman is the dominant sex. Men have to do all sorts of stuff to prove that they are worthy of woman's attention." (Camille Paglia, 1947–). The Italian-American professor appears to reflect on Italian culture. Marriage is a private matter between two people. It is a consequence of love, commitment, and relation. On the other hand, it is a public institution (Cott, 2000, Hilfer, 2003; Pluckrose and Lindsay, 2020; Soh, 2020). Forms of marriage in the United States have not only been embedded in national policy, law, and political rhetoric, but have had impact on some other countries as well. The model of consensual and lifelong monogamy based on Christian tenets and the English common law was wrecked with multifarious shapes of marriages. America has now motley legal forms of marriages. Marital policies reflect US moral and social standards, affect the citizenry, gender roles, and racial differences.

In modern times people choose to live together without marriage, marry late, and divorce. "It is capitalist America that produced the modern independent woman. Never in history have women had more freedom of choice in regard to dress, behavior, career, and sexual orientation." (Camille Paglia, 1947–). Woman's economic independence reduces the weight of staying together with a man in the choice preference and increases the weight of emotional satisfaction in maintaining the relation. Emotion is like cloud in sky. It is thus natural that when both man and woman are less tied together by economic benefits, they tend to separate as love is often too "expensive" for one side and does not naturally last long. As demonstrated in Figure 4.1 (Ortiz-Ospina and Roser, 2020), in 1920 marriages per 1,000 people in the US were twice as many as today. The long decline started in the 1970s and is still continuing.

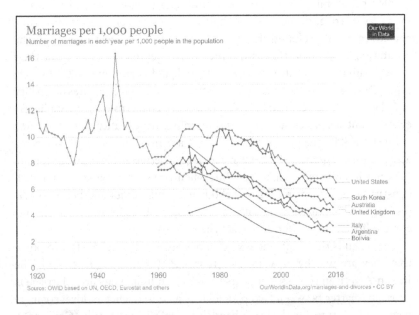

Figure 4.1 Dynamics of Marriage, Selected Countries

The age at which Americans are getting married is also going up. Cohabitation, which refers to an arrangement where two or more people live together without marriage, is common in America. For instance, the share of individuals between the age of 18 and 24 living with an unmarried partner rose from 0.1% to 9.4% over the period 1968–2018. The share of children born outside of marriage has increased substantially. Single-parent households have also increased. Most of these households are headed by women. They are mostly financially vulnerable. But they tend to be short-term as the remarriage rate among this type of households is high. It has also become common to see same-gender marriage in America — in 2004 it was permitted in only one state, and by 2015 in all fifty states.

Jordan Peterson (1962–) argued: "We're so immaturely cynical as a culture. We're not wise enough to look at an institution like marriage and to really think about what it means and what it signifies. It signifies a place where people can tie the ropes of their lives together so that they're stronger. It signifies a place where people can tell the truth to one another."

A high divorce rate follows American democracy and individualism, especially when America goes through fast economic progress and rapid enlarging income gaps. Romanticism increases weight of love in marriage and individualism lightens the weight of responsibility in family life. Secured economic conditions and pursuit of personal happiness creates a gender market with vivid dynamics of unification and separation. The American value of independence, pursuit of happiness, geographical mobility, and prosperity should have a natural equilibrium divorce rate in gender market, as demonstrated in Figure 4.2 (Ortiz-Ospina and Roser, 2020). America is not exceptional. Long-term trends of divorce and marriage rates are similar among rational rich countries. The same economic and emotional principles function in those countries as they are reading the same book, sitting in the same class, listening to the same music, receiving the same philosophy, watching the same film, living in the same style of housing, eating the same variety of food (as far as nutrition balance is concerned), having the same distribution between work and leisure (with adjustment by wage and wealth), and traveling to the same resort in this globalized world. Convergence in gender markets is the same as in other goods and service markets. The happy family is happy mathematically in the same pattern. Divorce's impact on personal growth and macroeconomic performances is generally situation dependent. For instance, after divorce, a person might be faced with new impasses and discover latent human capital not applied or found before in solving new dilemmas. As family is broken, separated members may need more goods and services than living together, which encourage macroeconomic performances and create job opportunities in society. Children of divorce may be disadvantaged in comparison with children brought up in stable families. But some children are quite successful in adulthood as people master assorted skills, values, and ideas with different family backgrounds. Children are often psychologically "normal" or even stronger and independent, risk-taking, entrepreneurial in a social, cultural, and institutional environment where divorce is socially acceptable and perceived natural. When man lived in wild, there was no institution like marriage. Natural man had no institutionalized responsibility. The monkey boss, like a father in some traditional society, takes care of his family because he is respected and obeyed and dominates the access to food and sex. In free society, fatherhood is no more respected and obeyed — a man may look so awful and powerless to their own well-informed children in a society where money and social status mean above everything else.

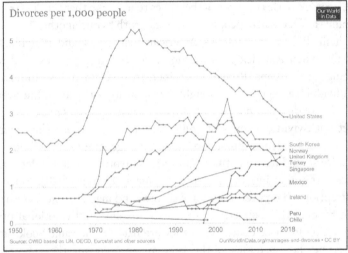

Figure 4.2 Dynamics of Divorce, Selected Countries

Divorce rate is related to other variables in the society. It is positively said that even half of marriages last forever. As demonstrated in Figure 4.3 (Ortiz-Ospina and Roser, 2020), this is true for the people who got married in the 1970s in America. The rate varies over generations. The young genera-tion's rates did not over-reach that during the 1970s. George Will (1941-) warns: "Some calamities — the 1929 stock market crash, Pearl Harbor, 9/11 — have come like summer lighting, as bolts from the blue. The looming crisis of America's Ponzi entitlement structure is different. Driven by the demo-graphics of an aging population, its causes, timing and scope are known."

Mankind is still too young to find a long-run equilibrium in gender market as modern societies are producing more technologies to satisfy desires of sex and sexuality and deal with personal and social unrests origi-nated from these desires. "Reduced to a miserable mass level, the level of a Hitler, German Romanticism broke out into hysterical barbarism" (Thomas Mann, 1875-1955).

Figure 4.3 Share of Marriages Ending in America

Hysterical barbarism is perhaps only transitory. One day a market equilibrium is achieved at which everyone can be at the romantic state where "Romance is the glamour which turns the dust of everyday life into a golden haze," (C. Gold Heilbrun, 1926–2003). Life is essentially dust. Dust can be very beautiful, at least, in very expensive modern museums in metropoli. Japanese art is excellent at turning a common rotten leaf into the most beautiful and memorial experience of life.

Romanticism under protection of law, which has not much to do with human nature and freedom, is a modern innovation. All rational and prosperous economies with romanticism are either importing a large portion of immigrants or are faced with serious dilemmas in association with falling populations. As economic income and education levels have evolved increasingly more unequal, how immigrants from poor economies are assimilated into rich countries are becoming global issues. In modern economies a poor immigrant will become another Einstein or bring more poor immigrants to a modern society. America is reforming its immigration policies to re-calculate national benefits and costs. Immigrants might contribute to American society far less than they cost because simple jobs can be replaced by robots and lifetime costs, associated with poverty, education, medical caring, and other social welfare, are rapidly increasing in developed economies. Moreover, it is a strict assumption that highly talented foreigners would choose America as the homeland like in the last century.

A society brainwashes the public with ideas, religions, or ideologies with the contents and spirits that it benefits the powerful group. People are addicted physically to drugs, emotionally to love, and mentally to assumptions/axioms/god. Addition to drug causes healthy, social, and economic disorders. It is not an easy matter to deal away with drugs especially for a country with long prosperity and freedom like America. Drug equips one to lead a fast, frivolous, and dissipated life. It has a great power over humans and the attraction naturally lasts longer than carefully-faked sexuality. It is a well-known history that opium made a great contribution to the history of China's humiliation from the 1840s till the 1910s. Different from addiction to drugs, societies with freedom and individualism "allow" young people to freely love as addiction to love usually does not last long, at least for most people. As family ties are broken, young people's relations might not destroy livelihood of parents as often in traditional societies with strong family ties. In modern societies people learn much from first love and many are not addicted again. For modern adults, love is a playful pleasure, without demanding final product, babies, as the fruit. On the other hand, humans are genetically structured with capacity to enjoy sexual playfulness almost without limits. It is due to biological evolution and gender strategy choice over history that sexual playfulness for the sake of sexuality might be continuously conducted. Family built by the same gender is becoming common in many Western societies. Affluent and educated people in modern societies still have something to do with sexual playfulness. Sex and sexuality distributions are not a main concern of fairness in modern democratic societies, at least in theory as issues are too private and too personal. Nevertheless, solid edifice is constructed on solid foundation. Whether family is still necessarily the foundation of a society with future technologies remain to see. Man has little idea about what technologies might advance individuals and the society to do without family. No animal like man can sexually, spiritually, ideologically, adapt to anything. Man is planning to immigrate to some remote plants after he is almost destroying his homeland.

4.3 Gender Games and Broken Families

> The root of the kingdom is in the state. The root of the state is in the family. The root of the family is in the person of its head.
>
> Mencius (372–289 BC)
>
> A son dealing with the troubles caused by his father. ... The position is perilous, but there will be good fortune in the end.
>
> A son dealing with the troubles caused by his mother. He should not carry his firm correctness to the utmost.
>
> The Yi Jing

"When the faith dies, the culture it produced begins to die, then the civilization goes, then, the population." (Pat Buchanan, 1938–). America is not afraid of decline of the population as it can cajole more to trek in. No one knows in what direction America will evolve even in near future as the majority of democratic America is no more Europe-based. It has now encouraged women and immigrants to make America great again as talented American men are interested in engaging in, except those indulging in playing alone by meditation (in a very high stage of mind maturity as Asian rich people had done over hundred years), financial gambling, political game, conducting social justice (lawyers), entertaining millions (superstars) and serving these stars, managing obedient servants (CEOs), writing popular books and easily accessible textbooks, and saving rich and aged people (medical doctors). Successful men are simultaneously relishing big money, great reputation, high value in masses markets, secured flows of happiness, and celebrated social networks. Thoreau (1910: 80) foresees the destine of modern man: "But lo! Men have become the tools of their tools.... We have built for this world a family mansion, and for the next a family tomb.... the effect of our art is merely to this low state comfortable and that higher state to be forgotten." "I have thought a sufficient measure of civilization is the influence of good women," Emerson (1803–1882) remarked. The question is how to define "good woman" and how many good ones one can find in a "mature" civilization. Influential women are usually, perhaps mistakenly and biasedly in the standard of current American state of mind, referred to being masculine.

Creativity hides destructiveness. Man's high creativity in the last two hundred years lows his own exchange value in gender market. "We owe to the Middle Ages the two worst inventions of humanity — romantic love and gun power," Andre Maurois (1885-1967) pointed out. Gun power liberated Han Chinese from being servants of China's "neighboring" nomads. Gun power rendered both the Great Wall and nomadic killing skills useless.

Gun power empowered the West in bridging the world. Mankind could not progress towards a nuclear-power-bolstered peaceful world without gun power between. Romantic love plays a significant role in reducing the global population and has made a great contribution to building prosperous economies. This positive role is still strengthening as more women are accessible to higher education in association with freedom of romantic love. "I don't know the question, but sex is definitely the answer," quipped Woody Allen (1956–).

America plays a major role in leading the world to new value systems, new sexuality, new types of gender relations, and new types of lifestyles. Almost any perceivable combination of human relations has been publicly and legally tried in the American style of freedom. Free America has brought mankind to a great variety of personal relations on a mass scale. No other human society has sustained so many varieties of human relations, relatively peacefully, within one system over such a long period.

Human relations can be created with, mathematically, almost unlimited patterns, but only very limited ones can be socially sustainable. Non-sustainable ones are relegated to museums, fiction novels, and the like, as they may be useful again as conditions are changed. Many values that mankind had collectively built over many centuries were broken by America in a few decades. East Asia has followed the American styles and is making great social progress in many ways. But these areas are faced with rapidly falling birth rates. Taiwan, Japan, and Korea might disappear as economic powerhouses as the population declines and might not be replaced. If the game is collectively played improperly, in the long term, a society may experience catastrophes as socioeconomic evolution is irreversible. America the Great, after WWII, has been through an era of exciting trials of heterogeneous human relations. Whether these support survival and sustainability, only time will tell. One result is obvious: America will no longer be white-dominated in the near future because the demographic changes are also reflected in changing voter priorities

A family based on romanticism requires more than a joyful friendship. Moral rules, duties, economic relations, social relations, and rights are mingled in varied proportions. When rights and duties are in harmony, social dilemmas can be fixed in a rational and certain manner. When they are in conflict, one society may prefer to apply duties above rights, and vice versa. Fukuyama (1992) concludes that in America men have perfect rights but no perfect duties to their partners. He looks at this as an Anglo–Saxon version of liberty. As human behavioral relations are articulated clearly and protected according to the written law, men would make decisions by obeying law, rather than ambiguously defining, or vaguely referring to, duties or respon-sibilities. Fukuyama argues that there would be reasonably many problems, such as the high divorce rate and the lack of parental authority, in a ratio-nally well-calculated and wealthy contemporary American family, as conse-quences of this law-based value. There are no stable ties between American families as all the members make their decisions based on liberal principles — each member of the family makes decisions like a member of a joint stock company with the utility which may or may not be dependent on ties of both duty and love. According to his analysis, a stable marriage should also be based on the "irrational (from the perspective of economic cost-benefit calculations) personal sacrifices" of the members of a family. Strong family life is maintained and transmitted across generations sometimes through sacrifices that some members of the family make for the sake of the family. But Americans, especially those who follow the liberal tradition, abrogate the terms of the contract when the obligations of family become more than what they bargained for.

Liberty and equality are the two most honored values in the American democratic tradition. American tradition believes that no one has a right to tell another how to live his life, and government has no business interfering in the private lives of citizens.

In the United States, there is less contact between people today than there was in the past. Increasingly, young people reject marriage, divorce easily, abandon their children, and have few friends. The great change in sexual morality is part of a massive change in the behavior on America.

The increasing numbers of single mothers and their dependent children are extremely vulnerable economically and socially. In recent years almost 30% of all children have been born out of wedlock. In 1993, over 46% of all families with children headed by a single woman lived in poverty; but only 9% of married-couple families with dependent children lived below the poverty line. Eleven per cent of the mother-only families were poor even though the mother worked full-time year-round (Rodgers, 1996:4).

According to Rodgers, mother-only families tend to be poor because: (1) women have lower earning potential than men on average; (2) single women with dependent children have high unemployment rates; (3) mother-only families have few income resources; (4) most of these families receive either no support from absent fathers or inadequate support; and (5) American public policies do not pay sufficient attention to families.

Between 1970 and 1993, the number of mother-only families expanded from 3.8 to 8.7 million. By 1993, almost one of every four American families with children was headed by a woman, compared one in ten in 1960 (the US

Bureau of Census, 1995). In 1993, some 17.9 million children lived with only one parent, 87% of them with their mother. Majority of mother-only families resulted from divorce and separation. By the 1990s, about half of all children under eighteen had seen parental divorce. Moreover, an increasingly large proportion of mother-only families were due to births to unwed women. In 1993, about 36% of all mother-only families were the consequences of out-of-wedlock births. Of the current generation of all the American children, more than half will spend some of their childhood in a single-mother household. Many American adults have abandoned their children. Many adults live alone (Klinenberg, 2013). America has gone through an abdication of parental responsibility in a scale unseen in human history. Younger generations are even less well socialized and more self-preoccupied than the previous generations.

Families have changed dramatically in the past few decades. Nonmarital childbearing is a common phenomenon as demonstrated in Figure 4.4. In recent years, almost 40% of children have been born to unmarried parents in America. The parents' ethnic backgrounds and education levels have significant impact.

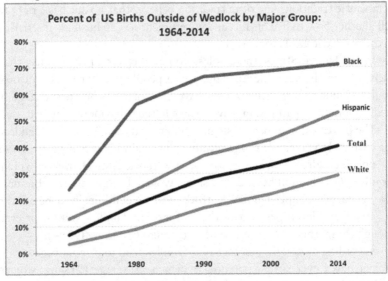

Figure 4.4 Dynamics of US Births Outside of Wedlock in Percentage, 1964–2014

4.4 Criminals in America

> The man who is fond of daring and is dissatisfied with poverty, will proceed to insubordination.
>
> Confucius (551-479 BC, 8:10)

Criminals are an integrated part of human society. More freedom simply implies less control or fewer constraints in choice. In *Meditation*, Marcus Aurelius said: "To expect bad men not to do wrong is madness." History shows that to expect the ignorant masses to choose virtuous and capable men as the leader is madness. Man is a learning animal whose behavior is controlled by rational calculations with hidden motivations, occasionally directed by uncontrollable emotions. Bad men can cleverly learn to appear good to achieve hidden motivations, as Xun Zi argued.

America clings to freedom in politics, freedom in wealth, and freedom in sex. The attitude against alien values is beneficial to America because the country has profound reasons for plundering and doing profitable businesses in global environment. Freedom encourages and facilitates people with animal spirits to do things which please them, at least, for a moment. It is supposed that men can form an orderly society through self-organization with profits as the final goal of human action. Nevertheless, freedom in association with individualism in sex and sexualism lead to broken family — the most essential and basic institution among high civilizations in history. In truly free society children livelihood can hardly be secured as some adults have little sense of family responsibility and inequalities in income and wealth make poor people have no means to properly bring up children. Mencius (372–289 BC, 11:7) reasons more than two thousand years ago: "In good years, the children of the people are most of them good, while in bad years most of them abandon themselves to evil. It is not owing to their natural powers conferred by Heaven that they are thus different. The abandonment is owing to the circumstances through which they allow their minds to be ensnared and drowned in evil." We still miss empirical confirmations on to what degree the broken family contributes the uninterrupted criminal rate in America.

Emerson (1803–1882) described American reality: "Good men must not obey the laws too well." This is a practically accepted definition of the good and practically active American man, as distinguished in behavior of Benjamin Franklin and Steve Jobs. This is the reality from many well-known American men in the past as well as in the present. In 1978 China opened its door to the U.S. and began to send students to study in America. In the early 1980s, young students, whose parents' monthly salary together were

US$20, knew almost nothing about the world. The Chinese government asked Chinese students in New York to keep minimum US$20 in pockets. They were taught that when being robbed, they might be shot to death if the robber did not find any valuable and felt frustrated with the failure in New Yorker's professionalism (New York's situation had been much improved in recent years). "We must reject the idea that every time a law is broken, society is guilty rather than the lawbreaker. It is time to restore the American precept that each individual is accountable for his actions." (Ronald Reagan, 1911–2004). The American society places a high premium on economic affluence. Merton (1957:169) says: "...success and failure are results wholly of personal qualities that he who fails has only himself to blame, for the corollary to the concept of the self-made man is the self-unmade man. To the extent that this cultural definition is assimilated by those who have not made their mark, failure represents a double defeat: the manifest defeat of remaining far behind in the race for success and the implicit defeat of not having the capacities and moral stamina needed for success... It is in this cultural setting that, in a signifi-cant portion of cases, the threat of defeat motivates men to the use of those tactics, beyond the law or the mores, which promise 'success.'" Thus, it may be that the American emphasis on individual success tends to lead individuals to commit crimes (Spence, 1985). Bell (1960, 116-7) argued that large-scale crime was a natural by-product of American culture: "The desires satisfied in extra-legal fashion were more than a hunger for the 'forbidden fruits' of conventional morality. They also are involved in the complex and ever shifting structure of group, class, and ethnic stratification, which is the warp and woof of America's 'open' society, such 'normal' goals as independence through a business of one's own, and such 'moral' aspirations as the desire for social advancement and social prestige. For crime, in the language of the sociologists, has a 'functional' role in the society, and the urban rackets — the illicit activity organized for continuing profit. . . [are] one of the queer ladders of social mobility in Amer-ican life." Free America had extreme high crime rate 5.3 even in 2017. In the same year some countries' criminal rates as follows: Panama (9.7), Uruguay (8.2), Argentina (5.1), Canada (1.8), Germany (1), Australia (0.8), Japan (0.2), and Singapore (0.2). The crime rate in America has fallen in recent years as demonstrated in Figure 4.5, even though the total number rose due to the population base was expanded.

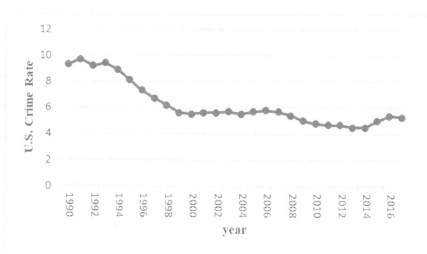

Figure 4.5 U.S. Crime Rate per 100K Population, 1990–2017

In recent years nearly seven of every thousand people in the United States is in a federal or state prison or local jail. The number rises to 11 of every thousand working-age adults. America has less 5% of the global population but its share of the world's incarcerated people is 20%. Like its Nobel prizes, American has much higher rate than the average rate in the rest of the world. Desirable numbers and negative numbers are often in close correlations statistically in aggregated levels. America's relative position in the world is illustrated in Figure 4.6. Although the rate has recently fallen, it is still leading the world. Contributions of military sector, dugs, prostitutes, crimes, and private guns to the US economy are so huge that the government would hardly do anything with its huge income resources. Each president reasonably borrows money and tries to neglect these issues. Mencius (372–289 BC, 1:7) mentioned importance of wealth for social harmony: "As to the people, if they have not a certain livelihood, it follows that they will not have a fixed heart. And if they have not a fixed heart, there is nothing which they will not do, in the way of self-abandonment, of moral deflection, of depravity, and of wild license. When they thus have been involved in crime, to follow them up and punish them — this is to entrap the people."

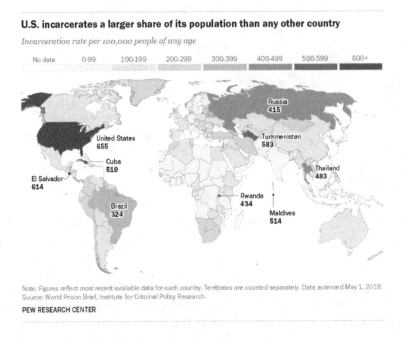

U.S. incarcerates a larger share of its population than any other country

Incarceration rate per 100,000 people of any age

| No data | 0-99 | 100-199 | 200-299 | 300-399 | 400-499 | 500-599 | 600+ |

Russia 415

United States 655

Turkmenistan 583

Cuba 510

Thailand 483

El Salvador 614

Rwanda 434

Brazil 324

Maldives 514

Note: Figures reflect most recent available data for each country. Territories are counted separately. Data accessed May 1, 2018.
Source: World Prison Brief, Institute for Criminal Policy Research.

PEW RESEARCH CENTER

Figure 4.6 Incarceration Rates of the World May 1, 2018

4.5 Multiculturalism with Immigrants

> Things joined by profit, when pressed by misfortune and danger, will cast each other aside.
>
> Zhuangzi (369 BC–295 BC)

Americans have been able to maintain an orderly society mainly due to abundant opportunities for wealth. As there is no solid reason for cultural assimilation, the harmony will be broken if there is no more easy money to earn. Rationalized criticism has high probability to be correct as imperfection is matter of fact in organic complex systems. In human life, imperfection is common if judged correctly, perfection is rare even if judged incorrectly. Poor and uneducated immigrants from poor countries came to the dream land with great dreams and hopes without knowledge, time, and sense of justice to see difficulties and tried their best to assimilate to the new foreign culture. Nevertheless, new global immigrants have different human capital from those before the 1980s. They have sharper and more critical eyes on positive as well as negative aspects on American society. They have already properly calculated how to get benefits legally merely by reading internets across the earth. Wolfe (1998) adumbrated how America was uncertain about many domestic issues. Many Americans crave for moderation, tolerance, accommodation, integration, and balance. But their behavior materializes collective disorder. For instance, they would bolster bilingual education programs, but only if they are short-lived. They encourage multiculturalism under the condition that ethnic identity is subsumed to the common American identity. "In America the majority raises formidable barriers around the liberty of opinion; within these barriers an author may write what he pleases, but woe to him if he goes beyond them," Alexis de Tocqueville (1805–1859) delineated American society.

America has made many great achievements, but also has been with botherations such as widespread discrimination, exploitation, violent anti-foreign movements, and a constantly renewed debate over equality, opportunity for a limited, and difficulties for national identity. Olzak (1992, 2006) applies ecological theories of competition and niche overlap to examine instances of ethnic collective action that occurred in American society around the turn of the 19th century. The causes of racial and ethnic confrontations, protests, riots, and attacks in the largest American cities are examined with causal dynamics between exclusion and repression. The intensification of ethnic competition generates collective actions by dominant ethnic groups that are designed to maintain their dominance and control. It is reasonable to expect that if competition becomes severe, ethnic boundaries will be salient, and ethnic collective action will spontaneously erupt. Ethnic conflict surges when barriers to ethnic group contact and competition begin to break down. Olzak tested relation between niche overlap and ethnic conflict. The event-history data involve 262 ethnic and racial conflicts that occurred in 77 large American cities from 1877 to 1914. It is concluded that low levels of ethnic and racial inequality will produce a high rate of ethnic and racial conflict. Low levels of occupational segregation tend to cause higher rates of ethnic conflict. If this conclusion is applicable to other situations, upward mobility of ethnic minorities in multifarious parts should be associated with intensified conflicts. In the United States, declining and low levels of segregation of the foreign-born will raise the rates of both conflict and protest. Competition for jobs during periods when ethnic diversity is rising would incline dominant groups to exploit organizations to restrain open rivalry. "These solutions," Olzak (1992:218) observes, "include passing rules restricting the rights of access to valued resources, as well as violence. In the United States, they sometimes involved reviving old systems of Apartheid, such as . . . disenfranchisement strategies."

"The Hispanic culture is finding its way into the American culture. Places like Miami are going to be centers for that influence — places like Los Angeles and, certainly, cities like Texas" (Randy Falco, 1953–). I noticed this phenomenon some years ago when I were twice circulating the United States with the Greyhound. Janet Mock (1983–) described: "I was a mixed black girl existing on a westernized Hawaiian culture where petite Asian women were the ideal, in a white culture where black women were furthest from the standard of beauty, in an America culture where trans women of color were invisible." America has gone through broken family. There is no strong reason to expect that racial assimilation will occur in American society. A country without family life can hardly have harmonious relations among various cultures with free association. The strong tends to be away from the weak while the weak pretends to think and live like the strong. In America, skin color generates a comprehensible and unerring identity for separation and unification. Profits are the most effective factor of assimilation. But the strong wants to take it all and monopolistic power and already concentrated wealth makes the strong to be stronger. When individualistic people lose family value and do not want to make further investment in family life, family is broken with high probability. This is similar for racial and inter-racial relations. As education is more widely disseminated, income gaps are widened, and people are more individualistic, it is reasonable to expect that American society is further divided, not only between races, but also within the race.

"The only sound foundation for a civilization is a sound state of mind." (E.M. Forster, 1879–1970). Disregarding (perhaps unconsciously) the history of slavery and colonization, Bell and Jayasuriya (1995:3) asserted that "Western political thinkers generally share a belief that 'all persons are by nature equal,' a principle of equal respect for the moral status and intrinsic worth of each person. . . . Needless to say, this principled commitment to equality has been imperfectly applied in practice . . . but at least at the level of theory most Western thinkers since the birth of liberalism in seventeenth-century England begin with an assumption that the interests of each member of the community matters, and matters equally ... help to explain the taken-for-granted, uncontroversial status of an egalitarian premise." The question for multiple cultures is what God implies for different people. British applied power, law, and knowledge to colonize the world; and now races once colonized by the English-speaker feel at home in places dominated by English language.

Williams (1960) listed eight traits of the American culture: "(1) It is organized around the attempt at active mystery rather than passive acceptance, with little tolerance of frustration, strong refusal to accept ascetic renunciation, a positive encouragement of desire, the stress on power, and the approval of egoassertion; (2) It emphasizes in the external world of things and events, of the palpable and immediate, rather than puts attention to the inner experience of meaning and affect. It is good at manipulativeness rather than contemplativeness; (3) Its worldview tends to be open rather than closed: it emphasizes change, flux, movement; its central personality types are adaptive, accessible, and outgoing; (4) In a wide historical and comparative perspective, the culture places its primary faith in rationalism as opposed to traditionalism; it deemphasizes the past, orients strongly to the future, does not accept things just because they have been done before; (5) Closely related to the above is the dimension of orderliness rather than unsystematic ad hoc acceptance of transitory experience; (6) With conspicuous deviation, a main theme is a universalistic rather than a particularistic ethic; (7) Human relations are based "horizontal" rather than "vertical" emphases: peerrelations not superordinatesubordinate relations and equality rather than hierarchy; (8) It emphasizes individual personality rather than group identity and responsibility." It is a broad characterization of American culture before the end of the 1950s. The traits listed do not mention racial issues — a main problem of America in the long term. It is quite easy to find some exceptions to each of these generalized formulations, as well as widespread alternative themes.

For people who emigrated to the United States after WWII from motley parts of the world, America has represented not only the land of opportunity, but also of equal opportunity. It has given every American citizen a promise that anyone, irrespective of racial background and current social and economic situation, can rise in station and achieve wealth and respectability. Over the years, these new Americans have come to hold many things in common. They have been assimilated into their homogeneous vision of American society. They have a common identity, a common English language, a common set of democratic ideals, a public life of participation in politics, government, and the economy. Ethnically diverse populations are indoctrinated with significant symbols of being American, such as the flag, the Declaration of Independence, the Liberty Bell, Abraham Lincoln's Emancipation Proclamation and Gettysburg Address, the Constitution, individualism, self-reliance, as well as a sense of "membership" in a superpower and the richest country on the earth. America tries to cultivate a patriotic and unified national culture to establish harmonious interethnic and interracial relations. Americans now share a popular culture created by consumer producers, advertising, and electronic media. In the 1950s and 1960s, African

Americans moved to assert their social and political rights. They articulated differences as a cultural asset rather than as a racial liability. The Black Civil Rights Movement achieved great successes with the Civil Rights Act of 1964 and the Voting Rights Act of 1965. These Acts dramatically expanded legal representation in America. In the 1960s, Mexican Americans began to underline their culture. In the latter part of the century, America allowed in large numbers of Asian and Latino immigrants and underwent rapid economic globalization and international mobility.

Americans have a dream — a dream of equal opportunity to accumulate wealth. Le Bon discussed behavioral implications of the crowd dream: "A crow is not merely impulsive and mobile. Like a savage, it is not prepared to admit that anything can come between its desire and the realisation of its desire." Ludwig von Mises (1881–1973) catered more dimensions of economic dynamics: "Economic prosperity is not so much a material problem; it is, first of all, an intellectual, spiritual, and moral problem." If economic prosperity brings about so many other issues, America is faced with new challenging in keeping peaceful co-existence of multiple races with sufficient large population of each race. Adam Smith held that selfish men can build a great and orderly society so far as free market conditions are secured. His theory is suitable for making British men feel good and even justified when colonizing various parts of the world and destroying other cultural heritages. "There is nothing in the world more shameful than establishing one's self on lies and fables," is what German von Goethe said about life. The 1998 Nobel Prize winner in economic sciences, Amartya Sen (1933-; 1999) deliberated upon the co-existence of multi-cultural world: "diversity is a feature of most cultures in the world. Western civilization is no exception. The practice of democracy that has won in the modern West is largely a result of a consensus that has emerged since the Enlightenment and the Industrial Revolution, and particular in the last century or so. To read in this a historical commitment of the West — over the millennia — to democracy, and then to contrast it with non-Western traditions (treating each as monolithic) would be a great mistake." An Indian scholar on history, like Chinese one, tended to think of history in a very long perspective. An American scholar has no time to form the preference yet and perhaps has no need forever. Mankind is entering new possibilities which man has never experienced.

Love creates happiness, but it is also associated with — for some people unbearable — costs. In racial assimilation, like any human relations, emotional as well as economic costs and benefits matter. There are costs and benefits in discrimination and assimilation. American culture advocates for, on the one hand, individualism, and on the other hand, has habits of rational calculations. There are neither strong cultural forces, nor emotional needs, nor religious unifier, nor economic benefits for racial assimilation in an individualistic, highly educated, and rational American society. The more prosperous and more educated America is, the more divided America might become. Americans are composed of the discriminated and discriminating ethnicities. Memory of hate tends to collectively last longer than any other emotion. According to de Crèvecoeur (Schlesinger, 1998:15), "From this promiscuous breed, that race now called Americans have arisen. . . . He is an American, who leaving behind him all his ancient prejudices and manners, receives new ones from the new mode of life he has embraced, the new government he obeys, and the new rank he holds.... Here individuals of all nations are melted into a new race of men." Old American immigrants were gradually and steadily losing its original cultural characters, perhaps most of them had never had much about their own cultural stocks. "The dominance of racism in American society —," Foner and Rosenberg (1993:1) chronicled, "resting upon centuries of federal and state sanction, legal segregation, biological 'proof' of ethnic rank, divisive hiring and discriminatory housing, the phobias and fulminations of presidents, the expeditions of the Klan, bias in school curricula, the propaganda in the press, and officially administered doses of hysteria which accompanied the birth of imperialism and the growth of US foreign involvement — is beyond doubt." Schlesinger (1998:18) recalled: "We must face the shameful fact: historically America has been a racist nation. White Americans began as a people so arrogant in convictions of racial superiority that they felt licensed to kill red people, to enslave black ones, and to import yellow and brown people for peon labor. We white Americans have been racist in our laws, in our institutions, in our customs, in our conditioned reflexes, in our souls." According to Shklar (1995:1), "America has in principle always been democratic, but only in principle."

The equality of political rights is the first mark of American citizenship; but the ideal was advocated in the presence of its absolute denial. Although American culture overtly rejects hereditary privileges, it has not managed to get beyond them in practice. Shklar (1995:8) wisecracks: "Americans have lived with extreme contradictions for most of their history by being dedicated to political equality as well as to its complete rejection."

4.6 Racial Assimilation with Economic Development and Education

> The key to growth is the introduction of higher dimensions of consciousness into our awareness.
>
> Laozi (6th or 4th BC)

Keynes quipped: "Americans are apt to be unduly interested in discovering what average opinion believes average opinion to be." Since he passed away, America has undergone great cultural changes. The Japanese American politician Mazie Hirono, who has served since 2013 as the junior United States Senator from Hawaii, has continued her preference for typical Japanese food: "One of my favorite Japanese food is called natto. It's fermented soybeans. I grew up in Japan eating natto. It's definitely an acquired taste. It's basically smelly." America today is patterned on something like tasty Indian cuisine — subtly mixed with numerous ingredients and perhaps one cannot even tell which are the essential ones.

Having passed through the period of linear advance and lived confidently as the superpower, America could have solved domestic conflicts relatively easily by delivering benefits to its citizens, importing goods and useful people (who would bring positive net-benefits to America through working or political contributions) and exporting miscellaneous expensive goods and garbage to the rest of the world. Mencius hints on the conditions for becoming a great country: "He who attends to his greater self becomes a great man, and he who attends to his smaller self becomes a small man." The Chinese ancient classics *Book of Rites* illustrates: "Through the perception of right produced by ceremony, come the degrees of the noble and the mean; through the union of culture arising from music, harmony between high and low. By the exhibition of what is to be liked and what is to be disliked, a distinction is made between the worthy and unworthy. When violence is prevented by punishments, and the worthy are raised to rank, the operation of government was made impartial. Then come benevolence in the love of the people, and righteousness in the correction of their errors; and in this way good government held its course." Mencius states: "The people are the most important element in a nation, the spirits of the land and grain are the next; the sovereign is the lightest." A nation is neither to serve a few rich with dirty hearts and nor to politicians without any decent principles to stick to. The duty of the state is not to make diligently working people pay taxes to biasedly benefit the privileged or the lazy parasites, but to deliver to all the people what they deserve fairly.

Mencius pointed out: "There is a way to get the empire — get the people, and the empire is got. There is a way to get the people — get their hearts, and the people are got. There is a way to get their hearts — it is simply to collect for them what they like, and not to lay on them what they dislike." Each part of society is complicated and interactions between parts are often incomprehensive. To keep persons healthy, society supplies medical doctors. Humans had more infectious diseases from animals. Almost 60% of bugs that infect humans originated in animals, New diseases, such as SARS, Ebola, and Zika (and the Covid-19 also?) originated in animals. Since mankind found the first virus in 1901, there are three to four new species still found every year. There are now about 220 virus species known to infect humans. It is suggested that about 300,000 pathogens have the potential from animals to humans. Man has evolved increasingly with more kinds of diseases partly as consequences of multiple cultural exchanges and doctors are specified in more fields. Each medical specialist knows his own field. People may have multiple defects in health and there are knotty relations between these diseases. Each specialist deals with his specified problem well but may worsen some other defects. It is often said that the Chinese medicine is effective for dealing with complicated health disorders as mystery compound of various materials physically neither cures nor worsen any illness but makes the patient to be addicted to a miracle. This is like current American democracy. Like physical diseases, social diseases are also diffused from one society to another. Each national ideology is associated with certain types of social diseases. Socialism, capitalism, Keynesianism, and some religions are evolved together with certain types of social diseases. No national game can eliminate all its social diseases as harmful parasites are a part of social organ. A society ruins when its social diseases have thriven too dominant. Social diseases, such as harmful social parasites, way of corruption, hypocrite "gentleman manner," illegal methods of consumption of sex and sexuality, tend to travel more fast than desirable things as they enable some people (or some gender) feel comfortable and more easily achieve their goals. For instance, in its earlier reform period, mainland China first underwent all kinds of social diseases accumulated in overseas Chinese, Korean, and Japanese societies as well as Western societies. All evils in Taiwan traveled to China very fast as Taiwanese businessmen are less influenced by the West and their styles more accessible (in comparison to Singapore and Hong Kong) to mainland Chinese. They speak both Mandarin and Cantonese. Some foreign social diseases are transitory in China, while other diseases will be rooted in Chinese cultural soil in reformed or adopted forms. When society is culturally mature, education is spread, and economy is developed, its social diseases associated with low classes are either obviously negligible or illegal, but social diseases associated with the rich, the powerful, the professional, and the elite are subtle, blurred and deeply hidden, and tend to saunter about long. Social diseases are also creation of civilizations and some of them, different from virtue, tend to survive in some societies even in the long term. Decent men die and their positive greatness die with them, but social diseases created by them loiter along with the society and even easily penetrate other societies. Everything is connected and mutually interdependent in the organ. This is a new challenge for co-existence among cultures in association with technological advances, information diffusion, and knowledge explosion. One society can be ruined with communications and trade if it has no ability to absorb positive elements from other cultures and has only potentials to allow social diseases to diffuse within the society. Mainland China got a lot of social diseases from the outsider but also absorbed positive elements in the last four decades.

Arthur Schopenhauer (1788–1860) described: "Suffering by nature or chance never seems so painful as suffering inflicted on us by the arbitrary will of another." In his *Lectures on the Philosophy of World History*, Hegel alleged that the dialectic of universal history reveals the development of consciousness of freedom and consequent realization of that freedom. Democracy in modern times is to create and maintain such a government. Rapid urbanization, industrialization, and immigration brought about great changes in education after 1865. Immigrants came to America in large numbers from many parts of the world. Assimilation through schools became increasingly important. Newcomers were expected to rapidly adapt to American life by learning English, American democracy, and basic skills needed for the workplace in schools. By 1880, almost three-quarters of school-aged children were in school, largely because compulsory school attendance laws had been adopted. Until the mid-1950s, the overt agenda included teaching girls to play a supportive role, Blacks to know their place, Indians to be civilized, and immigrants to be American workers (Mauk and Oakland, 1997:294). The civil rights movement from the mid-1950s began to scrutinize fairness and justice of this hierarchy.

Maslow's theory on human desires is quite interesting for looking at multi-cultural societies of America (Maslow, 1943, 1987). His theory of pyramid with five levels of needs holds that while people want to meet needs, these needs are successively ranked in a form of a pyramid as illustrated in Figure 4.7 (McLeod, 2018). The first four levels consist of deficiency (D–) needs and the highest one is called growth or being (B–) needs. People want to achieve the D-needs when they are not met. If these needs are denied long, people will strengthen desires intensively. Individuals tend to have lower needs first and then upgrade their demands after the low ones are satisfied. It is possible for one to have different levels of need at the same time. Cultural dynamics is characterized by nonlinear interactions: "Cultural dynamics are characterized not by a smoothly coordinated synergy of parts, a massive coalition of the whole, but by disjointed movements of first one part, and then the other. Some parts change very rapidly, while some others may be sluggish. Cultural changes do not always occur in order. They exhibit bifurcations and chaos. New orders are born from structural changes. Sometimes, cultural movement is well directed, while sometimes it may wander a long time before it is sure what to do. There is no simple progression from traditional to modern, but a twisting, spasmodic, unmethodical movement which turns as often toward repossessing the emotions of the past as disowning them." (Zhang, 1998:19).

Figure 4.7 Maslow's Hierarchy of Needs

"At once other (and "higher") needs emerge and these, rather than physiological hungers, dominate the organism. And when these in turn are satisfied, again new (and still "higher") needs emerge and so on. This is what we mean by saying that the basic human needs are organized into a hierarchy of relative prepotency" (Maslow, 1943:375). There are other needs such as cognitive needs (such as knowledge and understanding, exploration, meaning), aesthetic needs (such as appreciation and search for beauty), and transcendence needs (such as mystical experiences and religious faith) in human needs structure. Man finds the meaning of life in self-actualization and miscellaneous people are heterogeneous in needs of self-actualization. Although a government can create environment of freedom, varied higher needs do not converge among deeply divided and purposely separated people. This makes it a very frustrating task for the government to maintain a harmonious society with multi-cultural, especially, multi-religious peoples with high education. It is reasonable to expect that the more dimensions of freedom a society has, the more divided it appears. The more the society becomes divided, the more it is socially unsustainable, if it fails to identify some common enemy to unify its divided members. Efficiency and stability are often in conflict in human societies. Social and economic thinkers underline either efficiency or stability (order, harmony, continuation of culture), but the survival of an organic system needs some stabilizer factors. American has been united with multifarious fortune conditions. Without unforeseen fortunes, the American social machine might insinuate into a destructive track.

The "right" way to punish criminals varies among cultures. In *The Chrysanthemum and the Sword* published in 1946, Ruth Benedict (1974) listed many differences between gauges of right or wrong between traditional Japan and West. As living standards in many parts of the world are enhanced, American immigrants of motley cultures are no longer lowly educated and satisfied with American promise for a few hundred dollars per month through hard work. The same identity, the American flag, is a national symbol but has no well-defined contents as demonstrated publicly in numerous globally-broadcast occasions in recent years. Universal moral education cannot be effectively conducted even among rational civilizations because there is no such a universal theory — there is only collections of rational theories taught in isolation and conflict. Without a unification of theories, there will be clashes of cultures because they follow unrelated and even clashing dreams and rationalities. Camarillo (2013) examines how people of color adapted their lives in segregated settings by moving across color lines before the ending of WWII. Camarillo observes: "The great majority of African Americans, Mexican Americans, and Asian Americans in the nation's cities simply tried to make life livable for themselves and their families within a society that segregated them in neighborhoods, relegated them to particular types of jobs, and denied them equal access to public facilities.... Although less has been published about Mexican American and Asian American adaptation, the urban histories of these groups describe similar phenomena associated with adjustments to urban life." The United States is now more diverse and tolerant than ever, yet it is haunted by the threat of ethnic fragmentation (Rhea, 1997). The traditional primacy of the individual was bewildered by the values of ethnic identity and equal group status (Kim, 1999:592). Pluralism grasped group identity rather than universal belief as a primary construct of personhood. People are grouped in terms of social categories such as race, ethnicity, language, and national origin. Although Americans have faith in equality of human beings at birth, people's original natures are distorted and corrupted in the process of interaction with others (Tsuda, 1986). It tends to emphasize sameness within the group and ask for recognition of what they boast to be natural moral and intellectual rules for group distinctiveness (e.g, Williams, 2011; Sowell, 2019).

4.7 The Slovenian-American as First Lady and the American Dream

> The strength of a nation derives from the integrity of the home.
>
> Confucius (551–479 BC)

"As citizens of this great nation, it is kindness, love, and compassion for each other that will bring us together — and keep us together. These are the values Donald and I will bring to the White House" (Melania Trump). "Beauty is everywhere a welcome guest"— von Goethe confirmed the exchange law in gender markets. "I am sending you out like sheep among wolves. Therefore be as shrewd as snakes and as innocent as doves." (Matthew, 10:16). Albert Einstein is well known for his saying: "If I am proved correct, the Germans will call me a German, the Swiss will call me a Swiss citizen, and the French will call me a great scientist. If relativity is proved wrong, the French will call me a Swiss, the Swiss will call me a German, and the Germans will call me a Jew."

Hillary Clinton (1947–) unraveled the change in the American dream: "For centuries, New York has served as the gateway for millions of people from all over the world in search of the American dream. It only makes sense that it would now serve as a gateway for the world's greatest athletes." "Throughout history females have picked providers. Males have picked anything," (Margaret Mead, 1901–1978). Males did anything to provide a livelihood for women and family in traditional societies. Now women are as capable as men in collecting useful things, which is making men change their actions and strategies to survive.

Socialist China had been a reliable economic servant of America for the four decades since 1978. China played a role of female cleaner for America. Many pretty girls and women, not to mention smart and diligent young men, born in and brought up in socialist economies have been remodeled into great American citizens. It does seem that beautiful females from poor socialist economies are more quickly adaptive to advanced American culture than educated males from the same cultures. For the beauty and the talented brought up in poor socialist economies, America was the best place to improve their lives through their efforts and fortune. There are plenty of stories that celebrated Chinese "beauties" (in China's socialist standard in the 1980s and in 1990s) were married into America with men they had hardly known. Now the trend is still going on. Celebrated beauties and rich women have transfigured into American citizens with their rich mainland Chinese husbands and are still working in mainland China. America-born Chinese are very humble due to the discrimination environment they had been brought up and many of them tend to be more traditional Chinese even than mainland Chinese brought up in no discrimination environment (instead, they are in the position to discriminate others). America is now not so attractive for beauties in East Asia to find someone to get married and immigrate, but to buy houses as successful symbols and future retirement place for its advanced medical system, freedom and servants with their own native languages, secured places for their past wrongdoing in their home country, comfortable natural environment, and pension systems. Chinese, like any race on the earth, feel at home in America so far as they have money and can speak a little English. This is often reflected in Chinese and Korean social media and movies. When socially unfit rich pretties or rich "insane" boys cannot adapt to their own East Asian societies, they are often "immigrated" to America as a way to make up modern stories in movies and drams in China and Korea. Japan did not need this kind of fictions long time ago.

The American first-lady Melania Trump often spoke about unlimited love for the American dream and seldom anything positive about her own motherland. No other country, like the greatest America, can make one to forget and deny one's motherland so quickly and so thoroughly. She stated how she felt about becoming an American citizen: "... I arrived in New York City 20 years ago, and I saw both the joys and the hardships of daily life. On July 28, 2006, I was very proud to become a citizen of the United States — the greatest privilege on planet Earth." This is the charming of American culture — anyone successful in some affairs could heartily feel America as homeland. Melania Trump's statement might also be applicable to herself: "You cannot change a person. Let Them be. Let them be the way they are."

Trump's first wife was a Czech model. They got married in 1977 and have three children. His first wife became a naturalized American citizen in 1988 and divorced him in 1992 (publicly explained) due to Trump's affair with an actress who became his second wife. His second marriage was started in 1993 and broken in 1999. His third marriage was with Slovenian 'model' Melania Knauss (1970–) who was awarded U.S. citizenship in 2006. Slovenian-American Melania was the American's first lady. Melania, a non-native English speaker, is another showcase of realization of American dream. Her father was a member of the League of Communists of Slovenia. She was once a fashion model and engaged in business. She was born and raised in Slovenia. She started to work as a fashion model in New York City in 1996. She worked diligently in America. She married Trump in 2005 and was awarded U.S. citizenship the next year. She was quite supportive of her husband. During the 2015 presidential campaign, she publicly said: "I encouraged him because I know what he will do and what he can do for America. He loves the American people, and he wants to help". She charmed the world with her beauty and well-behaved quasi-European manner as America's first lady.

The American dream is a most suitable term to reflect the well agreed fact that America has been great, free, and fair country among the countries. Confucius measured the goodness of a country: "Good government obtains when those who are near are made happy, and those who are far off are attracted." America has been a dream land for people of many countries for over one hundred years (e.g., Samuel, 2012). People could pursue what they could hardly do in their own countries. The national prosperity, order and freedom have facilitated people to have decent jobs, succeed in business, own houses, receive higher education, and have conditions to feed and educate children well. Robert Reich (1946–) saw the dream: "The faith that anyone could move from rags to riches — with enough guts and gumption, hard work and nose to the grindstone — was once at the core of the American Dream." Suze Orman (1951–) commented: "Everybody in America started to define themselves by all these things they had around them. And all of a sudden it came tumbling down. So the old American dream has died...". The American dream has always flitted through American peoples' minds. Vision without action is a daydream. Chance for most Americans to realize American dream are low in comparison to the golden period of Great America. "Humankind cannot bear very much reality," said T.S. Eliot.

4.8 The South-African-Canadian-American as the Richest in America

> Human nature is evil, and goodness is caused by intentional activity.
>
> Xun Zi (298–238 BC)

The richest man in America on January 6, 2021, was the South-Africa-Canadian-American businessman Elon Musk, who holds three countries' citizenships. His wealth was estimated at $188 billion. His success, as it is told to us, is another beautiful story of the American dream. From a modest beginning he made it to the US, where in 1995, he and his two friends founded a web software company, Zip2. Before the company became successful, he had no money even to rent a small apartment. They could afford only one computer and he described the situation: "The website was up during the day and I was coding it at night, seven days a week, all the time." In due course, he found himself at the helm of PayPal. In October 2002, it was acquired by eBay for $1.5 billion in stock, of which Musk received $165 million.

Musk then founded SpaceX in May 2002, and quickly garnered a few contracts with NASA. On May 25, 2012, the SpaceX Dragon vehicle berthed with the ISS, making history as the first commercial company to launch and berth a vehicle to the International Space Station. SpaceX succeeded in many missions for men to conquer space. Musk has played a key role in the development of SpaceX, as the founder, CEO, CTO and chief designer. He was elected a Fellow of the Royal Society in 2018. He was already ranked 25th on the *Forbes* list of The World's Most Powerful People. His success is his spirits of adventures and capacity to explore what the mature American capitalism offers to him with his own words: "The problem is that at a lot of big companies, process becomes a substitute for thinking. You're encouraged to behave like a little gear in a complex machine. Frankly, it allows you to keep people who aren't that smart, who aren't that creative." He timely combined these well-trained, trivially-creative, and disciplined American gears to create great products and smartly bubbled market's believes in these products to earn huge profits. He describes his life in America: "I will never be happy without having someone. Going to sleep alone kills me."

4.9 Indian CEOs in American Multinational Corporations

> If you look into your own heart, and you find nothing wrong there, what is there to worry about? What is there to fear?
>
> Confucius (551-479 BC)

"It almost seems that nobody can hate America as much as native Americans. America needs new immigrants to love and cherish it," (Eric Hoffer, 1902–1983). In the modern world, the very talented in science and technology are welcome in most decent economies. Indian American female writer Bharati Mukherjee (1940–2017) asserted, "I am an American, not an Asian-American. My rejection of hyphenation has been called race treachery, but it is really a demand that America deliver the promises of its dream to all its citizens equally." Like people in Hong Kong and Singapore, which had been ruled by Britain, Indian people also feel quite at home in English-speaking parts of the world.

According to the American Community Survey (2018), the median household income was US$ 61,937 in 2018. Indian household income is the highest among the ethnic groups in the United States. Figure 4.8 plots a few groups' household incomes. Japanese household income is far lower than Indian, even though the variables in their original countries are the opposite. Chinese household income is almost equal to Japanese. This implies not only that immigrants' human capital before coming to the US might play an important role, but also the attractiveness of American economy for heterogeneous people in miscellaneous cultures.

For instance, high IQ people from Japan may have few incentives to work in America permanently if they are not interested in the academic world, where the discrimination cost is low and American research funding is relatively objective, fair, easy to get (for those who are capable) and generous. People with high IQs from India have strong incentives to immigrate to US. People with high IQs in Chinese societies (Singapore, Hong Kong, Taiwan, and some areas in mainland China) might like to have green cards or American citizenship so that their families can live in America and benefit from the US welfare system, and they can work in their own countries without paying discrimination costs while their family members enjoy American freedom with money earned in East Asia.

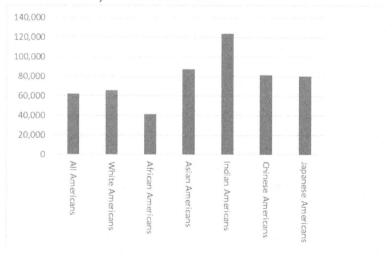

Figure 4.8 Median Household Income by Ethnicity in US in 2018, US$

India was a culturally rich country before the United Kingdom moved in, first under the English East India Company in the mid-1600s and then under direct rule by the British Crown in 1858. India declared itself a democracy in

1950; this has not economically upgraded the country (even in comparison with mainland China), but it has brought up and educated many talented people with English language. This prepares a great talent pool used to democratic values for import into the U.S. and Europe.

Historically India's close relations with the West are due to its geographical access to European countries with traditional transport. It was colonized by different European powers. Spices produced in India attracted European powers in the early stage of the West's global exploration. By the end of the 15th century the Portuguese established direct trade links with India. Since then, there were severe rivalries among the European powers in penetrating India. The Dutch Republic, England, France, and Demark-Norway had trading posts in India by the early 17th century.

Since then, many Indian states were increasingly opened to European manipulation through dependent Indian rulers. By the middle of the 19th century the British had gained direct or indirect control over almost all of India. India and America belonged to the same identity, British Empire. Contemporary Indians naturally feel at home in America and Britain. In 1947, India became independent and was partitioned into India and Pakistan (which was created as a homeland for colonial India's Muslims).

There is an increasing number of global CEOs of Indian origin (including born by immigrants), especially in American multinational corporations. These have included, for instance, IBM, the parent company of Google, Mastercard, Microsoft, Nokia, Harman International Industries, Palo Alto Networks, NetApp, Diageo, Wayfair, Adobe, Deloitte, Novartis, and Micron. Although the total number of immigrant corporate CEOs from people of color is still tiny and it is a recent phenomenon, it reflects a declining trend in the domination of white people in American business. Diligence, talent, tolerance of diversity — and affirmative action — and high discipline are obviously the main drivers of the trend.

CEOs of global companies are typically talented men good at manipulating human emotions. Like an Indian dish made of hundred species mixed, American and European multinational corporations are made up of a hundred races, multi-ethnic employees who are intellectually sophisticated, wealthy, and skillful at playing with flows of happiness. The white culture's strategy of divide and rule may lose its traditional comparative advantage as more people around the world have access to education and skills.

4.10 Chinese Restaurants in America

> To see and listen to the wicked is already the beginning of wickedness.
>
> Confucius (551—479 BC)

"If I knew for a certainty that a man was coming to my house with the conscious design of doing me good, I should run for my life." (Henry David Thoreau, 1817–1862). It is often plain to see the direction a group is heading, on the rise or falling, by observing how its diligent and talented people are treated. In earlier years, Chinese people came to America, knowing almost nothing about the country but going ahead and digging the land, searching for gold, constructing the railways, earning money, and going back home.

When I was first visiting America about 30 years, I wondered why white intellectuals were familiar with human rights issues in mainland China yet had almost no idea how Chinese Americans and Chinese with green cards were shielded by American human rights provisions, freedom, law, and democracy. Children and young people learn by observing reality rather than listening to hypocritical presentations with standardized assumptions and manipulated flows of emotions.

"Nobody is more inferior than those who insist on being equal," (Friedrich Nietzsche, 1844–1900). A very low portion of Chinese intellectuals who stayed in the West for a long period ended up trusting and respecting Western democracy. Deng Xiaoping, whose most important period of life was spent in France, saved China as he did not trust Western democracy but was deeply convinced of the positive role of both (Western) science and technology and the traditional Chinese bureaucracy based on leadership by a carefully selected elite.

Samuel Butler (1835–1902) described the mutual pleasure shared between man and dog: "The great pleasure of a dog is that you may make a fool of yourself with him and not only will not scold you, but he will make a fool of himself, too." Historically, Chinese culture has few good sayings about dogs, partly because the rice-paddy-locked Chinese (like the Koreans and Vietnamese; the Japanese were even poorer) were too poor and too densely populated to share food with dogs and to cultivate friendships with dogs as companions. Now, Chinese youngsters have completely changed their attitudes towards cats and dogs. Many of them give their attention and love to their pets rather than caring about their parents' welfare, as their parents and grandparents had done. They are cultivated with rich sympathies but living in a very lonely world.

Beliefs or assumptions lead to results. Rules that incorporate natural discrimination based on the model of Greek civilization explain the persistent discrimination against, and low education rate, of discriminated races or ethnic groups. I have mathematically proved that one race can benefit or lose from, consciously or unconsciously, practicing certain types of discrimination strategies. A specific form of discrimination (such as gender discrimination, racial discrimination, or club membership) is not definitively negative or positive with respect to certain aspects (such as consumer behavior, human capital accumulation, or happiness in the short term or long term) for anyone in the society. In the intellectual world, the discriminated Jewish in the white world have made great contributions to human progresses. The discrimination against Jewish in the West has benefited mainland China's contemporary economic progress and human capital accumulation. No race is benefiting from Jewish's intellectual contributions like mainland Chinese who has been devouring the global knowledge stock since 1978. This is how the modern world is connected.

"People who think they know everything are a great annoyance to those of us who do." (Isaac Asimov, 1920–1992). Chinese people have highest IQ among the populations in the world. Chinese people in Singapore, Hong Kong, Taiwan and in some regions of mainland China have demonstrated a capacity to achieve rapid economic expansion and become affluent even in terms of per capita income. Nevertheless, Chinese-American performance is much lower than expectations, at least the expectations of the Chinese themselves. Mainland Chinese are surprised to see so many Chinese restaurants in America supplying so much so-called Chinese food. Noticing Chinese restaurants, mostly with Chinese-American cooks and waiters, mainland Chinese often wonder why the high IQ race demonstrates such a low economic and social representation in free America. Simone Weil (1909–1943) breaks the cipher of the risk distribution for Chinese to make a fortune in America: "When once a certain class of people has been placed by the temporal and spiritual authorities outside the ranks of those whose life has value, then nothing comes more naturally to men than murder."

The international image of American civilization after the Cold War is that people of diligence and talent should politically, socially, economically, or academically succeed in American societies. To compare with African Americans, Chinese Americans had perhaps much lower social and economic status before WWII in the U.S.. Mark Twain (1835–1910) once said: "Never argue with stupid people, they will drag you down to their level and then beat you with experience." American political and public lives are now dominated by people good at arguing. Mark Twain published *The Treaty with China* (*New York Tribune*, August 9, 1868): "In San Francisco, a large part of the most interesting local news in the daily papers consists of gorgeous compliments to the 'able and efficient' Officer This and That for arresting Ah Foo, or Ching Wang, or Song Hi for stealing a chicken; but when some white brute breaks an unoffending Chinaman's head with a brick, the paper does not compliment any officer for arresting the assaulter, for the simple reason that the officer does not make the arrest; the shedding of Chinese blood only makes him laugh; he considers it fun of the most entertaining description. I have seen dogs almost tear helpless Chinamen to pieces in broad daylight in San Francisco, and I have seen hod-carriers who help make Presidents [by voting] stand around and enjoy the sport. . . . I never saw a Chinaman righted in a court of justice for wrongs thus done him. The California laws do not allow Chinamen to testify against white men."

Joh C. Chu (1979–, born in America), disclosed how he could make a success movie on *Crazy Rich Asians* (as the director): "The American culture is to pursue your own happiness, follow your dreams. The Chinese side is sacrifice everything for your family; it's all about the group. Those conflicting ideas were always a battle in my head." As a member of discriminated group, nothing but the family is the loyal center. Blood tends to be thicker than publicly diffused truth, especially for the discriminated. What American-Chinese dream about freedom of life appear constrained (or conservative) with comparison to overseas or mainland Chinese in, at least advanced — Chinese regions.

During the California Gold Rush (1848–1855), thousands of Cantonese came to America. They were mainly engaged in mining and railroad construction. American laws prevented Chinese immigrants from owning land. Chinese immigrants lived together in ghettos. They started their own small businesses such as restaurants, serving food according to the demands of customers from varied cultural backgrounds. Most of these restaurant owners were destitute before they came to America and were self-taught cooks. They created a cuisine with ingredients available in America and tastes unknown to their home country. Restaurants provided a way for Chinese immigrants to stay in the U.S. In most of the U.S., one can easily find "Chinese" restaurants, which serve Chinese cuisine adapted to American tastes. "France, and the whole of Europe have a great culture and an amazing history. The most important thing though is that people there know how to live! In America they've forgotten all about it. I'm afraid that the American culture is a disaster" (Johnny Depp, 1963–). The American taste for food has saved many a Chinese. America has consumed whatever cheap products East

Asia has supplied, starting from food cooked by Chinese in America, then Japan, late the four little tigers, and now China.

From the mid-19th centuries there were many Chinese immigrant workers in America. These workers were commonly counted on by employers as reliable workers. Chinese immigrants were regarded as contestants to white laborers. There was a variety of legal discriminations against the Chinese. The federal Chinese Exclusion Act of 1882 banned further Chinese immigration and naturalization. But the act allowed restaurant owners to have merchant visas in America. This sped up the opening of Chinese restaurants as a vehicle of immigration. Chinese restaurants provided a Chinese niche when the Chinese were not allowed to take most jobs either by law or ethnic discrimination. In the 1920s, Chinese cuisine had already been very popular (Lee, 2008; Liu, 2015). By 2015, there were 47,000 Chinese restaurants in the U.S.. The Chinese Repeal Act of 1943 replaced the Chinese Exclusion Act of 1882. The law was passed by President Franklin D. Roosevelt on December 17, 1943. It is the first time after 1882 that America allowed Chinese immigration and some Chinese immigrants already residing in the country to take naturalized citizenship. The ethnic Chinese were still banned against the ownership of property and businesses. In many states even Chinese-American (citizens) were not allowed to have property-ownership rights till 1965.

As people receive more education and secure their living, their cultural awareness and confidence will be changed. Daniel Chee Tsui (Qi Cui in *pinyin*, 1939-) is a case in point, illustrating the complexity of cultural identity. A Chinese-born American researcher, he received the 1998 Nobel Prize in Physics for contributions to the discovery of the fractional quantum Hall Effect. He was born into a needy family in Henan Province during the Second Sino-Japanese War. His parents had no education but he was sent to Hong Kong where he graduated from school in 1957; he attended university in the United States with a full scholarship, then stayed in the U.S. as a researcher. He joined Bell Laboratories, where the discovery was made for which he was awarded the Nobel Prize. Shortly after, he was appointed a professor at Princeton University in 1982. His colleagues and friends asked him why he had left Bell Laboratories and chosen to work at Princeton University. He did not know the answer with any degree of certainty. He reflected, "Perhaps it was the Confucius in me, the faint voice I often heard when I was alone, that the only meaningful life is a life of learning. What better way is there to learn than through teaching!" Contemporary Chinese people, both in China and outside China, had escaped from slavery not long ago and are culturally not yet much educated. A pig seems to be easily happy as their desires seem to be few and simple. But humans evolved vastly diverged when they get educated in ocean of knowledge with freedom of choice. There are new balance sheets with benefits and discrimination costs for Chinese Americans.

Human collective conscious consideration can be easily given up to follow the crowd. Le Bon stated: "An individual in a crowd is a grain of sand amid other grains of sand, which the wind stirs up at will." In *The Crowd*, Bon (1876: Preface) analyzed formation of characteristics of the crowd: "The whole of the common characteristics with which heredity endows the individuals of a race constitute the genius of the race. When, however, a certain number of these individuals are gathered together in a crowd for purpose of action, observation proves that, from the mere fact of their being assembled, there result certain new psychological characteristics, which are added to the racial characteristics and differ from them at times to a very considerable degree." An agglomeration of men manifests new characteristics from those of the individuals in the group. The collective mind is well-directed, and the conscious personality vanishes. Assimilation of multiple races is faced with even more challenging in from of enlarged inequality, losing equality of opportunity, fast growth of other countries, and digitalized well-connected world. Le Bon provided insights on the future of Chinese-American: "The masses have never thirsted after truth. Whoever can supply them with illusions is easily their master; whoever attempts to destroy their illusions is always their victim." America has supplied millions of Chinese great American dreams over many decades, and it is only in recent years that the illusion is broken for many talented Chinese. Many thousands of Chinese students educated in the best academic institutions in America have returned, some holding American green cards or citizenships, to China. In free world, foot can change direction of discrimination.

4.11 Costs of Social Parasites

> The coming of honor or disgrace must be a reflection of one's inner power. (1:5)
>
> Promote the worthy and capable without regard to seniority; dismiss the unfit and incapable without hesitation; execute the principal evildoers without trying first to instruct them; and transform the common lot men without trying first to rectify them.
>
> Xun Zi (298–238 BC, 9:1)

Human society is sustained not only by honest people, worthy leaders, diligent workers, and devoted scientists, but also lubricated and harmed by social parasites. The fittest group for survival in an organ can be dominated by parasites. "Creation destroys as it goes, throws down one tree for the rise of another. But ideal mankind would abolish death, multiply million upon million, rear up city upon city, save every parasite alive, until the accumulation of mere existence is swollen to a horror." (D.H. Lawrence, 1885–1830). A society is often weakened by overflows of social parasites. Nations vanish often owing to their inner inability to create new energy.

Darwin published his *On the Origin of Species* in 1859. Many insights of the theory of evolution by selection are also directly applicable to national survival in global rivalry. Natural selection refers to the process by which organisms transform as results of changes in heritable physical or behavioral traits. The organism is changed to better adapt to environment and to have more offspring. Evolution by natural selection is supported from a wide variety of scientific disciplines, such as development biology, genetics, geology, and paleontology. Man has collectively been the super-animal in the earth. Survival strategies of competition and co-operation, sexual attractiveness, gender division of labor and consumption, power structure, emotional attachments, social relations, family and mutual love and loyalty, love for children, devotion to their own children, grouping, organization, skill improvement under elder protection, learning through playfulness or games, social rules and "ethic" behavior, miscellaneous ways of cheating, can be found in wolf society, ant society, bee society, lion society, tiger society, or other animal societies.

Man is special, not yet fully proved, in that he can create knowledge, innovate, and use tools. Different societies are organized upon multifarious values and evolved with knowledge and tools. Like animal societies, human society as an organic system survives due to internal biological and social mechanisms and interactions with environment. Creativity, technology, social and economic structures, and environment interdependently evolve. As beauty is in the eye of the beholder, virtue is in the heart of the believer. Heart itself is not a predictable and controllable machine, but an organ creating chaos. According to the *yin-yang* vision of the universe, human heart is a boisterous oscillator between virtue and evil. Humans spend much money, time, energies, and other resources on manner, education, training, and practice to hidden evil aspects of the heart and to appear civilized. New generations construct their own hearts according to changed situations. One generation manufactures a respectable history in one land, while another generation leaves a shameful history in the same land. History is never the same as history is made of the heart and the heart is chaotic. But history may be similar somewhere and sometime as the heart may be similarly forged under the same sun with the same unknown human nature.

America was originally predominantly Protestant, and many of its business leaders have attributed their economic success to the Protestant ethic in Weber's terms (McClosky and Zaller, 1984:104). Protestantism was haunted by a fear of sinfulness and the need to enforce strict moral codes that would tame man's unlimited desires and passions. Bell (1996:289) saw: "The Protestant ethic as a way of life, then, was one of piety, frugality, discipline, prudence, the strenuous devotion to work, and delayed gratification." Its staunch moralistic orientation, the fear of the Dionysian spirit, and the insistence on subjecting human feelings and passions to rational control had a significant impact. American culture valued order, strict adherence to principle, and the importance of willpower and self-restraint, and was hostile to unchecked emotion, spontaneity, and playfulness. Earning a livelihood by work was perceived as pleasing to God. To be virtuous is to work hard with sobriety and thriftiness. According to Protestantism, one's economic achievements could be advanced as a symbol of one's moral standing. Artisans, merchants, and entrepreneurs were encouraged to amass large stores of wealth from the zeal and diligence of industriousness. The Protestants valued wealth not for the pleasures derived from holding it but as evidence of the arduous effort evinced in acquiring it. This process was admired, as it would tame passions, keep one occupied and insulated from immoral temptations, and instill good habits.

Somerset Maugham observed: "The common idea that success spoils people by making them vain, egotistic and self-complacent is erroneous; on the contrary it makes, for the most part, humble, tolerant and kind." Social parasites tend to be created and swell by attaching to successful people. The Protestant perspective on pursuit of wealth had important secular implications for early stages of industrialization. As Adam Smith shew, diligence and high saving propensity stimulate economic progress. Encouragement to channel one's energies into a form of disciplined economic endeavor plays an important role in improving productivity and increasing efficiency of economic performance. Adam Smith (1776) detailed the farmer's human capital structure in scathing terms: "The man whose whole life is spent in performing a few simple operations, of which the effects too are, perhaps, always the same, or very nearly the same, has no occasion to exert his understanding, or to exercise his invention in finding out expedients for removing difficulties which never occur. He naturally loses, therefore, the habit of such exertion, and generally becomes as stupid and ignorant as it is possible for a human creature to become. The torpor of his minds renders him, not only incapable of relishing or bearing a part in any rational conversation, but of conceiving any generous, noble, or tender sentiment, and consequently of forming any just judgment concerning many even of the ordinary duties of private life. Of the great and extensive interests of his country he is altogether incapable of judging; and unless very particular pains have been taken to render him other-wise, he is equally incapable of defending his country in war. The uniformity of his stationary life naturally corrupts the courage of his mind, and makes him regard with abhorrence the irregular, uncertain, and adventurous life of a solider. It corrupts even the activity of his body, and renders him incapable of exerting his strength with vigor and perseverance, in any other employment than that to which he has been bred.

"America gave the world the notion of the melting pot — an alchemical cooking device wherein diverse ethnic and religious groups voluntarily mix together, producing a new, American identity. And while critics may argue that the melting pot is a national myth, it has tenaciously informed America's collective imagination," Ivan Krastev astutely noted. However, a complex organ system incorporates many parasites. In general, a social parasite lives on the society and gets wealth, power, and sex at the expense of the society. Social parasites can be legal or illegal. Some of financial gamblers are parasites of national economies as they might make no real contribution to the society but get all the desirables into their own pockets. It is knotty to discern social role of financial gamblers or any social parasite as their benefits and costs to the society are so complicated that it is arduous to follow their cost-benefit tracks. A spoiled child who leads a wild and dissipated life might be brought up in good health and live singly till death without working once. He never-theless can make some contribution to the society if he brings happiness to his diligent and rich parents. If it is full of financial parasites and spoiled, lazy and irresponsible individuals, the society will lose morality, energy, and prosperity, and move towards ruin. Social and economic effects of financial gamblers and other types of speculators are so Gordian that they were illegal historically in some societies. In near future they may easily collect much more proportion of national wealth through modern technologies in free markets.

Xun Zi (9:1) advocates that society should be governed by capable men: "Although they be the descendants of kings and dukes or knights and grand officers, if they are incapable of devotedly observing the requirements of ritual and moral principles, they should be relegated to the position of commoners. Although they be the descendants of commoners, if they accumulate culture and study, rectify their character and conduct, and are capable of devotedly observing the requirements of ritual principles and justice, they should be brought to the ranks of a prime minister, knight, or grand officer." Presi-dent Trump didn't get the message. Selfish Chinese leaders could help their family members often in hidden and deceptive manner. It seems that Amer-ican way of social and political business costs the country much less than China's market-oriented business with Chinese characteristics. American family can continue its wealth, power, and sex over generations in multiple ways without any IQ-checking processes. Uneducated male children show off in public places with confidence as this is what the society admires. Traditional societies were often ruined by heritages of wealth and power. In modern times wealth heritage is often continued even by incapable children. There is a large supply pool of highly educated and well trained professional managers in labor market for management of family business.

Wealth and education are the basic determinants of America's polarizing society. Americans struggle to get into national top universities. Wealthy and upper middle parents live in the same zone which factually isolate schools from poor and racialized groups. Their children also receive expensive SAT test instructions and private tutoring. Many other practices facilitate their children to continue and move upwards their incumbent social and economic class by entering elite colleges before starting their professional career.

In 2019 a scandal of American universities shocked not only America itself, but also many young people who were building their American dream in other parts of the world. U.S. federal prosecutors charged 50 people for fraud schemes to get spots at Yale, Stanford, and other famous schools. Most the 50 charged are parents. Some of these, including actresses and business leaders, paid millions of dollars for bribing to make their children to receive passports to high social status. A teenage girl was recruited at Yale as a star soccer because of her parents' bribe. These young people are not necessarily converted into social parasites in the lifetime. But these kinds of parents conduct injustice and waste public resources and make life and dream of the youth born into the destitute more miserable and more hopeless. What the Swedish writer Ellen Key (1849–1926) described is applicable in some circumstances: "Countless are the women parasites who, to satisfy their craving for pleasure and luxury, impoverish father or husband. These lame limbs in the social organism, which themselves accomplish nothing, but for whom all other limbs work, are the most flagrant example of womanly immorality in the present."

Many American educational institutions are private. some well-known universities are profit oriented. Harvard University, with its over $36 billion endowment, Yale University over $27 billion, and Stanford University over $24 billion, for instance, could have easily continued their reputation with the dynamics of wealth accumulation and reputation building. These universities are also buying global talent at low prices. Private colleges and universities are classified as non-profit organizations, so they can avoid taxes on the investment earnings of their endowments. They don't pay property taxes or even sale taxes in cities and towns where they have real estate.

Thus, such private universities are massively subsidized. This implies that the system has an institutional bias. If the universities pay their taxes to the locals and the local governments encourage public education, inequality due to educational opportunity might be largely reduced in the American society.

Like parasites in human bodies, social parasites might make positive contributions to socioeconomic dynamics. Lawyers, medical doctors, and financiers are very expensive for society to keep. A great lawyer might be a great liar and his highly paid achievements lower morality of society. A successful medical doctor may be highly paid and not available to real workers but employed by the aged rich (due to heritage) without making any contribution to national future. High talent is wasted in multiple ways in serving social "parasites."

5. The End of Linearized and Simplified Ideologies

> The people are the most important element in a nation; the spirits of the land and grain are the next; the sovereign is the lightest.

Mencius (372–289 BC, 4:14)

Ideology is rule of social game. For common and unquestioning mind, this game rule is taken as truth and believed as granted to judge right or wrong of other people or other societies. In his lifetime a man may play miscellaneous games, in school, in workplaces, in gender relations and marriage, caring of children, and other numerous games in life. The basic motivation of gaming of each team is to maximize self-satisfaction. A team may be a nation, an organization, a firm, a family, club, or friends. Each social unit acts in such a way to maximize its goal, while its goal(s) itself is formed via games of its assorted members. A socialist or religious person may try all the ways to convert others to trust in what he believes disregarding consequences for other persons' lives. An organization makes its great efforts to maximize profits disregarding environmental effects on society. A president of a democratic society may not care much about his own country as his family business and children's futures.

The rules of America's national game were basically laid down by the founding fathers. Smith (1776 II: 129) judged early America: "To found a great empire for the sole purpose of raising up a people of customers, may at first sight appear a project fit only for a nation of shopkeepers. It is, however, a project altogether unfit for a nation of shopkeepers; but extremely fit for a nation whose Government is influenced by shopkeepers." By the end of WWII, America has already evolved a nation quite different from what

Adam Smith expected. Sigmund Freud (1856–1939) evaluated collective human nature: "I have found little that is 'good' about human beings on the whole. In my experience most of them are trash, no matter whether they publicly subscribe to this or that ethical doctrine or to none at all. That is something that you cannot say aloud, or perhaps even think." Man is physically addicted to drugs, mentally to ideas, and emotionally to love or hatred. Each kind of addiction can last a short or a long time, due to internal mechanisms or the external environment. Nations and races are addicted to their value systems. External forces and new factors often have little impact on the addicted values. As the values are quite stable over certain period, we can treat these values as "fixed reference point" in analyzing society.

Shklar (1998:157) disclosed almost invariant ideas for America: "The ideas born in the first fifty years of America's independent political life remain relatively unaltered and are as vigorous as ever." Alexis de Tocqueville (1805–1859) astutely characterized American culture: "The greatness of America lies not in being more enlightened than any other nation, but rather in her ability to repair her faults." As America was in its earlier stage of fast progress and expansion, it had reasonably high capacity to deal with new problems. America could repair its faults in business and social disasters because America was rich in resources, plenty supply of cheap immigrants, and not sophisticated socio-economic structures. A key obstacle to America being great again is its lost ability to repair its faults as the political, cultural, social, and economic systems have become knotty and interest groups dominate and control the complex systems.

5.1 Ancient Greek Democracy Based on Slavery and America's Democracy

> The respectful do not despise others. The economical do not plunder others.
>
> Evil exists to glory the good. Evil is negative good. It is a relative term. Evil can be transmuted into good. What is evil to one time, becomes good at another time to someone else.
>
> Mencius (372–289 BC)

Ancient Greek civilization assumes natural inequality and justifies slavery. The assumed unequal human nature seems still printed in the American cultural gene. Athenian democracy was the first democracy, existing around the sixth century BC in the polis (or Greek city-state). It was the city of Athens and the surrounding territory of Attica. Athens' political system was limited to male adult citizens. A foreign resident, whose family might have lived some generations in the city, was not a citizen. Slaves and women were not allowed to participate in politics. In the city state with a small population, there was a low portion of the population allowed to the democratic system while the rest was excluded (Thorley, 2005). During the 4th BC, the population of Athens might have been 0.25-0.3 million people in Attica, citizen families about 0.1 million, adult male citizens entitled to vote in the assembly only 0.03 million (Rothchild, 2020). Slaves might have outnumbered the citizens. Male adults were entitled to vote in Athens only after they had completed the required military training. It was estimated that only about 10% to 20% of the inhabitants participated in the government. Citizens who failed to pay a debt were also excluded from voting. One could claim citizenship only one was descended from two Athenian parents.

The most elementary bases of American civilization are liberty and democracy for specific people. The classical liberalism on which the United States has been constructed is a political ideology of the Enlightenment tradition rooted in European and Anglo-American philosophers such as John Locke (1632–1704), Adam Smith (1723–1790), and John Dewey (1859–1952). American political structure was influenced by Greek democracy which was constructed for an open, small island economy, without participation of a large portion of the population. America kept this tradition for quite a long time.

This cultural trait helps one to descry why Western countries have colonized so many parts of the world and most of these parts remain poverty-stricken. The division of man and slave is historically important for Western civilization and its stability and efficiency. The recent political and social movement of "Black Lives Matter" reflects the adapted and weakened manifestation of the traditional Greek social and political structure. Democracy is a rule of social games designed for open societies. When the same game is played domestically without a foreign enemy, this gaming tends to become self-destructive when it has multiple players shareing the same goal, same information, and same strategy. The democratic process is for political parties to calculate each other motivations and behavior and to brain-wash masses. As each side is equipped with huge funds and similarly talented people educated in the same knowledge reservoir and similar life processes, the American political game of electing president, like the final in the world football cup, has no certain winner until the last minute.

In the capitalist game, the distribution of income and wealth is a key determinant of social sustainability. No well-known political economic theory tells, in any sophisticated sense, how an economic system will evolve with income and wealth distribution in a democratic society. Adam Smith simply assumed away issues of dynamic distribution of wealth, while Karl Marx dealt with a simplified case which can be easily denied by people who trust market economics. Historically, all Western democratic societies with successful market economies colonized other countries. Kamala Harris (1964–) asserted: "Mitt Romney subscribes to the cynical logic that says the American dream belongs to some of us but not all of us." The American dream is effectively built on the separation. When the separation disappears, American people need to demonstrate how American dream can be realized with equal opportunities.

Colonization is an essential tool for modern Western civilization. It enabled the West to expand and explore not only their physical existence, but also spirits and mentality. Without this natural assumption, human history would be altered, for better or for worse. It is a "Greek Wall" of minds and cultural communications as it separates men between insider and outsider. Within America, people are consciously or unconsciously separated by the Wall. The Greek Wall will last as it is unconsciously rooted into Western civilization. It will not be gone with a few movements. American democracy has botherations in the global village as different countries have started not to perceive America the incontestable superpower in almost all kinds of games. Europe is becoming great again, East Asia is becoming affluent, Africa is winning America in many sports games, Russia is militarily strong, and rest countries are all improving in miscellaneous aspects with the same reservoir of global knowledge and information. America is slowly but steadily shrinking its direct influences on global affairs because of its financial burdens, and globalizing education and knowledge. Modern Western civilization has been maintained in open world so far, but Western civilization is now entering the global village.

5.2 Daniel Bell's End of Ideology

> Anciently, men had three failings, which now perhaps are not to be found. The high-mindedness of antiquity showed itself in a disregard of small things; the high-mindedness of the present day shows itself in wild license. The stern dignity of antiquity showed itself in grave reserve; the stern dignity of the present day shows itself in quarrelsome perverseness. The stupidity of antiquity showed itself in straightforwardness; the stupidity of the present day shows itself in sheer deceit.
>
> Confucius (551–479 BC, 17:16)

Confucius' above saying illuminates Bell's dynamic vision on capitalist evolution. Weber (1991) rationalized a long-term consequence of civilization: "specialists without spirit, sensualists without heart." It is not unique in the West. In each of Chinese dynastic cycles, the dynastic ending exemplifies Weber's description of stabilized personal types in professional markets. Jung (1989: 73) also unfolded the *yin-yang* dynamics of culture: "No culture is ever really complete, for it always swings towards one side or the other. Sometimes the cultural ideal is extraverted, and the chief value then lies with the object and man's relation to it: sometimes it is introverted, and the chief value lies with subject and his relation to the idea. In the former case, culture takes on a collective character, in the latter an individual one."

Daniel Bell (1919–2011) was born into a Jewish family in America. He was a sociology professor at Harvard University. One of his important work is *The End of Ideology: On the Exhaustion of Political Ideas in the Fifties* published in 1960. He argued that traditional humanistic ideologies in the 19th and early 20th centuries were no longer directing the future. "Sensible" people would not care much about political ideology. The polity of the future is to be developed from piecemeal adjustments of the extant system.

In *The Cultural Contradictions of Capitalism*, Bell (1978) asserted that in the 20th century capitalism had resulted in contradictions in the cultural, economic, and political spheres. He identified three pairs of cultural contradictions in contemporary capitalism, or the cultural *yin-yang* dynamics of contemporary capitalism (Bell, 1996:283). The first *yin-yang* relation is between asceticism and acquisitiveness. He held that the unbounded drive of capitalism came from the moral foundations of the original Protestant ethic. The asceticism of Calvinist and early Protestant thought encouraged development of modern capitalism. The asceticism highly valued diligence and work as a calling. It devalued consumption and thus enhanced savings. The value delayed gratification of impulses. Nevertheless, the value of diligence was gradually weakened, and people lost patience in consuming. Acquisitiveness has taken over asceticism. Gratification and consumption were also encouraged as Keynesian economics asks for. The second *yin-yang* relation is between bourgeois society and modernism. Modernism has become dominant force rather than the culture of bourgeois society. The third *yin-yang* relation is between law and morality. The market has emerged as the arbiter of all economic and social relations and people lost sense of shame as Confucius pointed out more than two thousand years ago. The recent American capitalism undermines the old Protestant ethic of thrift and modesty that had been credited as the reasons for its success.

5.3 Fukuyama's Last Man and the End of History

> The superior man indeed has to endure want, but the mean man, when he is in want, gives way to unbridled license.

Confucius (551–479 BC; 15:2)

After Bell's *End of Ideology*, another ending called *The End of History and the Last Man* (1992) was proposed by Yoshihiro Francis Fukuyama (1952–). His basic idea first appeared in *The End of History?* in *The National Interest* Summer 1989. "The first thing man will do for his ideas is lie," rationalizes Joseph. A Schumpeter.

A Japanese-American professor trying to penetrate the American culture may find nothing interesting but the notion of the last man imagined in Europe. Fukuyama was born in the United States; his father was a second-generation Japanese-American and his mother was born in Japan. He was classified as non-Western minority in America and was probably subject to racial discrimination in academic circles.

There is a deeply-rooted appreciation in the Japanese culture of "dying beautifully." The logic is that, if one is forced to live indecently, then the only hope is to live decently in the future. Japan was never invaded and occupied by any brutal force over a long period in its history. It was occupied only once by a foreign force, the United States. China was repeatedly invaded and occupied by foreign forces — some of these neighbors have since been "integrated" into China. Yet China survived over the centuries, perhaps much owing to its geography. The Japanese culture emphasizes a single clear ending: To die beautifully/dutifully. The national flower, *sakura* (cherry blossom), is considered to symbolize this attitude toward life. This unique value was formed in the poverty-stricken islands surrounded by bad-tempered seas. Japan is located along the Pacific Ring of Fire, which is the most active earthquake belt in the world. It bears heavy natural disasters yearly. But nature also supplies Japan with four beautiful seasons.

American social scientists, at least well-known ones, might not be intellectually interesting, but should be very smart when it comes to discrimination. Racial discrimination often helps a person to see clearly the negative sides of life and society. People who have been subjected to racial discrimination in a civilized society tend to have an objective and balanced perspective on life. Fukuyama received his Bachelor of Arts degree from Cornell University. His graduate training was in comparative literature and political science. His Ph.D. was in political science. He has been a professor mainly in the field of international relations in assorted institutions.

The basic idea of his influential book is that Western liberal democracies, free-market capitalism and lifestyle have come to the end point in socioeconomic evolution. In particular, the final form of human government is also at its end. When reading his *The End*, my first impression is something like "beautiful death," "death with dignity," "the last *samurai*" in Japanese culture or the last nomadic man — "nomadic" mean being freely alone and freely self-sufficient in the forest. In ancient Confucianism, which the Japanese studied over a thousand years, human life is not an ending but a process of creating and progressing or constructing and improving. Thus the name of the Japanese university, *ritsumeikan* (a university for creating and establishing life). Creativity never leads to the last or final anything. After publishing *The End of History*, Fukuyama was criticized from various perspectives and he modified his conclusion. But a modification not originated from inner reflection or intuition causes more confusions.

Edgar Allan Poe (1809–1949) sees perfect man neither in the present nor in the future: "I have no faith in human perfectibility. I think that human exertion will have no appreciable effect upon humanity. Man is now only more active — not more happy — nor more wise, than he was 6000 years ago." In Greek tradition, the valuation of national welfare and rights excludes slaves and foreigners. It does seem that the Japanese-American Fukuyama structurally follows this Greek tradition of measuring the degree of civilization and judging the usefulness of an ideology.

Friedrich Nietzsche (1844–1900) is well known for saying: "God is dead.... What festivals of atonement, what sacred games shall we have to invent?" In fields of academia, multifarious impossibility theorems were published in the last century, such as Arrow's impossibility theorem and Gödel's incompleteness theorem. Nothing was meaningful, lasting, or final according to this trend of impossibility. One might simply interpret the end of history, a result of academic fashion, as an impossibility theorem in human progress.

The concept of the Last Man implies the impossibility of becoming more human. It is not intellectually challenging but it got social attention. If there is not yet a universal acceptable concept of what is called being "human," one may naturally doubt how one can know wha is the last man. Man is created by man — there cannot be the last man, as long as man's creativity is not ended. Man is organic and evolutionary. Man is a culturally created imagination. The ideal or respectable man in one culture may be nothing but a laughingstock or a barbarian in another culture, or in another time in the same culture. Modern knowledge in social sciences complicates man's ways to deceive, urban life involves adaption and preparation to lie all the time, and internets wash the brain. Fukuyama's last man was first caught by a crazy man, Nietzsche.

Fukuyama, educated with a traditional linearized vision of evolution, as a member of discriminated minority, reasonably saw evolution as heading towards an ending. Meaningful chaos with order is impossible in traditional Western rationality. He conceived that the American liberal democracy has ethically proved itself, politically and economically, a better system than any of the alternatives. One would be flabbergasted at his blindness to historical facts, not to say the logical consistency of sustainability of American democracy.

Sustainability means survival of an organic system. The rest of the world has paid high costs to sustain the "successful" liberal democracy. Since the very day of the French Revolution, the current democratic societies with economic prosperity colonized and enslaved one non-Western society after another (Japan is the only country which also suffered from nuclear bombs). The two rich East Asian economies, Japan and South Korea, are still "servants" to America and can allow themselves no free mind. Democracy is born in co-existence with slaves. No one yet has rigorously proved the sustainability of a decent democracy without discrimination since the first day it was proposed.

The world has been dominated by liberal democracy since the end of the Cold War and the fall of the Berlin Wall in 1989. President Ronald Reagan ended one world but launched the inner decline of America. He was a second-rate actor but a first-rate American President. He once quipped, "Going to college offered me the chance to play football for four more years." America does not need a properly educated president.

According to Fukuyama, the eventual triumph of Western liberalism is illustrated as follows: "What we may be witnessing is not just the end of the Cold War, or the passing of a particular period of postwar history, but the end of history as such.... That is, the end point of mankind's ideological evolution and the universalization of Western liberal democracy as the final form of human government."

No one yet has proven how Western liberal democracy can sustain a stable and healthy world. The universalization of Western liberal democracy is a childish belief; one does not get any clear answer to questions about how it works economically, politically, culturally, emotionally, sexually, and biologically. Belief is belief. Any intellectual with some emotional capacity can easily make up a belief system based on day dreams, at least in modern times when we have access to such a with huge stock of rational knowledge. Democracy is neither theoretically checked nor historically valid. A democratic society theoretically as well as practically degenerates, like any type of society. Society is organic. The fittest individuals survive. But no one has yet proven what would constitute the fittest. Man is still alive and in the process of becoming, not yet at the status of being.

Fukuyama imagined that as the Soviet Union collapsed, the last ideological alternative to liberalism disappeared. While he was perceiving the collapse of communism as marking the triumph of American ideas, the rest of the world was experiencing both the decay of Western ideas and the collapse of socialist ideas.

Socialism exists due to the powerful and effective existence of capitalism. When socialism collapses, the self-destructiveness of dynamics implies that Western democracy destroys itself. America collapses from within when it lacks the opposite force, socialism, to sustain its energetic dynamics. China does not play with America using socialism gaming, even if America keeps trying to seduce China to do so. The collapse of socialism also implies the start of decay of America. Fukuyama's argument is based on his belief that the main determinant of economic inequality has little to do with the legal and social structure of Western societies. If the assumption is invalid, and economic inequality does have a significant impact on the practical, functional efficiency of the legal and social structure of Western societies, all his arguments are meaningless as inequality destroys societies as human history repeatedly shows. America is too young to have fully practiced its inner mechanisms of socioeconomic dynamics.

5.4 Huntington's Clash of Civilizations

> What you do not want done to yourself, do not do to others. (15:24)

> It is easy to hate and it is difficult to love. This is how the whole scheme of things works. All good things are difficult to achieve; and bad things are very easy to get.

> Confucius (551-479 BC)

Unlike Bell and Fukuyama, whose ethnic backgrounds are easy to research on-line, I could not clearly identify Huntington's racial identity after extensively searching. His emphasis on conflicts of civilizations reminds me of the saying, "Those are at war with others are not at peace with themselves." (William Hazlitt, 1778-1830). A still-energetic male raver should feel pleasant witnessing conflicts and can hardly be at harmony within himself.

Samuel Huntington (1927-2008) was an American scholar on international affairs. His *The Clash of Civilizations and the Remaking of the World Order,* published in 1996, after Fukuyama's *The End*, is still influential in interpreting international relations. As an American political analyst, he was largely preoccupied with America as a superpower. Western history is often portrayed by the struggles between monarchs, nations, and ideologies. The end of the Cold War implies the ending of ideologies. International political games need new targets and new rules. Moreover, non-Western civilizations are no longer exploited recipients of Western countries. Non-Western countries have gradually and steadily emerged as important actors in world history.

Huntington's popular term reminds me of an Edgar Allan Poe (1809–1949) joke, "I have great faith in fools; self-confidence, my friends call it." As politics is a matter of playing on people's emotion, the importance of searching for a commonly hated target is more attractive than that of looking for an economic partner, for the reason deduced by Tocqueville: "In politics, shared hatreds are always the basis of friendships."

Caribbean cuisine is sometimes used as a symbol of contemporary American culture. The cuisine is a fusion of European, African, Amerindian, Cajun, Creole, Latin American, Indian, South Asian, Middle Eastern, and Chinese inputs. But hot pot might be a better exemplification in the sense that motley peoples share their multifarious foods in one base broth, within one round pot which symbolizes reunion. People satisfy their personal preferences by adding their own chosen materials and cooking them to their own preferred degree. Hot pot is a most popular form of social gathering among young generations in China. There is no need for harmonizing tastes because the goal of gathering is achieved. There is no communication among groups of people, as a national superpower is secure and individual profits are earned, at least, for each group on average.

Clashes imply destructiveness as well as creativity. Clashes of civilizations also contain the possibility of the creation of a higher rational value system as the base, where multifarious emotions and religions interplay. Any ideology fixed is nothing but a temporary rule of the game for human society. It is a sign of barbarianism for one country to use such a temporary rule and apply it as a universal truth. A single rational system in association with heterogeneous religions has been the Chinese type of civilization over many hundreds of years. Mankind can theoretically co-exist in harmony, as man is not simply an animal, killing others for the group benefit, with a natural inclination for religions, values, and habits, he is also rationally educable. As killing other humans is no longer economically and sexually beneficial, owing to advances in technology, knowledge, and values, mankind has theoretically high possibilities to co-exist in peace.

A man who is addicted to the superiority of a particular culture would interpret exchanges between multiple cultures as cultural clashes. The belief in one's own culture or in one's own god occurs anywhere, either due to pure belief (addiction), contents of education, or lack of observations and practices. Clashes of cultures theoretically imply many possibilities — wars, convergence, mutual separation, creation of a higher integrated culture, and the like. Clashes of civilizations seem to have low probability as a civilization could destroy all mankind in a few hours with certainty. Quarrels between contemporary civilizations are like quarrels between old women in South China's countryside. Nothing happens but wording. America could have used military forces only on those areas which had no effective nuclear bombs. In Huntington's work, one feels an implicit concern about the continuation of America's greatness. Even he admitted importance of non-Western civilizations, for him they are only additional important actors joining the West to shape and move world history. In the aged man's assumed world, he had little idea about how modern technologies can shape man, society, and the world in the future. In his 2007 *God and Gold: Britain, America, and the Making of the Modern World*, Huntington argued that the Anglo-American tradition of world power from the seventeenth century to the present is due to the individualism inherent in British and American beliefs. This is a historical fact (without referring to the other countries' costs by colonization and slaves). The Anglo-American tradition of world power is due to the mighty or the guns if one is asked to single out the most important determinant for the Anglo-American world power.

The British system was an effective combination for robbing as well as improving the world. Great empire built with freely conquering and invading includes some individualism as the Mongolian empire or other nomadic societies neighboring China did. With regards to the West's future, Huntington argued for the importance of reaffirmation of the Western identity. As his main concern is reaffirmation of the Western identity, he could easily identify motley reasons for clashes simply because it is easier to find emotional reasons for conflicts than for mutual understanding and harmonious relations. This wolf-like strategy is recognized by Confucius more than two thousand years ago: "It is easy to hate and it is difficult to love." By creating the outsider (defining others as slaves in Greek and predators in nomads), one can do whatever on the outsider — a wolf strategy for survival. The wolf can hardly be friends of humans, but the dog is always a lovely animal for mankind in the long term. Wolf disappears, but dog, the weakest of the same kind survives with man's love. Modern technology has changed meanings of geography and time on formation of future cultures.

The Clash was basically constructed on the contemporary American vision of the world and partially supported by biased empirical data. Huntington asserted that the world is moving into a period of civilizational collision. He is convinced that once the age of ideology was ended, the world would revert to normal states of affairs with perhaps dream-based and drug-addicted cultural identities. He is of the opinion that the primary identification of people will not be ideological but cultural. The world would not be in harmony but characterized by conflicts among the cultural groups people identify with: religions, tribes, ethnic identities, customs, values, institutions, nations, or even civilizations.

For instance, global conflict would arise not between socialism and capitalism but among the major cultural groups: Western, Islamic, Confucian, Japanese, Hindu, and others. For instance, Christianity (a basis of Western civilization) and Islam are both missionary religions in the sense that they seek to convert others; "all-or-nothing" religions in the sense that both sides believe that only their faith is the correct one; and teleological religions in the sense that their values and beliefs are the goals and purpose in human existence. In Japanese and Chinese cultures, this kind of mentality is interpreted as forcing one's dream upon others. The rice-paddy-based Japanese and Chinese civilizations were not geared to invade neighbors (modern Japan tried to do it but failed miserably), the isolated civilization needed a tolerance for multiple ideas. As the world is collected like a village, humans born with sense of shame "should" behave differently from the traditional world in which each community or country could easily self-glorify, and make up lies about its potential enemies.

In short, Huntington's basic assumption was that human rationality will give way to irrationality.

Wrong assumptions lead to invalid conclusions. As far as Chinese civilization is concerned, Huntington's arguments make little sense. What Chinese intellectuals are reading and what students are learning from are, except for works on the Chinese language and literature, products of the Western civilization. Even the national ideology of contemporary China, Marxism (which has been wrongly interpreted and misleadingly applied on Chinese soil), is a product of the Western civilization.

When I was entering university in 1978, young people who wanted to major in Chinese language, history, Chinese Marxism, or culture in higher education institutions were generally perceived as intellectually inferior. Mathematics, natural sciences, and Western social sciences — mainly Western products in modern times — were considered intellectual and useful.

Two decades ago, I concluded that America might be anti-China not because of some Chinese anti-Americanism, but because China could be Americanizing too fast. *Hermann Hesse* (1877–1962) says: "If you hate a person, you hate something in him that is part of yourself. What isn't part of ourselves doesn't disturb us."

Trade conflicts have rationally occurred between China and the U.S. Trump correctly informed the Chinese that American confidence and the American way of doing global business were unsustainable. China has learned quickly from the conflicts during Trump's term, which in some ways at least may seem to have been more honest (straightforward) than some other presidencies.

Modern trade economic theory as taught in Western classrooms has little to do with global trade. Traditional economics does not give answers to benefits of free trade between China and U.S. as the two economies do not satisfy the requirements in mainstreams of (popular) trade theories. Trade wars may bring about mutual harm. As China is not a market-dominated economy and the US is faced with predicaments of unemployment and trade deficits with the rest of the world, the net impact of trade wars on any side is hard to calculate.

Trade wars between the two countries might be analyzed like quarrels between husband and wife — the results might economically benefit both, harm one and benefit another, or hurt both. There is no certain consequence with trade wars, except that people of both sides comprehend much about each other and mutually hate more strongly as natural law of humanity predicts. Strength and character of a race, like a person, are not only formed and influenced by environment, but also determined by its inner character. As many aspects of the environment are globalized, inner features of each culture affect its way in contributing and converging (or separating from) rational mainstreams of global cultural stocks.

Chinese intellectuals have largely failed to appreciate the positive aspects of Chinese culture since the West opened China's door by force in the 1840s. Observing behavior of Chinese people, not only in mainland China, but also in the U.S., Taiwan, Hong Kong, and Singapore, Western powers have used force and religions and ideologies to influence other countries. In the last half century, America has enabled the world to be digitally-connected, nuclear power diffused, and knowledge dispersed; but any positive progress begets its destruction. America has benefited greatly from its progress, but also deepened its own self-destructiveness. Man evolves with weapons and technology. The Canadian psychologist Jordan Peterson (1962–) might give the Harvard international relations professor a useful lecture, starting with: "To me, ideology is corrupt; it's a parasite on religious structures. To be an ideologue is to have all of the terrible things that are associated with religious certainty and none of the utility. If you're an ideologue, you believe everything that you think. If you're religious, there's a mystery left there."

Like sports, a society's games are judged, largely, by its ideology and value systems. There was no reason for early America to play games without freedom as the country is so vast and people were so few. One does not judge the performance of a table tennis player by the rules of football. Similarly, one does not judge the performance or behavioral excellence of a man in one social system according to an ideology not accepted in that society. There are "universally" acceptable human behaviors, like eating rice and flour, universally condemned behavior like arbitrarily killing babies, and universally appreciated behavior like taking care of aging parents in trouble. A possible clash of civilizations is a possible crisis for mankind, but crisis implies possible fortune, too, as the Chinese proverb says. Good fortune is often grasped by a prepared mind.

5.5 Mutually Debilitating American Core Values

> Great knowledge sees all in one. Small knowledge breaks down into the many.
>
> Zhuangzi (369–295 BC)
>
> Those who cultivate more confusion for profit should understand this: we will name their names and shame them as they deserve to be shamed.
>
> Bob Dole (1923–)

The essence of greatness is harmony in variety. The natural freedom American culture clings to has a low probability of leading to harmony. Pure competition leads to extremes — extremely beautiful or extremely ugly. In *The Turning Point*, Capra (1982) epitomizes the dynamic vision of Chinese thought: "The Chinese philosophers saw reality, whose ultimate essence they called Tao, as a process of continual flow and change.... All developments in nature — those in the physical world as well as those in the psychological and social realms — show cyclical patterns. The Chinese gave this idea of cyclical patterns a definite structure by the polar opposites yin and yang, the two poles that set the limits for the cycles of change... It is important, and very difficult for us Westerners, to understand that these opposites do not belong to different categories but are extreme poles of a single whole. Nothing is only yin or only yang." The Chinese vision connotes that social development embodies sensitive relations between change and order and between destructiveness and constructiveness. Technological changes in last few decades have begotten structural changes in socioeconomic structures and human relations. Material relations between people and nations have been fundamentally altered.

Adam Smith advised light regulation of colonial trade by parent countries. He recognized that Europe's discovery of the New World had brought wealth and prosperity to the Old World, even though he weighed lightly the catastrophic disasters on the people of the New World. After the benefit-cost analysis, he rationally concluded the impossibility of keeping all the possible benefits of colonies and rising costs of empire (e.g., Williams, 2014).

In *The Wealth of Nations* published in 1776, Smith justified colonization: "It is not contrary to justice that ... America should contribute towards the discharge of the public debt of Great Britain." He calculated the British cost as follows: "If any of the provinces of the British empire cannot be made to contribute towards the support of the whole empire, it is surely time that Great Britain should free herself from the expense of defending those provinces in time of war, and of supporting any part of their civil or military establishments in time of peace, and endeavour to accommodate her future views and designs to the real mediocrity of her circumstances." Another important political economist, John Stuart Mill (1806–1873) also extensively discussed issues related to colonization (e.g., Bell, 2010). His idea about liberty: "The liberty of the individual must be thus far limited, he must not make himself a nuisance to other people". But his whole life had justified the British's colonization. Many Western rational thinkers had a different conception about humanity in the standard of ancient Confucianism or modern rationality. That is perhaps the reason that British gentleman-scholars could sing songs of liberty like a passionate youth believes in the continuation of pure love forever. He defended colonization and advocated to create permanent "civilized" communities in North America and the South Pacific. He considered colonization as a solution of social botherations in Britain.

American news media often mention the number of American lives lost during a given war, but the loss of Vietnamese lives, or Afghan, for instance, is almost never mentioned. Western civilization has a traditional way of counting human lives — both owing to religion and to endured mutual fighting and killings. There are many American movies made of the Vietnamese war. For some, the war seems to amount to nothing but a costly entertainment set in a poor country far away, made by the most civilized and greatest country in human history.

"Harmony makes small things growth, lack of it makes great things decay." (Sallust, 86—c. 35 BC). The Chinese social order kept by the Chinese communist party within which no man even properly understands the party's doctrine (except Mao's idea "governing by the barrel of a gun") has expanded a great economy. Things occur with its own mechanisms beyond the uneducated mind's comprehension.

The great America which lacks social harmony is deepening its self-destructiveness. In contemporary America, great affairs related to sex, sexuality, and its related products such as family, relatives, and gender relations seldom infiltrate analyses of social and economic functioning. The family is outside the main concerns of classical economists.

In Chinese tradition of historical thinking, it is neither religion nor technological change but gender relations that is treated as a determinant of the fall of a dynasty. In America, women's labor participation and higher education have created another level of social and economic complexity. Contemporary creation, distribution, and consumption of wealth, power, and sex have evolved so complicated that no theory has a whole picture about how they evolve interdependently over time. If America falls rapidly in the near future, a main determinant might be the broken family and poverty resulted from and caused by this.

"An American cannot converse, but he can discuss, and his talk falls into a dissertation. He speaks to you as if he was addressing a meeting...," Alexis de Tocqueville rendered an early American characteristic. The 2020 United States presidential debates highlighted the cultural continuation. "Men are especially intolerant of serving and being ruled by, their equals," says Baruch Spinoza.

Globalizing democracy in association with digitalized information leads to intolerance of any single superpower. Carl Jung, who was interested in the *Yi Jing*, rationalizes the pattern of life: "Shrinking away from death is something unhealthy and abnormal which robs the second half of life of its purpose."

Henrik Ibsen (1828–1906) taught what America should do in this global village: "It is inexcusable for scientists to torture animals; let them make their experiments on journalists and politicians." When Ibsen was writing, the economist had little influences on world affairs as today. "The Tragedy of our time is that those who still believe in honesty lack fire and conviction, while those believe in dishonesty are full of passionate conviction" (Fulton J, Sheen, 1895–1979). The phenomenon is perhaps not limited to "our time" as any country which has a period of high civilization has experienced it. There is a natural equilibrium in high civilization because one who knows tends act as little as possible, while one who knows little will passionately act in a complicated situation. No culture with history of higher civilizations could have avoided the status of the civilized equilibrium, as no aged man can avoid slow but steady degeneration, if not a sudden death.

There are three common desires in a human society — desire to own wealth, desire to be powerful, and desire to have sex and establish and extend sex-based trustful networking. The core values of production and consumption of these goods and services in the United States are correspondingly democracy, free market, and individualism (human rights, gender equality, liberalism, romanticism ...). The desire for sex seems to be relatively easily solved by freedom of choice and free market mechanism in a modern society with huge wealth and modern technology. Even the Chinese Communist Party "allows" gender market to self-organize with freedom between heterogeneous genders (not yet modernized to the same gender and marriage between the same gender) with legally free and low-cost divorce. Chaos in gender market, different from chaos in financial markets, does not create panic in society in the short term. The impact of freedom and chaos of sex and sexuality need generations to be seen in macro levels.

Max Weber (1864–1920) studied the role of culture on industrialization in *The Protestant Ethic and the Spirit of Capitalism* (1904). He was convinced that capitalism requires both an instinct toward self-aggrandizement and a willingness to channel that instinct into constructive values such as diligent toil at one's calling, self-denial in the private use of capital, investment, sober economic calculation, efficiency, frugality, and scrupulous adherence to contracts. Protestantism was, according to Weber, crucial to the development of a climate in which these and other values intrinsic to capitalism could develop. He suggested a deterministic link between the Protestant ethic and Western capitalism. Newtonian way of thinking tells unique correspondence between the principle and the phenomenon. Newtonianism also implies that the path of history is unique and pre-determined. There is no role of fortune or luck in main paths of history in this world vision. Modern science, not to mention the Chinese bible *Yi Jing*, has a different view on social and economic evolution. Chaos, multiple possible paths, bifurcations, and catastrophes are normal in evolution.

America underwent a decline in religious observance and increased secularization partly in association with expanding rational education, industrialization, consumer cultures, self-seeking pleasure principles. Real religion and knowledge of the Bible diminished to an almost negligible point (Bloom, 1987:56). Nevertheless, many Americans are members of specific religious groups and are very interested in spiritual matters. Americans commonly believe that religion is important in human life. The absence of any civil religion in the US Constitution has led many to assert that there is no civil religion in America. "We must face the fact that the preservation of individual freedom is incompatible with a full satisfaction of our views of distribution justice," admits Austrian-born British F.A. Hayek (1889–1992), who received Nobel prize award for his analysis of the interdependence of economic, social, and economic institutional phenomena. His *The Road to Serfdom* influenced one generation's views about socialism. It is evident that free market and capitalism are not necessarily associated with distribution justice. In the case of America, it is to what degree that freedom will bring about distribution injustice.

"The whole dream of democracy is to raise the proletarian to the level of stupidity attained by the bourgeois," as the Frenchman Gustave Flaubert (1821–1880) deduced. Freedom includes free markets, free speech, and free choice of lifestyles under law. Democracy is supposed to mean, basically, that the political power is determined by the majority. This itself contains the possibility of excluding freedom of opinion and benefits of minorities. If the majority likes a government which wastes public money for national pride and takes money from the talented and diligent minority to distribute to the lazy to enforce equality for the sake of equality, the elected government may harm the country in the long term by destroying economic freedom through democratic freedom.

Democracy has a strong inclination to heavily tax teachers and diligent workers in the middle class rather than fairly tax the rich, as the former are obediently diligent and the latter pony up the campaign funding that enables individuals to control operation of democratic systems.

American has reached an impasse on reducing poverty. The poor have nothing to lose but to demonstrate in streets, peacefully or violently, against injustices hidden in American society. The government takes in needy immigrants to do low jobs and, also makes the country look nice in global images, even though immigrants have a long way to achieve a social status not discriminated. As the world is full of poverty-stricken people (the American poor have far more than the middle class in many parts of the world), America has been able to attract a large inflow of immigrants. In recent years, diligent Europeans, have had little incentive to emigrate to America. Immigrants to America are now mainly people of color.

The American government is basically influenced and directed by powerful elites and has not much to do with majority of American people. In association with widened economic inequalities America tends to be ruled by the few (oligarchy) or by the top rich (plutocracy).

Capitalism is the foundation of economic operation in America. It is commonly expected that the two values would bolster the national harmony in a healthy interdependence: democracy enhances capitalism by guaranteeing a desirable social and economic environment for material prosperity and capitalism capacitates democracy to deliver political and social goods to its citizens. Nevertheless, in modern economies, men learn quickly as they consume more and produce more. A prosperous capitalism capacitates people to judge political, social, and economic affairs. Democracy attributes equivalent value to all people and people judge and value differently with multi-cultural values. Capitalism establishes the reward system that encourages individuals to earn and amass as much wealth as possible, while democracy places a value on enabling everyone to gain at least a proper livelihood. From the viewpoint of capitalism, free market is economically efficient and socially fair; while from that of democracy, popular majorities have the right to override market mechanisms when necessary to alleviate social and economic distress. Man's action is networked politically, economically, and sexually, in a single organ. Pure separation of political and economic systems is not yet possible. If scale and scope economies occur in economic markets, wealth is naturally concentrated in a few families. These few families dominate the main operations of markets with monopolistic power. Hence, free market creates monopolistic group of people who influence political operations, through controlling media to manipulate and brain wash the public and "bribe" politicians — through invisible networking of human relations — to further increase their economic power. It is often those who are cruel in heart and gentlemen in demeanor who control the wealth of nation in market economy in the long term. Businessmen with cruel hearts have comparative advantage over those who are virtuous. People can easily make-up to behave gentlemen or lady in public so far if they are endowed with huge money and education opportunity from childhood. People with cruel hearts have more strategies to choose in the game than those who are virtuous. National power tends to be finally grasped by those without virtue. Power networking tends to be composed of obedient servants, cunning administrators, and evil leaders. If a nation is ruled by evils, it will not sustain a virtuous government as networked groups will only operate for its own survival without caring about people's lives.

Democracy satisfies a strong passion for equality. It is bolstering the American dream of heterogeneous immigrants being legally equal. Free market encourages people to pursue self-interests. It is basically assumed that one's income is proportional to one's effort. The traditional value of diligence pays in a traditional free market in which the income is basically determined how much one digs land a day. In traditional economies, income differences within the country and between countries are not huge, except that one gets wealth additionally by plundering or exploiting. Modern technology fundamentally changes growth and distribution of wealth and income in capitalist societies. Society is composed of not only positive contributors, but also social parasites. Social parasites, dependent on which type, may have positive or negative contribution to pleasure or pain to different members of the society. For instance, some people might fake reasons to receive government welfare help or other people's taxes. Some people born into a rich family might not work whole life and extravagantly play around. Their expenditures provide job opportunity, and their behavior might give pleasures to, for instance, their diligent parents. Each type of behavior has miscellaneous implications. Rich "parasites" of American society could also interfere other people's lives and distort operations of market mechanism through, for instance, power of inherited capital. Social parasitism is perhaps dispersed widely in American society in miscellaneous forms in hidden ways.

"Men are mistaken in thinking themselves free; their opinion is made up of consciousness of their own actions, and ignorance of the causes of which they are determined." (Baruch Spinoza, 1633–1677). Unlimited space in America allowed immigrants from the cultures in the midst of the Enlightenment to develop an unlimited taste for freedom. This spirit of freedom is different from the spirits of nomadic people, Europeans, and rice-paddy East Asians.

American freedom is now undermined by increased inequality. The rich and politically powerful classes indulge in nepotism to a degree unheard in American history. Americans used to have confidence in upward mobility through education, diligence, and wealth, but decreasing returns on education and corruption of the academic world have reduced the promise of this avenue upward. The opportunities available to American children are now strongly related to their parents' income and education. Other countries provide more dreams and opportunities for young people, even if they are born poor, with parents having little education. In America, as Formisano (2015: 31) brought up: "about 62 percent of children born in the top fifth stay in the top two-fifths, while 65 percent born in the bottom fifth stay in the bottom two-fifths. More mobility occurs in the middle, but not as much as in comparable countries." In recent years the mobility of the middle is not so much upwards as downwards.

"In politics stupidity is not a handicap." Napoleon Bonaparte's insight still applies to Western politics. In mature politics, honesty equipped with virtue and deep insight tends to be handicap. Democracy is desirable in principle. But democracy might bring self-destruction so that other parts of the society suffer. It is one thing for a young man to have ideal or pure dream; it is quite another to actualize the dream.

Realization of meaningful dreams results from combination of passion, belief, persistence, and talent with the help of environment and fortune. This is similarly true for a nation. Nations write similar dreams, ideals, goals, religions, and ideologies. But a few can stay at developed states. Plato sees the dynamics of democracy: "Democracy passes into despotism."

Aristotle makes a more detailed prediction: "Republics decline into democracies and democracies degenerate into despotism." Karl Marx wrapped up: "Democracy is the road to socialism." America has perhaps already moved toward despotism after the national wealth is concentrated in a few families. Social and economic predicaments involved in America's biased distribution of wealth are more serious now than China's despotism. In mature and democratic America, diligent, obedient, and talented people are paying taxes and bear national debts as the destitute has nothing to lose and the rich knows how to avoid taxation.

"Can capitalism survive?" Schumpeter (1942) asked in the opening of his book *Capitalism, Socialism, and Democracy*. "No," he averred, "I do not think it can." Schumpeter considered three processes in a capitalist system. First, the capitalist economy undermines the entrepreneurial or innovative function. Innovative forces are valued as the essential feature of capitalism. In association with successful innovations, enterprises are augmented. The bureaucratic administration of large enterprises has internal mechanisms to make innovation automatically and to substitute the activities of committees and teams of experts for individual initiative. Secondly, capitalism tends to erode its own institutional framework by destroying the protective strata. The strata include, for instance, the gentry, small businessmen, farmers, and others. Capitalism also weakens individual proprietorship in favor of a more diffuse kind of ownership in the modern corporation. Thirdly, capitalism is associated with an increasingly strengthening rational criticism against its own social system. There will be an army of intellectuals interested in social unrest. Due to these forces, capitalism would inevitably sustain a socialist form of society which divides the capitalist society.

American civilization is weakening precisely due to its greatness. For Chinese *yin-yang* world vision, self-destruction is a natural process of creativity and construction.

The *yin-yang* vision visualizes fairness in a whole framework. Liberty versus slave, democracy versus hypocrisy, individualism versus cruelty (to the outsider), and the like, are the two sides of the same coin. If the positive side is strong, the negative side is seemingly weak for a while but will rebound so that the organic system is dynamically balancing. Lipset (1996) cogently demonstrated that the organizing principles and the institutions of the United States include many negative traits. It is not by accident that America is now characterized by income inequality, high crime rates, intolerance toward political and ethnic minorities, deepened cold feelings towards each other, un-trustful human relations, lack of public spirit, hypocrisy, and low levels of electoral participation. These phenomena are inherently linked to American values and institutions.

It is plain to the world that America has destroyed many traditional values and is faced with serious social dilemmas. If individual freedom has no boundary or even direction, the assumption of evil human nature leads to the conclusion that American people's sense of duty as citizens and sense of shame tend to evolve into chaos, if not quickly degenerated.

Keynes argued: "Capitalism is the astounding belief that the wicked of men will do the wicked of things for the greatest good of everyone." American democracy implicitly contains the astounding belief that a most uncultivated man might make the most selfish decision for the good of America. American freedom in gender market implicitly contains the astounding belief that the most sexually attractive of women may commit the most romantic adultery for the good of everyone. The adultery can be verified even in the long term so far as one changes the concept of fairness in gender market. In *The Elephant in the Brain*, Simler and Hanson (2020) depict a common human trait: "Human beings are primates, and primates are political animals. Our brains, therefore, are designed not just to hunt and gather but also to help us get ahead socially, often via deception and self-deception. But while we may be self-interested schemes, we benefit by pretending otherwise. The less we know about our own ugly motives, the better — and thus, we don't like to talk, or even think, about the extent of our selfishness. This is 'the elephant in the brain.'"

5.6 The End of Rational Simplicity and Colonization-Convenient Thinking

> The people may be made to follow a path of action, but they may not be made to understand it.
>
> Confucius (551–479 BC, 8:9)

> The beginning and ending of all things are nothing but integration and disintegration. ... If viewed from the causes of what is hidden and what is manifest, from the principle of life and death,

and from the features of positive and negative spiritual forces, the Way of Heaven and Earth can be understood.

Ch'eng I (1033–1107, Chan, 1963: 571)

Until a few decades ago, Newtonianism had been the principal paradigm in traditional sciences. Political and economic Newtonianism dominated mainstreams of rational approaches to human societies. Chaos theory and nonlinear science provide alternative perspectives on socioeconomic evolution (Prigogine and Stengers, 1984; Peitgen, et al., 1992; Prigogine, 1997). The founding fathers of the United States were strongly influenced by Newtonianism in their approaches to politics (Striner, 1995). Newtonian metaphors were pervasive forms of intellectual discourse in 18th century thought. Adam Smith was the follower of Newtonianism. His economic equilibrium theory and the invisible hand are consequences of the traditional scientific vision. Political laissez-faire is also from this linearized world view. The theory leads basically to a conclusion that equilibrium establishes itself. Educated with Newtonian vision, American thinkers would treat democracy, market economy, and individualism as separated systems and each system would achieve its optimal equilibrium (or balanced path). This is typically British mentality about individual and society. For instance, traditional "American economics" (after WWII most influential economists in the West have been American) makes up all kinds of stories to identify such an equilibrium. Traditional theories in politics, economics, and sociology were developed in isolation and each field was dominated by Newtonian dynamics.

The great America was once renowned for certain qualities that Confucius attributed to men at an early stage of socioeconomic development: "The purity of traditional man showed itself in a disregard of small things; ... the stern dignity of traditional man showed itself in grave reserve; ... the stupidity of traditional man showed itself in straightforwardness...." But contemporary America is politically, socially, culturally, and economically far more complex than before WWII. Its social and economic networks have contained many "dark holes." Traditional economic ideas, political thought, and social theories are not effective to explore the complexity of American society.

In the last few decades, the world has seen rapid development of nonlinear science, widespread use of computer, and economic globalization. Traditional sciences, including economics, were created with worldview of linearity, simplicity, and stability, and cannot explain, even in an approximate sense, the complexity of fast changing reality. On the other hand, new science, with names such as chaos theory, catastrophe theory, complexity, synergetics, and the like, has important implications for understanding global change.

Infinite linear progress of a society does not exist in this world view. Opposite forces, as portrayed in the Yi Jing, exist for any change and internal dynamics does not move the system to one direction to its extreme before it tends to return. Changes take place in human groupings as well as in individual life. The spirit of change shifts in flow, and no one can stop. Man is born to have an inner dynamic nature biased toward change. The Chinese does not see life as immobility or stationary pendulum (like Adam Smith) but in constant change, regularly or irregularly. The Yi Jing does not imply any predetermined destiny. It does not limit free will (this kind of freedom can be identified both in Taoism and ancient Confucianism). Rather than predicting certainty, it suggests alternatives and probable consequences of human actions.

The collapse of socialist economies and implementation of market mechanism in socialist China and Vietnam and the expansion of government intervention in capitalist systems epitomize cyclical features of the *yin* and the *yang*. The structural transformation between socialism and capitalism is due to the internal mechanisms of social evolution. The socialist collapse is by its enforced stability and "femininity" (strengthened "*yin*"); the steadily increased government intervention in capitalist systems is caused by the inherent instability and "masculinity" (strengthened "*yang*") in capitalism. Neither *yin* nor *yang* alone is desirable from the humanistic perspective. Only a mixed economic system is sustainable; and there is no single stationary point for maximum welfare.

In principle, the future is completely determined by the past; but small uncertainties are amplified, with the effect that even though the behavior is predictable in the short term, it is unpredictable over the long haul. Chaos theory deals with those systems that have fluctuations about the fixed level of the periodic cycle, and that appear to be so irregular that it may be perplexing to associate them with any underlying stationary or periodic process. There are mysterious situations in which fluctuations are found even when environmental parameters are maintained at a level as constant as possible and no perturbing influences can be identified. Influenced by Newtonian science, traditional social scientists dismissed the notion of nonpredictability as a cheap evasion. But "Both extremes — " as Walter (1994:19) says, "passionate romantic or cool logician — reveal a paucity of perspective in the West for more than 2,500 years. It has split us into romantic versus classic, liberal versus conservative, left versus right, heart versus head. But it is possible to encompass both poles within a larger, transcendental third stance.

This paradigm is cradled in chaos theory, that amazing new science of the 20th century. It reveals the *I Ching* [i.e., *Yi Jing*] to be a model of chaos patterning in microcosm. It even connects science to spirit."

The American intellectual world has been addicted to British Newtonian linear mentality. Linearized vision makes it convenient for the superpower to play with the world. Applying simplified rules and easy-to-implement versions of such intricate concepts as human rights (without deeply examining the meanings of becoming human and being human), young America got by. But a "linearized rule" is not suitable for highly culturally cultivated and well-educated human societies. Self-destructiveness and globalization results in long-term issues for America to continue its prosperity with fair, at least socially tolerable, distribution of wealth, power and sex, as well as its role of leading the world.

6. America's Deepening Destructiveness in the Global Village

> The evil of men is that they like to be the teachers of others.
>
> A man must first despise himself, and then others will despise him. A family must first destroy itself, and then others will destroy it. A kingdom must first smite itself, and then others will smite it.
>
> Mencius (372–289 BC)

Self-destruction is a part of evolution. Man's physical power and wealth have been becoming less useful and less valuable in gender markets due to the past achievements of his passionate energy and creativity. Creativity results in destruction in business and innovation does not necessarily enhance social welfare and living conditions of the population. Most profits brought about by American great innovations do not end in the pockets who make them. Democracy has exposed its weak points even since the day it was conceived in small islands in Greek. Freedom in the market leads to concentration of national wealth into a few families.

Due to its spirit and way of business, America has played a great role in connecting the world. The rest of the world has benefited from the peace, security, and access to larger markets. Due to American greatness, the epoch of rational simplicity dominated by Western civilization is ending and the world is entering nascent globalization of rational civilization(s). Mankind is steadily climbing toward a more sophisticated stage of civilization, without having been set back by any catastrophes, yet.

6.1 Self-Organization of Human Societies with Creation and Destruction

> If men of virtue and ability be not confided in, a state will become empty and void. Without the rules of propriety and distinctions of right, the high and the low will be thrown into confusion. Without the great principles of government and their various business, there will not be wealth sufficient for the expenditure.
>
> Mencius (372–289 BC, 14:12)

Wealth, power, and sex are created, maintained, distributed, and utilized with different mechanisms. Their applications have motley effects on social and economic evolution. Modern Western civilization has theoretically separated the three variables with three separate institutions, free market, romanticism (in association with individualism and liberty), and democracy. America has relatively and effectively applied three separate values and institutions to three apparently separate markets. There are dynamic interactions between the three institutions in the same organ, but they are separated in modern scientific theories. Conflicts among them have increasingly turned out more evident after America has tasted the best time with (spiritually) young and energetic people. Peter Drucker spoke of what will happen in a free society without genuine leadership: "Only three things happen naturally in organizations: friction, confusion, and underperformance. Everything else requires leadership." America has a strong tendency to produce people of friction, confusion, and underperformance, irrespective of its very talented experts in many fields and its high national productivity. Trump's presidency might symbolize the bifurcation point of America's golden age — the last president of America's golden era and the first president of America's decline. This is not a personal but organic phenomenon.

Schumpeter is well known for saying: "At the heart of capitalism is creative destruction." Young Schumpeter (1934) is mostly concerned with positive consequences of destructiveness. The young mind has "shallow" understanding about how the social organ would work together. Aged Schumpeter sings different tune with more balanced but dark conclusion for American capitalist culture. American has entered a mature stage of civilization with American liberty: at the heart of capitalism is concentration of wealth in a few hands; at the heart of the American Romanticism is the broken family; and at the heart of the American democracy is huge stock of lies.

"The progress of the human race in understanding the universe has established a small corner of order in an increasing disordered universe," said Hawking (1988: 152). Economic theory reaches a similar conclusion about possible number of rational societies. Any civilization embraces self-destructive mechanisms for continuation with its past pattern because of human creativity and natural conflicts within humanity. "It is lamentable, that to be a good patriot one must become the enemy of the rest of mankind." (Voltaire, 1694–1778). "Men are trained to kill and slaughter people for their territory, in similar ways that animals protect their own territories. Financial gamblers now hurt families on a scale and at a speed unprecedented in history. Nations have their heroes. This is how nations evolve together — killing or co-operating according to national interests.

Lipset (1996) sees the American culture as the most individualistic, religious, optimistic, patriotic, and rights-oriented; the culture also demonstrates the opposite extremes. America is wealthy in real income terms, productive as reflected in worker output, high in proportions of the highly educated population in the total population. America also has the highest crime rate; has the most people locked up in jail; and has the most lawyers per capita of any country in the world.

6.2 America's Declining Relative Economic Power

> Riches and honors are what men desire. If they cannot be obtained in the proper way, they should not be held. Poverty and meanness are what men dislike. If [the former] cannot be obtained in the proper way, [the latter] should not be avoided.

Confucius (551–479 BC, 4:5)

The American "Goddess of Pop" Cher (1946–) recalls, "I remember a great America where we made everything. There was a time when the only thing you got from Japan was a really bad cheap transistor radio that some aunt gave you for Christmas."

As the world has advanced peacefully, prosperously, and with low-cost connectivity, the opportunities for greatness in absolute terms have changed. The U.S. government has run out of money and has huge debts. It can no longer maintain — much less upgrade — public infrastructure, general education, and science and technology after it meets its military expenditures and commitments to public health, pensions and social welfare. Many Americans have no private savings to speak of, nor can they rely on the government to secure their livelihood.

It begins to appear that, in the long run, it is not so beneficial for great powers to invade and plunder other countries to solve their own economic and social dilemmas. Europeans colonized the world. America took in huge numbers of immigrants annually. Philosopher Karl Popper has a very influential book, *The Open Society and Its Enemies*. He could not image the closed society and its enemies, which America is faced with now.

Another Jewish public figure, economist Paul Samuelson (1915–2009), makes fun of the great nation: "What I say is, 'If you're so rich, how come you're so dumb?" By the same token, "The Nobel is a ticket to one's own funeral. No One has ever done anything after he got it," observed T.S. Eliot (1888–1965). This is applicable to a great country as well. Once it is sure of its superpower, it slithers into decline. A civilization evolves to be great not only because of its own internal strength and virtue, but also because of luck.

After World War II, America has made the world more closely connected, with regards to mutual understanding, global justice, shared information, and wide dissemination of knowledge. The success also destroys traditional American values. Civilization is the stock accumulated over its history. People who are born into a given civilization might contribute nothing significant to that civilization but many miserable memories may be left for its later generations to disguise. The opposite is also possible. The Trump generation which experienced the greatness of America in almost every field and which has little idea about modern industries, science, technology, and the progress made in other countries, understandably feels full confidence in America becoming great again. Nevertheless, examining the human capital of people aged 30 or younger, and comparing America to the rest of the world, one might wonder how America can maintain its superiority (even in relative terms) even in the near future.

America's productivity fell in the late 1970s, in absolute terms. There were multiple determinants for the productivity slowdown. The loss of the work ethic, excessive government regulation, low savings rate, little emphasis on science and mathematics in school, insufficient investment in communication and transportation infrastructure were listed as main factors. This deceleration was, however, followed by fast progress. The rise of per capita income from 1984 to 1994 was almost 20% faster than the period 1963–1983. After such a prosperous period, many Americans have become used to leisure activities, an unlimited variety of consumer goods and services, and unprecedented pleasures.

America's modern development, as a by-product of European expansion and conflicts among the Europeans, is not special in economic history. East Asian development and Singapore have been passing along a similar path to national prosperity. The idea that people can freely pursue their own interests and society will somehow be advanced is not an American innovation, but it seems to have worked for a while in America.

America's economic power is now challenged by many countries. In 2018, its nominal GDP and PPP were $21.44 trillion; the corresponding variables for China are respectively $14.14 trillion and $27.31 trillion, for Japan $5.15 trillion and 5.75 trillion. China's PPP has exceeded America's for some years already. In 2018, America accounted for 15.2% of global gross domestic after adjusting for PPP. It is expected that the share would decline to 13.86 by 2024. Figure 6.1 plots the dynamics of share of America's economy in the global economy during the period of 1960 to 2014. In half a century, the share would fall from 40% to near 20%.

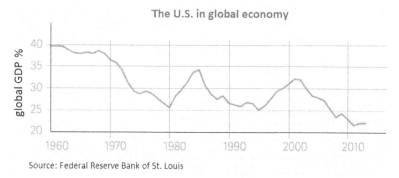

The U.S. in global economy

Source: Federal Reserve Bank of St. Louis

Figure 6.1 Falling Share of U.S. Economy in the Global Economy

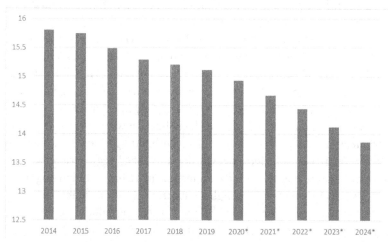

Figure 6.2 Falling Share of U.S. Economy in the Global Purchasing Power

Figure 6.2 exhibits the changing share of America's economy in the global economy during the period of 2014–2024 (the data from 2020 to 2024 are estimated).

The main features of American civilization can be "replicated" easily. Other regions could easily compete with America if peace is kept and the investment environment is secured.

6.3 America of the People, for the Rich, and by the Rich

> It is not difficult to govern. All one has to do is not to offend the noble families.
>
> Mencius (372–289 BC)
>
> When a country is well governed, poverty and a mean condition are things to be ashamed of. When a country is ill governed, riches and honor are things to be ashamed of.
>
> Confucius (551–479 BC, 8:13)

Desmond Tutu (1931–) described the behavior of Europeans in Africa: "When the missionaries came to Africa they had the Bible and we had the land. They said 'Let us pray.' We closed our eyes. When we opened them we had the Bible and they had the land." and "In the land of my birth I cannot vote, whereas a young person of eighteen can vote. And why? Because he or she possesses that wonderful biological attribute — a white skin." It is reasonable for the powerful Americans to advocate for the American dream, as it is the safe way to enrich themselves.

"It is impossible to understand the history of economic thought if one does not pay attention to the fact that economics as such is a challenge to the conceit of those in power." (Ludwig von Mises, 1881–1973). Market mechanism as escalator works effectively for some societies in some stages of socioeconomic development but will not work properly in other stages.

White civilization is built on Greek civilization with religion and racial discrimination as the key elements of social building. Education is deeply involved with the evolution of a culture and social segregation; one can reasonably expect that the U.S. government is more interested in upgrading weapons rather than in making higher education equally available to heterogeneous populations. The United States is spending billions of dollars to compete with Russia and China militarily, but not educationally. Instead, America is educating perhaps millions of mainland and overseas Chinese. Russia's portion of adult population with a university education is higher than America's. The American dream through education is no more typically American, as many other countries are doing better.

Lao Zi (6th–4th BC?) compared long-term social evolution with a subtle trap: "When cleverness and knowledge arise, great lies will flourish. When relatives fall out with one another there will be filial duty and love. When states are in confusion there will be faithful servants." Keynes described: "The political problem of mankind is to combine three things: economic efficiency, social justice and individual liberty." Academic political economy exists to find out how economic efficiency, social justice and individual liberty can be achieved under various circumstances. Politics should be about how to produce, distribute, and consume three things: wealth, power, and sex in varied time scales. As society is organic, maintaining one-subsystem does not betoken that the other subsystems are trivial. One may have a good heart but without teeth. One might hear, see, and listen well but has no brain to understand anything. It is also possible that no part of the body has any serious defects tested with most modern medical instruments, but the man suddenly dies. Sustainability of the great power is not only a matter of wealth and power, but also minds of peoples.

"In bourgeois society capital is independent and has individuality, while the living person is dependent and has no individuality." (Karl Marx, 1818–1883). Applying Marx's observation to contemporary America, we see that the rich are independent and free, the poor are dependent on the rich, and are manipulated and brain washed by the rich. Camille Paglia (1947–) pictured: "Americans? Though they claim to speak for the poor and dispossessed, Democrats have increasingly become the party of an upper-middle-class professional elite, top-heavy with journalists, academics and lawyers."

American Identity has been repeatedly emphasized. The identity is constructed on individualism rather than distinctions based on ethnic and other social categories. America wanted to create a universal belief for a national benefit. Belief cannot be rationally based, and irrational belief cannot be sustainable in the global village. "The Principle on which this country was founded and by which it has always been governed," Franklin D. Roosevelt said in 1943, "is that Americanism is a matter of the mind and heart; Americanism is not, and never was, a matter of race and ancestry. A good American is one who is loyal to this country and to our creed of liberty and democracy" (Schlesinger, 1998:43). When speaking of American citizens' "primary allegiance to the values America stands for and values we really live by," President Clinton stated, "long before we were so diverse, our nation's motto was E Pluribus Unum — out of many, we are one. We must be one — as neighbors; as fellow citizens; not separate camps, but family" (Kim, 1999:598).

But the meaning of family is meaningless (in the traditional sense), if not contradictory, in terms of being united. Children learn by observing reality. Parental adultery is already "routine" and children learn family values from their own families. Hearty investment in the family life by either party is very risky as the accumulated stock has great probability to be enjoyed by some other man or woman. Man needs a public spirit to be loyal to the family. "The prejudices of ignorance are more easily removed than the prejudices of interest; the first are all blindly adopted, the second willfully preferred." (George Bancroft, 1800–1891). Before WWII, most of Americans had little education. Their common interest was were money. People could easily adopt to the American culture.

National history is often a collection of partial and biased stories for illustrating its glory, encouraging positive thinking (in free environment), and justifying the power with examples of virtue and great achievements. Rational civilization is full of stories made up from various sources and cherry-picked and manipulated social and economic statistic data without reliable sources. The contemporary American culture is characterized by propaganda rather than a religious fever or extreme passion for a rational and reliable ideology. This cultural formation has been portrayed by *Propaganda* in 1928 by Edward Bernays (1891–1995), an Austria-born Jewish American. He established a systematic way for leaders and industrialists to manipulate or/and control the masses without their knowing about it. He was Sigmund Freud's nephew.

Seeing that human action is driven by irrational forces, in his influential *Propaganda* he proposed his method of propaganda through understanding the group mind. He dubbed his method "the engineering of content". Of course, the method, like lethal weapons, has no moral direction in the sense that it can be applied for any purpose. He succeeded in launching his most famous campaign by convincing women that smoking cigarettes as a sign of female empowerment. He is frequently quoted saying: "The conscious and intelligent manipulation of the organized habits and opinions of the masses is an important element in democratic society.... In almost every act of our daily lives, whether in the sphere of politics or business, in our social conduct or our ethical thinking, we are dominated by the relatively small number of persons... who understand the mental processes and social patterns of the masses. It is they who pull the wires which control the public mind. Those who manipulate this unseen mechanism of society constitute an invisible government which is the true ruling power of our country."

"All successful people are standing on ground that is crumbling beneath their feet" (Joseph Schumpeter, 1983–1950). The American rich are supported by American poor as well as the poor of the rest world. As more of the poor of the rest world is escaping from poverty, many of American poor feel more miserable than they expected, as many of them had escaped their own country to enjoy the American dream.

It has often been argued that the widened gaps between the rich and poor are partially due to processes of globalization and rapid technological change. In America large inflows of immigrations might also have played a significant role. Workers in any part of the world are confronted with increasing competition from other countries and machines. Advances in technology have potentials to lower real wage of any sector in any part of the world. Global freedom of capital implies that capital owners can move their wealth easily to wherever the returns appear likely to be the highest.

Immigration also makes a contribution to income distribution. The increase in the relative supply of less-skilled workers tends to depress wages at the bottom of the pay scale. The increase in talented workers makes high-paid jobs more competitive, too; thus the salary for top computer specialists ids driven down b newcomers who have some of the needed skills

America has many structural obstacles in facing with new challenges both domestically and internationally. The rich control political power and own high proportion of national wealth. America has been converted into a country of the poor (and a shrinking middle), for the rich, and by the rich. Many social conflicts are fundamentally related to economic performance and trends. American policies, institutions, and economic arrangements that had enabled America to build enormous industries have proved less effective to promote economic advancement and enhance income of low-income people.

It is now faced with the paradox of a declining sense of moral obligation and a heightened awareness of distributive justice. The accepted belief that freedom will enhance people's welfare is faced with great tests that America has never known before.

Human evolution does not easily and randomly allow greatness to be repeated in the same place as the greatness is maintained by unstopped destructiveness and — as far as macro social phenomena are concerned — is associated with biased distribution of wealth, sex, and power. If one observes monkey societies across the world, one will see great differences in strategy of domination and distribution of sex and food.

Azar Nafisi (1948–) said: "The negative side of the American Dream comes when people pursue success at any cost, which in turn destroys the vision and the dream." A sense that there is a biased distribution of power, wealth, and sex can give rise to the belief Bernie Sanders (1941–) expressed: "For many, the American dream has become a nightmare."

As America's domestic constructive success is slower than its destructiveness, it needs a fluke of fortune, like the two World Wars, to rejuvenate its greatness. Immediately after these wars, Europe was in devastation and East Asia in initial learning process, not to mention that many developing economies had just escaped from colonization. America became the leader.

Upward social mobility is an important part of the American dream. Highly concentrated wealth and biased income distribution build barriers for those who follow. Today's education system is not only very costly, it seems full of corruption. Academic corruption and unwritten rules in the academic world cannot be breached. Children born rich nowadays have their future advantage secured. There are many reports of successful Americans who allegedly indulge in crime to satisfy their unlimited desires.

Some rich businessmen are not satisfied with wealth and sex alone. Equipped with money, they want their shallow and long-term socially destructive views and visions to influence society. They obviously have multiple ways to influence political power. In the early 2021, tech companies, such as Twitter Inc., Apple Inc and Amazon.com Inc, Facebook Inc, Alphabet Inc.-owned Google, decided to limit President Trump's mainstream social media. They were also joined by smaller tech companies. The most powerful man on earth could not get his message out, owing to a few businessmen's decision.

Lincoln's "of the people, by the people, for the people" has encouraged people not only in America, but also people outside America, to make their countries more democratic and more equal. Contemporary America is distancing it capacitated itself from the ideal. Franklin D. Roosevelt pointed out: "True individual freedom cannot exist without economic security and independence. People who are hungry and out of a job are the stuff of which dictatorships are made." "What is most important for democracy is not that great fortunes should not exist, but that great fortunes should not remain in the same hands. In that way there are rich men, but they do not form a class," Alexis de Tocqueville commented on how to maintain a healthy democratic society.

The rich of America have close relations within the rich through marriage, family relations, business, and politics. Henry George observed the historical lesson: "What has destroyed every previous civilization has been the tendency to the unequal distribution of wealth and power." Julius Caesar described sources of social disorder: "It is not those well-fed long-haired men that I fear, but the pale and the hungry-looking." What Sigmund Freud (1856–1939) elucidated may be allied to America's long-term dilemma: "A civilization which leaves so large a number of its participants unsatisfied and drives them into revolt neither has nor deserves the prospect of a lasting existence." Or, perhaps Isaac Newton's description of the visible, physical world, is apt: "What goes up must come down."

The United States is faced with escalating predicaments caused by poverty. The concept of absolute poverty is often defined as the failure to satisfy a minimum standard of nutritional requirement. The definition itself involves human perception and emotions. To determine how a society should weigh its member's suffering or happiness is an important issue in understanding the measurement of poverty. It does not seem that we can have a rationally trustful weight system. In practice, the measurement often reflects customs, political conflicts, and human perception in general. In the *Wealth of Nations*, Adam Smith outlined the situation necessity: "By necessaries I understand not only the commodities which are indispensably necessary for the support of life, but whatever the custom of the country renders it indecent for creditable people, even the lowest order, to be without. A linen shirt, for example, is, strictly speaking, not a necessary of life. The Greeks and Romans lived, I suppose, very comfortably though they had no linen. But in the present times, through the greater part of Europe, a creditable day-laborer would be ashamed to appear in public without a linen shirt, the want of which would be supposed to denote that disgraceful degree of poverty which, it is presumed, nobody can well fall into without extreme bad conduct. Custom, in the same manner, has rendered leather shoes a necessary of life in England. The poorest creditable person of either sex would be ashamed to appear in public without them."

Households become poor under all sorts of political, economic, psychological, social, and cultural mechanisms at different stages of economic development. One observes poverty in agricultural, communist, industrial, and post-industrial economies. Famine and mass starvation still happen in some parts of the world. Although the United States is the richest nation in the world, a substantial proportion of the American population lives in poverty. The U.S. poverty rate fell almost by half between 1959 and 1974, mainly due to the economic expansion and public social welfare programs. Throughout the rest of the 1970s, the poverty rate remained almost stationary. Since 1980, the overall poverty rate has increased. According to Rodgers (1996), progress against poverty declined dramatically with the main reasons being that (1) the wages of less-skilled workers were relatively reduced with regards to higher-skilled workers; (2) real spending on welfare was reduced; and (3) the proportion of the mother-only families in all American families was increased.

Modern (mainstream) economics has little insight into the dynamics of inequalities and poverty in America. Dynamic distribution issues among heterogeneous social groups are not even a concern of mainstream economics. Massive amounts of data and an expansion of research techniques related to the causes and consequences of poverty had been accumulated in the US (O'Connor, 2001:1).

Globalization tends to enforce convergence of wage rates in the world. This also implies that if America continues is to conduct free trade policy and have domestic free markets, payments of jobs in, for instance, manufacturing, tend to converge with some other countries. A Chinese businessman, Ma Huateng (1971–) described speeds of American and Chinese markets: "In America, when you bring an idea to market, you usually have several months before competition pops up, allowing you to capture significant market share. In China, you can have hundreds of competitors within the first hours of going live. Ideas are not important in China — execution is."

The impact of Chinese markets on America's economy has been well addressed in recent years. Other economies stir or are whipped by American economy in assorted goods, services, resources, and professionals in various forms through motley channels. America cannot influence the world in the simple manner as during its golden time. Dan Lipinski (1966–) sketched the structure of American economy: "Small businesses are the backbone of the American economy and employ almost half of the working population. Yet because of their size, they rarely have access to the same information security resources as large firms." These small firms are vulnerable in global markets if America continues to be closely connected to global economies with free immigration.

6.4 A Thucydides Trap Between America and Other Powers?

> When right government prevails in the world, princes of little virtue are submissive to those of great, and those of little worth, to those of great. When bad government prevails in the world, princes of small power are submissive to those of great, and the weak to the strong. Both these cases are the rule of Heaven. They who accord with heaven are preserved, and they who rebel against Heaven perish.

> Mencius (372–289 BC, 7:7)

> The least of things with a meaning is worth more in life than the greatest of things without it.

> Carl Jung (1875–1961)

Mo Zi (c. 470–391 BC) perceived a globally peaceful world in which each country has the ability to destroy invaders. This idea has gradually become a possibility owing to the diffusion of nuclear power. Since Spain started to connect Europe to the rest of the world, one Western country after another has dominated the globe. Great countries based on plundering and invading need enemies for their own sustainability. Albert Einstein is historically wrong: "Peace cannot be kept by force; it can only be achieved by understanding." He is never right at anything about human social life as he, like Lao Zi in ancient China, thinks common humans as worthless pigs or fishes. Peace can be kept by equal destructive forces.

The Cold War was idiotically serious, impotently lovely, and more peaceful than it might have been, if not for the "nuclear deterrent." The Cold War guaranteed a peaceful period between great nations. Technologically simple, WWII delivered the global power to America. A technologically advanced WWIII between America and Russia/China might pass the global power to India or Africa in future.

"Men fight... because they are convinced that the extermination of adversaries is the only means of promoting their own well-being." (Ludwig von Mises, 1881–1973). The first lesson of globalization for Americans should be that it cannot gauge its own future without locating itself within the changing global political and economic structure.

Digitalization picks up all trivial matters which devalue the great or the respected and diffuses them immediately across the earth. A way to maintain personal or national progress within the global village is to keep its root as illustrated in the ancient Confucian doctrine, *The Great Learning* (505–435 BC): "It is only the truly virtuous man who can love or who can hate others. To see men of worth and not able to raise them to office; to raise them to office, but not so quickly; this is disrespect. To see bad men and not be able to remove them; to remove them, but not to do so to a distance: this is weakness. To love those whom men hate, and to hate those whom men love: this is to outrage the natural feeling of men. Calamities cannot fail to come down on him who does so.' Thus, we see that the sovereign has a great course to pursue. He must show entire self-devotion and sincerity to attain it, and by pride and extravagance he will fail of it."

Owing to the history of mutual killing, European civilization evolved a collective preference for "scrupulousness" with a single religion or dominant ideology. The singleness is necessary for a society whose key target is to protect itself and to exploit others. As a rule of the national game, having one ideology is far better than multiple ones for teamwork.

"Americans love to fight. All real Americans love the sting of battle," General George S. Patton generations. American man now has become far "softer" than Patton's generation could image. "America is a country founded on guns. It's in our DNA. It's very strange but I feel better having a gun. I really do. I don't feel safe, I don't feel the house is completely safe, if I don't have one hidden somewhere. That's my thinking, right or wrong." (Brad Pitt, 1963–). This is the home of 330 million Americans. One feels necessary to have guns within one's own home. That is not a home country, in any meaningful sense. Contemporary America, as a nation, will not feel safe if it is not sure being capable of killing all of humanity overnight. This is the national spirit or the cultural gene of the invader.

In the 1960s–1970s, America was believed to be the only country filled with happiness. "Contempt for happiness is usually contempt for other people's happiness, and is an elegant disguise for hatred of the human race." (Betrand Russell, 1872–1970). Man has a great capacity of not only self-deception in personal or Freudian intrapsychic level, but also in collective level. "Men hate the individual whom they call avaricious only because nothing can be gained from him," Voltaire (1694–1778). He could have been describing a source of great America's complaining about the rest of the world.

China is built on a cultural basis different from imitative Japanese and from the quasi-nomadic and quasi-European Russian culture. The extensive quotes from ancient Confucianism so far in the book demonstrate some cultural traits. The Chinese *yin-yang* theory does not justify any man-made ideology with a single God or goal. Any single-ended ideology is not sustainable in the long term. China is a civilization which devoted much of its energies on constructing and maintaining the Great Wall against nomadic neighbors. China does not have passion to diffuse some religion to other societies simply because it does not create any spiritually or ideologically addictive one. China's loyal center is fundamentally blood-related and has little to do with management and beliefs in national levels. For an almost "isolated" rational civilization constantly faced with the fate of being invaded by neighboring nomads, no religion fits for social harmony and national survival. Chinese civilization imported Buddhism to satisfy religious needs of Chinese people. Its Confucianism and Taoism "satisfy" needs of rationality and free spirit.

Michel de Montaigne gave a sustainable formation of gender gaming: "A good marriage would be between a blind wife and a deaf husband." Like a well-cultivated couple with multiple interlinked interests, they will not easily start to talk about divorce; but once they start to discuss the end, it tends to take a long time, with ambiguous consequences, like Brexit.

Tocqueville (1805–1859) said: "There are two things which a democratic people will always find very difficult — to begin a war and to end it."

There were relatively good relations between China and America in the four decades from 1978. Since President Trump took the national power, America has changed its attitude to China. China is now perceived as a new threat. Rice-paddy farmers emphasized social stability. They would fight to the death if they were aware of some probability of a victory. America's wars with Japan, Korea and Vietnam show the common character of these rice-paddy farmers as fighters. Land was life, but human lives had no high value, as life would be cheaply reproduced and continued (in comparison with land) in these traditional societies.

Cultural value is a joint product of nature and man. Confucius (13:9) told the Chinese to be prepared before going to war, not to throw their lives away: "Let a good man teach the people seven years, and they may then likewise be employed in war. . . . To lead an uninstructed people to war is to throw them away." During the period 1978–2018, China has produced a historical miracle by using the opportunity offered by America in a way pointed out by the ironic Oscar Wilde: "There is nothing in the world like the devotion of a married woman. It is a thing no married man knows anything about." Mainland China, at least the people of my generation, have appreciated, loved, and respected America as it has symbolized the most precious value of mankind, freedom, that China had never had. It is owing to this passionate and unconditional appreciation of American civilization that Chinese people can now dream about building their own country and making it beautiful in a profound sense. Education may be misconducted, but the consequences of learning are irreversible for a person, as well as for a race or nation who has studied diligently.

"The Thucydides trap" is often mentioned lately in studies of international relations, especially when referring to conflicts between America and China (e.g., Allison, 2018; Chan, 2020). The term implies that when a rising power rivals a ruling power, wars tend to occur between them. As far as game theory is concerned, this kind of games occurs not only between nations, but also between families in a village, gangsters in a city, firms in an industry, regions in a large area or so on.

Since Trump became president, conflicts between America and China have increasingly become multi-dimensional and severe. China has learned much in the last few years about modern societies since. Trump's 'honest' lies about China as one of the greatest powers in human history has made the Chinese people have, for better or worse, more confidence in the Chinese government. Trump's leadership has further polarized American society, but it has solidified the power of China's government.

Modern people are supposedly educated in rational thought. They will not so easily give life to a deposed cause in which they have no true belief, no interest, no net benefit, and no understanding. Hemingway (1899–1961) long ago described the modern meaning of wars for the individual: "They wrote in the old days that it is sweet and fitting to die for one's country. But in modern war, there is nothing sweet nor fitting in your dying. You will die like a dog for no good reason." Bertrand Russell (1872–1970) illustrated the point: "I would never die for my beliefs because I might be wrong." Confucius expressed it in another way, "if I know truth, I might peacefully die tonight."

Society consists of various macro levels of subsystems, such as agriculture, government, industry, education, academics, and the like, and each subsystem consists of various micro systems, such as individuals, households, and firms. The American military sector bolsters its superpower status in the world. Its expenditures are huge. Empires were often ruined fast when they started to decline economically but continue their military expenditures. If the military expansion does not return a profit, the national decline would be sped up.

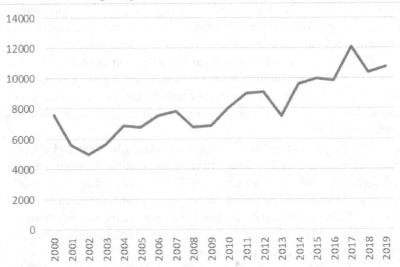

Figure 6.3 U.S. Arms Exports, 2000 to 2019, in 1990 million U.S.D.

Figure 6.3 shows U.S. arms exports from 2000 to 2019, based on the known unit production of a core set of weapons. In 2019 global arms trade is about 200 billion US dollars and the US shares 80 of the total trade. It exported four times more arms to the other countries than the next nine countries combined. America has a strong motive to perpetuate political, cultural, and military conflicts and instabilities so far American is the superpower and dominates the global military trade. It sells somehow outdated weapons and uses the profits to re-invest in advanced technologies and has more power to make regions unstable in its preference. Positive trade-offs between global political instabilities and military production have continued.

"The direct use of force is such a poor solution to any problem it is generally employed only by small children and large nations." (David Friedman, 1944-). A threat of the direct application of force is the way for America to continue its military profits. It makes better economic sense for other countries to buy the useless stock of goods than to feel their impact.

The superpower position benefits America in all fields of economics. Its share of global arms exports is about 80 % annually during the period of 2007 to 2017 and 140 billion US dollars (Figure 6.4). Giant companies adopt all methods to encourage the government to make the world profitably untrustful and unstable.

There are positive trade-offs between military production, economic benefits, and global power. The superpower position facilitates America to station their young men abroad. In the 1960s and 1970s, some areas around American military bases in the world played the role of using up leisure time of American young soldiers (reducing social burdens and contributing social order within America). After WWII, America played some war games, outside America, perhaps having solved more domestic military, economic, and political issues than making positive contributions to global peace. The world might advance toward a better place if each nation solves their own botherations as free market mechanism implies. "When the rich wage war, it's the poor who die" (Jean-Paul Sartre, 1905-1980). In future, it is the rich, the elite, and the powerful to lose or even to die first as they are occupying expensive and important places.

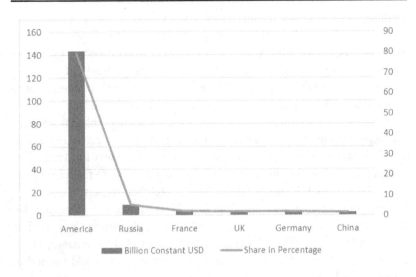

Figure 6.4 The Top 6 of Average Annual Arms Exports, 2007 to 2017

6.5 People of Color as the Principal New Immigrants, and Global Respectability

> Friends are the siblings the Heaven never gave us.
>
> Mencius (372–289 BC)

> There are three friendships, which are advantageous, and three which are injurious. Friendship with the upright; friendship with the sincere; and the friendship with the man of much observation — these are advantageous. Friendship with the man of specious airs; friendship with the insinuatingly soft; and friendship with the glib-tongued — these are injurious.
>
> Confucius (551–479 BC, 16:4)

In *The Ancient Regime*, Tocqueville (1732–1799; 1988: 86) described the difficulties of assimilating discriminated people with the mainstream: "It was no slight task to reunite people who had been strangers to each other, or foes for so many centuries. It was very difficult to teach them to come to an understanding for the transaction of their common business. Division was a comparatively easy achievement. We have furnished the world with a memorable illustration of the difficulty of the reverse process. When, sixty years ago, the various classes into which French society was divided were suddenly brought together, after a separation of several centuries, their only points of contact were their old sores; they only met to tear each other in pieces. Their rival jealousies and hatreds survive to this day."

Scale and scope economies are the basic factors for the rich (who owned big companies) to increase profits. The rich who control American politics would not be against immigration so long as the social order and security of rich areas are secured. As America has ever more people of color, it implies that it can hardly "borrow" the respectability created in Europe in future. As France and Germany come back to greatness in Europe (it does seem that Germany has never fulfilled its ambition to be the greatest, and might try to do it again in the near future), the English-dominated world is becoming more diversified in association with its relative decline.

The Yi-Jing-formed civilizations like the Chinese, Japanese and Koreas, cannot easily follow the British-American linearity once they become culturally more sophisticated and economically prosperous, and militarily secure. America needs to further create and sustain cultural stocks for global respectability and trustfulness if it wants to keep its superpower position. People don't respect trivial word gaming. America may lose cultural and social respectability in the global village when it does not deliver to the world a solid symbol sustainable in the future. No trust, no business.

National trust is based on many factors. Postman (1985) discussed how national assimilation and trust are affected when politics, religion, journalism, education are a part of entertainment industry. Technology is a part of cultural evolution and the world view of people on the earth is shifted with these changes. This kind of effects do not occur only within America. Whatever happen in America is simultaneously a part of global entertainment. Any country is challenging with its global image and respectability in the global village. America's national image built on big data of its hybrid population is now becoming confusing in the global village.

The great French mathematician André Weil (1906–1998) gives his evaluation of immigration policy: "First rate mathematicians choose first rate people, but second rate mathematicians choose third rate." Exchanges in human capital and ideas are nonlinear. His sister Simone Weil (1909–1943) recognizes the economic law in trade: "Beauty always promises, but never gives anything." The powerful show off and charge high rates but deliver little.

Society may be in a Malthusian trap or face civil wars for quite a long period. It may undergo a fast linear expansion over a certain period. It may also oscillate around a high level of development before making a further progress or linearly declining.

Micro-level chaos is a main feature of socioeconomic evolution in any stage of life. Like a man, a country based on a given ideology also has stage of life. The greatness of a culture or nation, like female beauty, is only transitory. For a society with large population with various preferences and abilities, to have a stable desirable path of economic prosperity with social harmony and mutual benefits is, mathematically, an event of low probability. An open prosperous and strong society needs an enemy — and a servant.

If one defines America as an individualistic, liberal, democratic, fairly equal, and competitive-market-dominated society, America is socially and culturally ending its middle age and entering the stage of aging. The probability of fast growth is quite low at this point. America is still wealthy, but the huge wealth is concentrated in a few hands. America has been a great country and the old generations could have been rightly proud in the world. It is doubtful about how young generations could earn special attention and respectability in the global village.

Individualism, and especially freedom in gender games, are breaking up the traditional family structure and reducing birth rates in association with prosperity and social and economic security. This occurs not only in the West but also in East Asian societies. As conditions become similar, behavior patterns become convergent among humans. East Asian societies have converged towards the West rapidly because East Asia had been educated rationally long before America was even found by non-Americans. Some affluent East Asian regions are faced with the fate of eventual disappearance if socioeconomic trends are linearly developed.

In America, ethnic differences have a similar meaning as in other rational cultures. As America has the common goal of profit maximization among assorted ethnic groups and the opportunity is secured by the teamwork, immigrants make an effort to seek the common interest together. Immigrants before WWII had little education and cultural cultivation could be easily mingled together with mutual prosperity and upwards movement. Cultural differences, especially among Europeans who were enemies before they immigrated to America, did not matter so much.

As demonstrated in Figure 6.5, the German-American population is larger than British-American. But one seldom hears about German impact on American civilization, even though German civilization may be more sophisticated than the British melting-pot. Most important thinkers of modern times are German. But due to anti-German sentiment associated with WWI, many German names were Anglicized and the use of German language declined. German immigrants spoke English and were educated with Newton and Adam Smith (rather than Leibniz, Einstein, and Kant). German "intellectual favor" almost "disappeared" in America.

People of color were treated together as racial minorities and had little voice in public life in early American society.

Figure 2.
Fifteen Largest Ancestries: 2000

(In millions. Percent of total population in parentheses.
Data based on sample. For information on confidentiality protection,
sampling error, nonsampling error, and definitions, see
www.census.gov/prod/cen2000/doc/sf3.pdf)

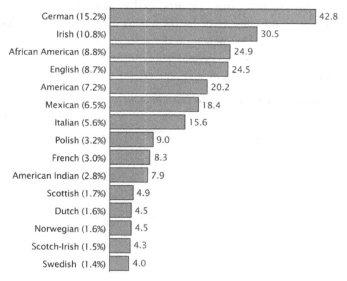

German (15.2%) 42.8
Irish (10.8%) 30.5
African American (8.8%) 24.9
English (8.7%) 24.5
American (7.2%) 20.2
Mexican (6.5%) 18.4
Italian (5.6%) 15.6
Polish (3.2%) 9.0
French (3.0%) 8.3
American Indian (2.8%) 7.9
Scottish (1.7%) 4.9
Dutch (1.6%) 4.5
Norwegian (1.6%) 4.5
Scotch-Irish (1.5%) 4.3
Swedish (1.4%) 4.0

Source: U.S. Census Bureau, Census 2000 special tabulation.

Figure 6.5 Original Countries of American Immigrants

After WWII, situations have been much changed. People of color have become increasingly conscious of their own racial identity due to changes in politics, education, economic opportunity, and communications with their own original cultures.

There are many hundred paths and traps, to be a naturalized American, legally or illegally. Civilization, like making a dish of food, is a dynamic combination of various elements in balances. The dish's value also depends on the cook's skills, timing of eating, and the taste of consumer. For instance, the white civilization is not highly evaluated by the Japanese consumer, even though some of its components are highly valued and symphonized into the Japanese life, sometimes in an adopted idiosyncrasy.

Minorities have been successful in vast areas that people of color consider their own cultures as important as European cultures. "As a child of West Texas, I identify with Hispanic culture every bit as much as I do North American culture," stated the American actor and film director Tommy Lee Jones (1946–). "Growing up, my parents were very much about the Egyptian culture. They never really wanted to assimilate in American culture," related the American film and television producer Sam Esmail (1977–).

As plotted in Figure 6.6, the population of non-whites is now almost equal to that of whites. The difference is that the younger population of non-whites is much larger than that of whites. As the whites have not saved much, who will pay social welfare costs for them in the future? That is challenging for America. As Asians have higher propensities to save and to receive higher education, they might disproportionately grow in near future to pick up the slack in national savings, tax income, and talent.

In U.S., most common age for whites is much older than for minorities

Number of people of each age by race/ethnicity, 2018

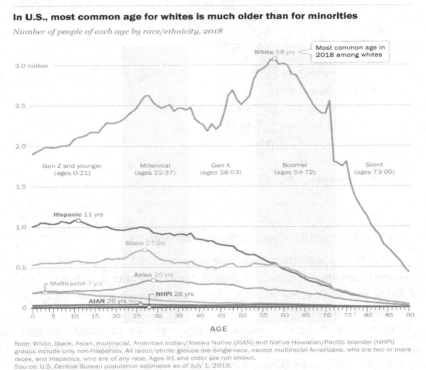

Note: White, black, Asian, multiracial, American Indian/Alaska Native (AIAN) and Native Hawaiian/Pacific Islander (NHPI) groups include only non-Hispanics. All racial/ethnic groups are single-race, except multiracial Americans, who are two or more races, and Hispanics, who are of any race. Ages 91 and older are not shown.
Source: U.S. Census Bureau population estimates as of July 1, 2018.
PEW RESEARCH CENTER

Figure 6.6 Ethnic Population Components across Ages

Skin depth is deep enough for poor and uneducated immigrants, but perhaps not when it comes to highly educated and properly cultivated ones. It does not seem to be very hard for educated professions (with globally identical rational knowledge, computing skills, and English as a working language) to assimilate into American civilization, which is so far essentially a "replicator" of European (English-based) civilization. It remains to be seen what are the implications of increasing proportions of people of color in the long term.

If they face little language barrier, many of these people feel at home in the U.S. Like mercenary soldiers, perhaps a high proportion of them have no strong national or cultural identity. This also implies that they can be easily attracted by other countries with better conditions than America. Many of professional businessmen and scholars in mathematics and natural sciences feel at home in many parts of the world as long as the pay is high, the living environment is comfortable, and the work environment is pleasant. British culture has dispersed as a "common" culture partly because many parts of the world belonged to the British empire.

Bertrand Russell (1872–1970) characterizes the spirit of social relations in American society: "In America everybody is of the opinion that he has no social superiors, since all men are equal, but he does not admit that he has no social inferiors, for, from the time of Jefferson onward, the doctrine that all men are equal applies only upwards, not downwards."

Reduced costs of transportation imply increasing complexity of movement of goods and people. Oil produced in many parts of the world can be safely and cheaply transported in many other parts of the world. Fruits and many other goods supplied in land-locked countries can also be consumed in remote places.

The global education that America has promoted, and global connectivity that America has culturally and technologically brought about, guarantee that immigrants can either directly bring the best American elements to their "home" country or indirectly encourage young people in the home culture. This is quite different from what immigration implied for America even a few decades ago. In many poor parts of the world, one can easily find some America-educated people who organize companies to produce, or who become politicians. With digital means and low-cost movement of people and goods, various parts of the world are further diverged in some perspectives, but converged in many others. This betokens that American supremacy in some special fields can be imitated and even outstripped by others.

For instance, Africa is challenging in the sports in which African-Americans are strong. White Europeans, Canadians, and Australians can naturally take profitable parts of the economy from white Americans. East Asian countries where the populations have highest average IQs are exposed to rivalry with America in technology. China is learning from America so rapidly in culture, political gaming, technologies, and many other fields that America tries to stop China's Americanization (in the name of being against Communism).

The tradition of encouraging immigrants to strengthen the nation and further enrich the incumbent rich is still carried on but seems to have been recently slowed down. Figure 6.7 exhibits the dynamics of foreign-born civilian population and its share in America during the period of 1900 to 2019. The share was high in most years and during the Cold War period the share was relatively low.

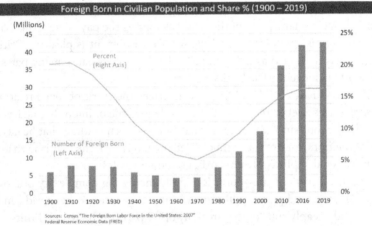

Figure 6.7 Dynamics of American Population Components

In recent years, more immigrants came from developing and non-Western societies, rather than European countries, as illustrated in Figure 6.8. In the figure "other Latin America" refers to Central America, South America, and the Caribbean. This occurred after the end of the Cold War when Germany and other Western societies had recovered from the devastations of WWII. America began to lose its "absolute attractiveness" to white people. White people might not pay "discrimination" prices and adjustment costs in a foreign country. It is expected that some white people might migrate back to Europe in the future, since the European countries are now relatively stable and prosperous places.

As people of color will soon exceed the white population, the direction of American democracy is increasingly uncertain. Memory is not symmetrical between the discriminator and discriminated. Hate is deeply rooted and secretly kept in the collective mind.

America has taken in more immigrants of people of color to sustain its economy with higher returns for the rich. Racial assimilation with increasing inequalities and poverty is a great challenging question for America, if opportunities for profit and upward mobility do not grow.

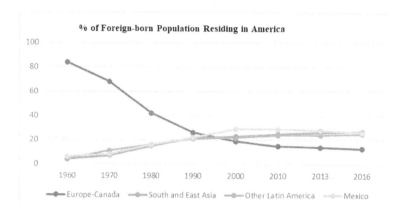

% of Foreign-born Population Residing in America

Figure 6.8 Origins of the U.S. Immigrant Population, 1960–2016

From 1921 to 1965, America had policies such as the national origins formula which checked immigration and naturalization opportunities for people outside Western Europe. Exclusion laws from the 1880s excluded largely immigration from Asia and quota laws from the 1920s restricted Eastern European immigration. By 1965 these rules were annihilated. The Immigration and Nationality Act of 1965 abolishes the system of nation-origin quotas and equalizes immigration policies. This explains new waves of immigration from non-European nations. The ethnic components are changed.

Since then, foreign-born immigrants have rapidly increased, affecting job opportunities for America-born minorities and immigrants, residential patterns, social mobility, and voting behavior.

In 2016, as recorded in the Yearbook of Immigration Statistics, America took in 2.18 million immigrants, of these 20% were family-sponsored, 48% the close relatives of American citizens, 13% refugees, and/or asylum seekers, 12% employment-based preferences, and other miscellaneous reasons. Most are family-based and from developing countries. This seems to be the trend as poor countries have poor connections and they are intimately tied together.

For instance, a retired Chinese (or any poor economy) woman might immigrate to America in the name of her only successful, diligent American son. The almost penniless old woman will live the rest of her 30 years under the American welfare system. When this kind of case occur rarely, it is insignificant. But now, people, poor or rich, skilled or unskilled, in the entire world calculate costs and benefits to move to any accessible places.

The Americans are sociable in their companies, voluntary associations, churches, and the like. They are good at creating and operating private organizations. They are skillful at forming and being free from associations and clubs. "Class consciousness, weak enough in the United States to begin with, has been almost obliterated by the multiplication of particularistic communal mysticisms subsidized by the very government and white overclass that they purportedly threaten. Far from being revolutionary, identity politics is merely America's version of the oldest oligarchic trick in the book: divide and rule." (Lind, 1996:141).

It is generally believed that immigration to America benefits the national economic performance and average Americans. Crime rates among foreignborn immigrants were lower than among the locals. Many immigrants tend to be very adventurous, innovative, and industrious.

But immigrant segregation has risen a recent decades. Immigrants with low socioeconomic status tend to have close relations with people with the same ethnic origin and concentrate in densely populated areas with convenient public transit. Due to their low education, and professional, cultural and linguistic barriers, new immigrants have more Herculean tasks in joining mainstreams of American societies. Moreover, it is argued that lowskilled immigration makes positive but little impact on the average American. Immigrants tend to do types of work that natives may be unwilling to do at that pay rate.

As life expectancy increases, an unskilled immigrant's life-time benefits and the education costs of educating their children, might be quite different from what have been so far. Other nations are also changed economically, culturally, and politically. For instance, some immigrants from mainland China are highly educated, successful, and rich. They come to settle in America not for the American dream, as they have already realized the dream, as far as work and money are concerned, in their homeland. They do not trust equality of opportunity but enjoy comfortably living a free life under protection of American law. They do not live in China Town but purchase big houses and their children graduate from Harvard, MIT or other top universities. Some corrupt Chinese officials immigrated to America, living luxury life without any working history in America. They might never be American in any sense. It is unknown whether their children will be assimilated, as their family network is still rooted in mainland China and they may not need to do business with non-Chinese Americans.

6.6 The Average IQ Population in the Global Village

> To have faults and not to reform — this, indeed, should be pronounced having faults.
>
> Confucius (551-479 BC, 15:30)

Stephen Hawking (1942–2018) cannily noted, "People who boast about IQ are losers." On the individual scale, his criterion is equally applicable to diligent geniuses or highly educated hypocrites. As far as macro phenomena are concerned, the average IQ is a main determinant of economic development, especially in knowledge-intensive and mentally-demanding economies (Herrnstein and Murray, 1996; Jones, 2015; Murray, 2020). As demonstrated by Jones, modest differences in national IQ can explain most cross-country inequalities. A higher IQ score is associated with, usually, better test performances, being more patient, higher cooperativeness, and better memories. Within the same country, IQ scores can be used to predict individual wages, information processing power, and brain size. If one is living near people with high IQs, one gets a positive environment for individual improvement (Cavanagh, 2019; Epstein, 2019). Through division of labor, the worker bees within the same profession produces collectively the hive mind which automatically enhances the national productivity of the sector. The sector can maintain its global comparative advantage after the hive is built and each worker has only a tiny impact on the system. As the world has entered the digital epoch with increasingly more dominant scale and scope economies, intelligence and cognitive skills are a key to national progress. Positive spillovers across economic sectors and heterogeneous households require capacities of information processing. An effective democracy also requires people to judge properly without being manipulated by cunning politicians. America is an extreme exception in IQs as it has sucked in many highly talented and already successful foreigners. If it fails to enhance the average IQ of the U.S.-born population, America will have problems to maintain its superpower position in future.

A great artist is capable of animating different emotions by the "same" phenomenon, while a great scientist is capable of creating the one law for multifarious phenomena. Life can be approached only through endless processes of aggregating and disaggregating, as it is lived as a particularity in generality and on transition within permanence. Immigrants mix everything as a hot pot with wealth as the key determinant of social achievements and with selfishness as the key motivation.

George Orwell (1903–195) averred: "Each generation imagines itself to be more intelligent than the one that before it and wiser than the one comes after it." The American-Italian feminist academic and social critic Camille Paglia (1947–) wonders whether America would come to the historical turning point like the civilization where her grandparents were born: "Are we like late Rome, infatuated with past glories, ruled by a complacent, greedy elite, and hopelessly powerless to respond to changing conditions?"

The conundrum for the single superpower is that it was born beautiful and rich and will be eventually aged and sentimentally fragile. The American actress, playwright, comedian, and sex symbol Mae West (1907–1980) brandished her attitude: "It's not the men in my life that count, it's the life in my men." To keep its great power status, it is not past power, the wealth of the aged, and the glory of history that matter, it is the human capital of youth in the country that counts. It is a sign of decline that it wants to enjoy glory and comfort but has lost inclinations and energies to sustain its past diligence and frugality. A nation which has neither honesty nor courage to admit its past mistakes is not strong enough to correct them and will not make sincere efforts to make any essential progress as a decent human society. America's greatness is not an exception to the common pattern of civilizations. America's superpower has been a transition from an uncultivated land toward a long-term equilibrium. Leo Tolstoy starts *Anna Karenina* with "All happy families are alike; each unhappy family is unhappy in its own way."

In traditional China and the cities of Greece and Rome, education trained the individual to subordinate himself to the collective interests and to become a "fixed" element rather than an autonomous personality in society. Athenian education strove to produce cultivated souls capable of enjoying beauty and the joys of pure speculation. Rome's educational purpose was to guide children to be men of action, devoted to military glory, indifferent to letters and the arts. In the Middle Ages in Europe, education was all Christian. In modern times, the sciences assume the key place in education. Education is to train professional "soldiers," killing people without mercy and feeling. Financial bankers, who might be the most trivial type of humans for racial survival, are typical examples of professionals. They take away people's livelihood without mercy through the so-called profession for the sake of the profession. Artists induce young girls to get pregnant out of so-called love for the sake of love, without thinking of social duties and the consequences of producing "bastards". The action is conducted owing to the male nature. Consequences are conducted according to individualism and freedom under law. Profession for the sake of profession is the fundamental for operating a social machine with human emotions as lubrication. Too much oil stops the machine. Too much fake news, too many accumulated political lies, too many human parasites, and too much human deception will ruin democracy, but a society absolutely without these social wrongdoings might be unhuman and so boring.

Bill Gates, who is making a fortune from scams across the globe, is making a straightforward calculation: "The malaria parasite has been killing children and sapping the strength of whole populations for tens of thousands of years. It is impossible to calculate the harm malaria has done to the world." Malaria might have done more positive things for human survival than the computer, if one has a bit luck to live another one hundred years. Economic theory easily proves that mankind might have had only one-tenth of the current population without malaria.

Everything is connected to everything else. His wealth enables Bill Gates to judge confidently about any public affairs. That is the power of wealth, not the power of the brain. In America, when a successful businessman makes up a story, everyone believes it. That is another way to build a bubble civilization.

America's past wrongdoings are known globally, but who cares as its greatness keeps on growing, and is evident and undeniable. However, for America to continue its absolute superiority in science and technology, it needs to bring up talented youth or to absorb foreign talented. America-born youth is losing its comparative strength in academic performances and competition in science and technology. Confucius (551-479 BC) taught: "It is not the failure of others to appreciate your abilities that should trouble you, but rather your failure to appreciate theirs." America-born students do not compare with those from developing, not to say developed, countries who receive higher education. A human society, if freely evolves, will evolve back into a degenerating society if it fails to bring up its youth passionate with discipline and knowledgeable with sense of justice.

Immigrants in recent years are not progressing the way they used to; new immigrants seem to be making only marginal, if not net negative, contributions. American greatness is reflected in its global companies, sports, movies, mass cultural products, high-tech products, Nobel laureates, luxury lifestyles, high incomes, and high GDP. The shining greatness shadows many negative aspects, such as crime, corruption, broken families, and the like.

One key variable is its very low (among the developed economies and East Asian countries) average IQs as listed in Table 6.1. This is a result of social and cultural structures. America has absorbed many highly talented individuals among all the countries who have bolstered is greatness. American freedom and discrimination also imply that if one is behind, society will not give enough attention to their social, educational, and economic conditions. Especially racial discrimination implies that the dominant race(s) naturally, consciously and unconsciously, neglects social upwards mobility through education of discriminated races. Germany, UK, France, and the United States all have colonized others with the strategy of separating and ruling. They are also romanticism-dominated cultures in association with falling birth rates. Irrespective of their glorious achievements, their average IQs are low.

Most of these immigrants work in low-paid jobs and live separately from the mainstream. No high hope there will be any great success in upward mobility. There are always important unseen or purposely neglected trade-offs within human social organic systems. Table 6.1 also lists sex times per year across (selected) cultures. The explanation of the result is given by Sechiyama (2014). France and America have the same level of IQ and almost equal amount of sex. Although China and Japan have the same average IQ, it seems that Chinese enjoy far more than Japanese such low-cost and easily conducted pleasures. There are unseen nonlinear, perhaps even unstable connections between the mind, emotion, and economic conditions which require further research.

As its superpower status is created and sustained by a combination of international immigrants and multiple cultures, it is reasonable to expect that America's strong points based on individual achievements can be copied and re-immigrated back to its original sources under peace and improved connectivity between countries. In recent years, one finds great sportsmen in Africa, great achievements in science and technology in Europe, great imitators, huge innovations, and successful industries in East Asia, and many excellent achievements in various parts of the world, which are competitive with or even more advanced than America. After WWII, it is not only America that has gone through a sustained period of prosperity and peace, some other countries have also had a peaceful, orderly, and economically-secure environment for their people to achieve success in multiple fields.

Economic convergence in terms of per capita income has taken place not only in immigrant-based economies such as America, Canada, New Zealand, Singapore, Taiwan, and Hong Kong, but also European economies and Japan that were destroyed by WWII. China is speeding up its process of escaping from the middle-income trap. Its highest average IQ, elite-based bureaucratic system, market-mechanism with a strong government sector, and largest population encompasses a high possibility of sustainable development. No one knows the economic and environmental implications if China achieves per-capita income even a half of America in the near future.

Table 6.1. Average IQs, GDP per Capita, Happiness Indexes, and Frequency of Sex

Country/Region	IQ rank (IQ)	GDP per capita (US$) in 2017	Happiness rankings	Sex (times per year)
Singapore	1 (108)	57,713	34	73
Hong Kong	2 (108)	46,194	36	78
Taiwan	3 (106)	n.a.	26	88
South Korea	4 (106)	29,742	57	Na
Japan	5 (105)	38,428	54	45
China	6 (104)	8,826	86	96
Switzerland	7 (102)	80,190	5	104
Germany	15 (100)	44,769	15	104
United Kingdom	16 (100)	59,720	19	118
France	26 (98)	38,477	23	120
United States	27 (98)	59,532	18	118

America's superiority is already gone, compared to its golden period, when one looks at each sector of society. That is the reason that Trump's "again" aroused the American heart so much. America has its wealth over-concentrated in a few families, which leaves the American dream much more onerous to realize by all the rest.

Exploring their political skills, monopolistic powers in goods markets, monopsony powers in labor markets, and human networking established among the rich, they take away whatever profits that diligent and decent workers create.

6.7 On Spengler's The Decline of the West

> While they have not got their aims, their anxiety is how to get them. When they have got them, their anxiety is lest they should lose them. When they are anxious lest such things should be lost, there is nothing to which they will not proceed.
>
> Confucius (551–479 BC, 7:26)

> Opportunities of time vouchsafed by Heaven are not equal to advantages of situation afforded by Earth, and advantages of situ-

ation afforded by the Earth are not equal to the union arising from
the accord of Men.

Mencius (372–289 BC)

It might be helpful to deviate from the main road for a while to see from
another perspective America's "deepening self-destructiveness" through
an influential book on the rise and fall of civilizations. In *The Decline of the
West* (1918–22), Oswald Spengler argued that civilizations and cultures are
subject to the same cycle of growth and decay as human beings.

In the modern West it is generally believed that progress in civilization
is linear, in the sense that everything is improved over time. We know more
about nature through scientific advances. Inventors create new tools to
further exploit and dominate the world. Artists brandish more varieties of
creative expression. Civilization should progress towards a point at which
all social conflicts are solved by knowledge and technology. There would be
no social and economic classes.

Spengler admitted that every civilization has its twilight period during
which it preserves the form of its central Idea, but loses the content, the
essential spirit. He long ago held that Western Man is a proud but tragic
figure. Although he strives and creates, Western Man is far from his goal.
Spengler accepted the end of other civilizations in the following sense: "Here
then, I lay it down that *Imperialism*, of which petrifacts such as the Egyptian empire, the Roman, the Chinese, the Indian, may continue to exist for
hundreds or thousands of years...is to be taken as the typical symbol of the
end. Imperialism is *Civilization* unadulterated. In this phenomenal form of
the destiny of the West is now irrevocably set. The energy of culture-man is
directed inwards, that of civilization-man outwards...".

In economist terminology, an absolute culture-man is concerned with
maximizing inner value, while an utter civilization-man is concentrated
on maximizing exchange value. According to Chinese cycling of the human
mind, there is an oscillation between the culture-man and the civilization man. A simple society is composed of culture-men, while a sophisticated society is called civilization. Spengler alleged: "In the history, the
genuine history, of higher men, the stake fought for and the basis of the
animal struggle to prevail is ever — even when the driver and the driven are
completely unconscious of the symbolic force of their doings, purposes and
fortunes — the actualization of something that is essentially spiritual, the
translation of an idea into a living historical form. This applies equally to the
struggle of big style-tendencies in art, of philosophy, of political ideals and of
economic forms. But the post-history is void of all this. All that remains is the

struggle for mere power, for animal advantage *per se*." The American history does not seem to avert the track of a civilization.

He considered that civilization is what a culture becomes once its creative impulses wane and become overwhelmed by critical impulses. The intellect rules once the soul abdicated. Culture is the becoming, civilization is the thing become. For him, "Plato and Goethe stand for the philosophy of Becoming, Aristotle and Kant the philosophy of Being... Goethe's notes and verse ... must be regarded as the expression of a perfectly definite metaphysical doctrine." Men like Rousseau, Socrates, and Buddha mark the point where their cultures transformed into civilization. Each buried centuries of spiritual depth by revealing the world in rational terms. Becoming is the basic element and being is static and secondary. Civilization is the destiny of every culture. The transition is not carried out by choice. It is not the conscious will of individuals or groups of individuals that decides. Civilizations are what cultures become when they are no longer creative and growing. According to Spengler, the imaginative Greek culture declined into practical Roman civilization. He had a low opinion of civilization, even they made great expansion and successes. That expansion was not real growth. For him, Roman world domination was not an achievement because the Romans faced no strong resistance to their domination. They simply occupied what lay open to everyone.

Spengler highlighted the will to power in Western civilization as a driving force of progress: "If, in fine, we look at the whole picture — the expansion of the Copernican world into that aspect of stellar space that we possess today; the development of Columbus's discovery into a world-wide command of the earth's surface by the West; the perspective of oil-painting and the theater; the sublimation of the idea of home; the passion of our civilization for swift transit, the conquest of the air, the exploration of the Polar regions and the climbing of almost impossible mountain-peaks — we see, emerging everywhere, the prime symbol of the Faustian soul, Limitless Space. And those specially Western creations of the soul-myth call 'Will,' 'Force' and 'Deed' must be regarded as derivative of this prime symbol." The will to power, the will to sex, and the will to wealth are nature of humans. Man, after all, a special animal with various capacities for knowledge creation and application and tool construction and utilization. The modern civilization accentuates the will to get power; but the will to sex will withdraw powerful man back to the ground, and the will to wealth will make humans mediocre. Power without sex, how a boring or mad life; wealth without sex, how a meaningless and childless life; Sex without power or wealth, how an unstainable relation. Life is sex, life is power, and life is money. A full life is a subtle combination of the three lives. Modern chaos theory confirms that only the three wills can interdependently create world with an unlimited complexity.

He perceived that blood is the only power strong enough to conquer the dominant power of modern time, money. "Blood" is a race feeling. For him, race has nothing to do with racist and ethnic identity. A race is united in outlook and is connected to a landscape. Each culture is advanced or degenerated in a specific geographical area. It is defined by internal coherence of style in terms of art, religious behavior, and psychological variables. Space is thus a key to cultural formation. Culture is organic. Higher culture is an organism, with its coherence and maturity in its own right. It is characterized by its capacities of sublimating the various customs, myths, techniques, arts, and peoples into a single historical tendency.

A race has roots like a plant. He points out: "If, in that home, the race cannot be found, this means the race has ceased to exist. A race does not migrate. Men migrate, and their successive generations are born in ever-changing landscapes; but the landscape exercises a secret force upon the extinction of the old and the appearance of the new one." He does mean that a race is exactly the same like a plant: "Science has completely failed to note that race is not the same for rooted plants as it is for mobile animals, that with the micro-cosmic side of life a fresh group of characteristics appear and that for the animal world it is decisive. Nor again has it perceived that a completely different significance must be attached to 'races' when the word denotes subdivisions within the *integral race 'Man.'*"

Spengler is also convinced of that that agglomeration of people into mega cities speeds up the destruction: "What makes the man of the world-cities incapable of living on any but this artificial footing is that the cosmic in his being is every decreasing, while the tensions of his waking-consciousness become more and more dangerous.... the city's history ... growing from primitive barter-center to Culture-city and at last to world-city, it sacrifices first the blood and soul of its creators to the needs of its majestic evolution, and then the 1st flower of that growth to the spirit of civilization — and so, doomed, moves on to final self-destruction." For Spengler, democracy is simply the political weapon of money and media are the tool through which money operates a democratic political system. Through the media, money is transformed into power — the more money is spent, the more intense money influences on the political system. Democracy requires universal education for the shepherding of the masses. People who originally considered education to be solely for the enlightenment of each individual pave the path for the media and eventually lead to the rise of Caesar. The concentration of wealth in a few families, according to him, makes political competition to revolve around questions of money. This is not a corruption of democracy because this is the necessary end of mature democratic systems. The complete penetration of money's power throughout a society is a completion of transforming culture to civilization. He wrapped up his contemplation on democracy: "Through money, democracy becomes its own destroyer, after money has destroyed intellect." When money dominates the society, who would care about high intellectual achievements?

6.8 America's Deepening Self-Destructiveness

They must often change, who would be constant in happiness or wisdom.

Asked what he thought about the poor man who yet does not flatter, and the rich man who is not proud, Confucius replied: "They will do; but they are not equal to him, who, though poor, is yet cheerful, and to him, who, though rich, loves the rules of propriety."

Confucius (551–479 BC, 1:15)

A man who has no laws at all is lost and guideless. A man who has laws but does not understand their meaning is timid and inconsistent. Only if a man abides by laws and the same time comprehends their wider significance and applicability can he become truly liberal and compassionate.

Xun Zi (298–238 BC, 1:10)

The genius Hawking had the pleasure of free playfulness with theoretical physics as a matter of course, with inborn confidence: "We are just an advanced breed of monkeys on a minor planet of a very average star. But we can understand the universe. That makes us something very special." The British knew the origin of species, perhaps assumed. In the West after the Enlightenment, natural scientists could fortunately wholeheartedly and honestly look after truth while playing for the sake of playing. In political sciences, truth is like an indestructible chewy toy for dogs. The bone has been thrown around by numerous types of dogs (the powerful). Each dog satisfies its idiosyncratic pleasures by playing and biting miscellaneous parts of the bone. Then the dogs are gone but the bone remains.

Human society rarely allows people to study the truth about humanity for the sake of understanding humanity. Original contributions to the field consist in designing new rules (such as creating religions, ideologies, alternative values of sex and sexuality, tax systems, and the like). Important creative ideas are associated with social destruction or revolution, if they are actually implemented. Marx's ideology of communism was one example, not to mention various religions that have been created in different cultures — and often exported, that is, created in order to be introduced or imposed into different cultures. Original ideas or theories about humans and human society are often socially destructive.

Bill Gates (1955–) asks for a change in the world: "We have to find a way to make the aspects of capitalism that serve wealthier people serve poorer people as well." No macroeconomic economist has offered any valid idea how to achieve such dream conditions.

In historical perspectives, the American civilization is perhaps a slightly degenerated but equally peacocky form of the British civilization, somehow mixed with French and German traits. Contemporary America is portrayed by Chris van Allsburg (1949–): "Santa is our culture's only mythic figure truly believed in by a large percentage of the population. It's a fact that most of the true believers are under eight years old, and that's a pity." Popular figures in America are aged wealthy politicians, financial gamblers, and producers of flows of pleasures. "Beauty is in the strangest places. A piece of garbage floating in the wind. And that beauty exists in America. It exists everywhere. You have to develop an eye for it and able to see it." (Alan Ball, 1957–).

But it needs an educated mind to understand why a nation is rarely truly great twice. No great empire or country is great twice before having passed through self-humiliation and deep ruination after the first greatness. China was perhaps not an empire but only a "country," one that has cyclically evinced great and inferior (the oscillator between master and slave) due to its unique geography and engenderment of great ancient thinkers. Young people have little idea what Trump meant by saying, "America (is/was) great". He lived through the epoch when America was home to global superstars in almost all fields and was experiencing the global expansion of American companies.

Many aging non-American people might now feel that life is like a cloud, when they watch the ever-shifting images of American superstars in the 1970s–1990s in movies and dramas. America's super companies nowadays needs the government's strong — sometimes even unjustified — support and protection, just to survive against global competition. "The American Dream has run out of gas. The car has stopped. It no longer supplies the world with its images, its dreams, its fantasies. No more. It's over. It supplies the world with its nightmares now: the Kennedy assassination, Watergate, Vietnam." (J.G. Ballard, 1930–2009).

From the Vietnam War and until today, America has remained the greatest country. However, looking through the lens of an economist, the signs are no longer positive. Signs of marginal values are often more important than average values. The relative decline in national global position is not only owing to political power, but is also caused by gender relations, ethnic relations, economic forces, and other forces within the society. There are internal self-destructive mechanisms in greatness. Let's look at some of them.

Individualism is a key value of American liberalism. It is generally perceived that a fair society and basic liberty of the individual are necessarily bolstered by equal rights and equal opportunity for all individuals. America lends an opportunity for cultivating talents and applying skills and knowledge. This feature attracts all races of the earth to freely profit from one's own efforts, especially when most parts of the world were unable, or simply failed, to provide opportunity due to collective inefficiency, greed, and stupidity, wars, natural disasters, over-population, and the like.

As each year so many people settle in America from elsewhere in the world, one might reasonably ask what it means to be American. Mauk and Oakland (1997:4) corroborate the view that the concept of being American has varied: "The notion of what constitutes 'American' has had to be revised over time. This process reflects both a materialistic/practical reality and an idealistic/abstract hope. Racial differences have demonstrably presented the greatest barriers to national unity."

In many parts of the world, societies are diffused with multiple, easily available types of materials — drugs for physical addiction, various rational ideas and ideologies for mental addiction, and multiple types of romantic objects and religions for emotional addictions. As ideology is the rule of social games, there is no universal ideology, like there is no universal religion or a drug that everyone will be addicted to.

The American concept of freedom is so abstract and so admirable that it may mean little for most, at least properly educated, common adults. "One of the characteristics of North American culture is that you can always start again. You can always move forward, cross a border of a state or a city or a country, and move West, most of the time West. You leave behind guilt, past traditions, memories." (Isabel Allende, 1942–). America is now domestically well-connected and internationally it is the focus of the world. The traditional American way of starting again by "leaving guilt behind" does not work effectively anymore. Official documents follow us throughout our whole life.

Great America has pushed the world to a turning point for socioeconomic structural changes in the flow of human history. Due to democratization, freedom and easily available information, any seemingly powerful and respectable status in one rational value system might be mocked in the light of another rational value system. Popular theories and ideologies on humanity and society accepted by America have proved partial and non-universal. One country can hardly brainwash all others with one unproven belief or a faith. In the global village, a politician's hypocrisy cultivated in one environment may appear comical to the rest of the world.

People do not deem another person great for unproved reasons. They have a natural inclination to perceive others as inferior. Self-confidence is nowadays called positive thinking, and a positive attitude is strongly encouraged, if for no other reason than to create flows of happiness and self-confidence in all the developed economies. But if America wants to linger on as a superpower, the younger generations need to earn it, as greatness cannot be passed on.

Changes have taken place in all areas of America society. For instance, in 1940, the top problems in the public schools were listed as talking out of turn, chewing gum, making noise, running in the halls, cutting in line, dress code infractions, and littering. In the 1990s, the top concerns were drug abuse, alcohol abuse, pregnancy, suicide, rape, robbery, and assault (Bennett, 1994:9). American kids learn in broken families and are brought up in a society full of crimes and laughable politicians. The world has changed so fast that adults now have little idea even about the major problems in the schools. There is little sign that young generations of Americans can earn American greatness in the near future irrespective of its huge stocks of culture, politics, knowledge, technology, and wealth. America could have imported foreign talents for increasing its greatness and foreigners have made net positive contribution to social and economic growth. Economic equations are shifted now. "Everything in the world may be endured except continual prosperity" — was von Goethe hinting at the root of self-destructiveness of America's economic superpower? No foreign country need deceive the educated and high-livingd Americans, they are so good at deceiving themselves.

"Insane sects grow with the same rhythm as big organizations. It is the rhythm of total destruction," (Theodor W. Adorno, 1903–1965). The cultivated are low paid and highly taxed, the stupid consume public resources of education and public offices, the workers complain about low pay all the time without thinking about work and duty, the cunning gamblers in the financial markets play with the average man's livelihood without mercy, students sleep or play in the classroom, rich social parasites boast uninhibitedly of their unimaginable wealth, artists destroy traditional moral codes in the name of freedom without producing anything meaningful, expensively trained and highly disciplined soldiers become psychologically sick after only a few days on a real battlefield, professors remain silent when faced with truth, the lazy are given social security, the irresponsible seek public welfare, the barbarians are over-protected by the law, the human-rights activists have no proper concept of being human, the environmentalist pollutes the environment far more than common citizens, the animal lovers give more attention to their beloved pets than their own aged parents, men and women conduct adultery shortly after the wedding, partisans have no sense of justice (not to say shame), and people shoot others for no reason.

All of these are not specific to America — wrong-doings crop up in other societies. But if the proportion of such people is high, the society is ruining itself. One parasite is detrimental in one body, while it is salubrious in another. If detrimental parasites overflow in an organ, the self-organizing system will naturally dysfunction. Parasites are not only domestic. Their consumption behavior causes global problems as well. Global pollution might destroy the earth in near future, as argued by some scientists. Bill Gates, who enjoys his private jet, revealed that Americans "put out a lot of carbon dioxide every year, over 26 billion tons. For each American, it's about 20 tons. For people in poor countries, it's less than one ton. It's an average of about five tons for everyone on the planet."

John von Neumann (1903–1957) warned against the unstopped linear technological change and economic dynamics led by America: "The ever accelerating progress of technology ... gives the appearance of approaching some essential singularity in the history of the race beyond which human affairs, as we know them, could not continue." America is the dominant player in the middle of this change. Moral codes, social values, human relations, worthiness, and respectability have undergone structural transformations in speed, scale, and scope that have never been seen throughout all human civilization. As with any revolutionary change in an organic system, the originator cannot control and predict consequences. It is often the weak, cunning, crazy, lying, shorty, and neglected that take the fruits of chaos.

A free world is like a wild forest: some are prey, some others are predator; prey and predators often co-habit in mutually beneficial relations. The Jew Karl Marx only imagined struggles and conflicts between classes. One who follows the rule of evolution will survive, one who does not will perish in the long term. Even mankind might perish if it does not follow rule of existence, as is evident with nuclear power, over-population, pollution, limited resources, and non-cooperative survival games among countries.

Mankind has enough capacity to destroy itself by all these means, or by viruses, or over-consumption, or diffusing hatred among races with their dream-based beliefs. American civilization is staunchly directed by profit. Man is selfish. Sympathy is important but only secondarily, as far as national survival is concerned. American society has been constructed and moved towards maximizing profits. White people and people of color have admired and loved this vast land of full opportunities. But there is no deep communication, not to say conformity, within America. Although diversity is counted on as a great source of strength, justice and fairness have not been fully pursued as a society. Diversity is constructive when each variety's positive energy is well synthesized with the other varieties. Great diversity contains self-destructive elements when conflicts occur in large scale and scope.

Genuine freedom and great opportunities for upward social and economic mobility were once relatively easily accessible to all citizens in America. Many dirty and low-paid jobs were filled by new (legal or illegal) immigrants who may feel they have already moved up just by entering America. The world was separated, compartmentalized, and people in one box had little idea what was going on within the other boxes. It was simply blind trust in America for many immigrants from poor countries. Millions entered America with unlimited hope and knowing almost nothing about reality.

As each box is opened by modern technology, the American dream is made and realized differently now. *The Doctrine of the Mean*, one of Confucian classics, talks about sincerity in human affairs: "Sincerity is the end and beginning of things; without sincerity, there would be nothing." A society which has freedom but fails to cultivate and respect sincerity will obviously lose its respectability. Without respectability nothing is worthy as being human. In American culture, one often hears about freedom and human rights, but seldom sincerity and being human. Falsifying statements (lies in Kant's sense) are everywhere in American life. Honest sincerity, which one might find, somehow, in the American founding fathers' generation, is no longer a main characteristic of America. Like any civilization which has evinced prosperity and power, it has strengthened self-destructive forces and weakened creative constructiveness. A culture which does not create sincere people with originality and strong character has nothing to remember, as things done without sincerity can be either imitated or improved, or simply forgotten or merely laughed away, irrespective of its ephemeral glory. This is what Mencius implies: "Sincerity is the way to heaven."

Aristotle predicted a long-term convergence of global mediocre as democracy becomes a global phenomenon: "Democracy arises out of the notion that those who are equal in any respect are equal in all respects; because men are equally free, they claim to be absolutely equal." A national ideology is usually a rule at the macro level and often has little to do with truth and justice at the micro level. American politics plays with democracy (there are multifarious manifestations of democracy in Western civilization).

Science and technology have brought great progress in human life. Technology is replacing human labor and services in many fields. Some humans are already playing with the technology to change our genetic structure. This could be used to improve talent by mutating the gene structure — whether man does this or something else, is another question. On the other hand, it is reasonable to ask why globally important decisions are made by ignorant, uncultivated, and aged politicians, or by ambitious billionaires, rather than by clean, most knowledgeable, and fair robots in the near future.

The world might be dominated by the nations which have most advanced robots. A man from any race is becoming incapable, if not useless, in front of a robot almost in any field of knowledge, physical work, solving well-defined problems, and complex calculation. How well they can handle making judgements of human affairs remains to be seen. Even emotional demands might be satisfied by robots in future, if a society permits it.

Science and technology have so far had limited ability to make man happy. Freud (1951:46) reflected on the issue in the 1920s: "In the last generations man has made extraordinary strides in knowledge of the natural sciences and technical applications of them, and has established his dominion over nature in a way never before imagined. The details of this forward progress are universally known: it is unnecessary to enumerate them. Mankind is proud of its exploits and has a right to be. But men are beginning to perceive that all this newly won power over space and time, this conquest of the forces of nature, this fulfillment of age-old longings, has not increased the amount of pleasure they can obtain life, has not made them any happier." His insightful assessment is too old fashioned in the light of possibilities of future technologies. Man is a super animal because of his capacity of collective creativity, restoring and diffusing ideas, learning, and using tools. The global village implies that any young man in the world, if he is talented and keen to get educated, can have opportunity to achieve his goals with few geographical limitations.

It is common to meet young men born in the middle classes of developing economies like Vietnam and Cambodia who have far more knowledge of mathematics, computers, and the sciences than young men from American middle-income families. Harvard and MIT can collect the globe's talented young people and retain the globe's talented professors. But America is going to have a hard time to keep the most value-added and practically useful people because countries like China and India, not to mention other European and East-Asian economies, will be competing now, too.

"Just as a cautious businessman avoids investing all his capital in one concern, so wisdom would probably admonish us also not to anticipate all our happiness from one quarter alone" (Sigmund Freud, 1856–1939). Even for many brilliant people in China and India, America is becoming a place to receive education, to raise their kids for a good education, and to spend holidays in as a resort, to get citizenship in order to securing a retirement haven, rather than a country for their ambitions and a dreamland for professional pursuits and business successes.

Talented Chinese of East Asia will choose to work in Chinese societies in East Asia as a confident boss, rather than be a smiling servant facing discrimination in the American labor market. This, of course, does not occur only to the Chinese. Economic principles are as universal as laws of physics. The law of equalizing prices (more generally, equalizing utility levels when applying to migration) for freely mobile inputs has important implications for America to be great again. Of course, America's aged generation, like Trump, can easily continue the story of American greatness, as old saying observes that a man does not learn anything new after the age of 30. In his 1890 *The Principles of Psychology*, William James concluded: "In most of us, by the age of thirty, the character has set like plaster, and will never soften again." Neuroscience has also confirmed this.

The middle-aged, the young, and the children in America do not exhibit any special feature that would give one confidence that America will be great again anytime soon. In *Trust: The Social Virtues and the Creation of Prosperity*, Fukuyama (1995:11) underscored: "the American Problem" is the inability of the US to perceive its own society correctly. There is perhaps no society which can perceive itself correctly. Tocqueville (1835:123) disclosed: "Nothing is more annoying in the ordinary intercourse of life than the irritable patriotism of the Americans. A foreigner will gladly agree to praise much in their country, but he would like to be allowed to criticize something, and that he is absolutely refused."

It is necessary to emphasize patriotism. Even Chinese people recently admitted as American citizens show patriotism towards their own country, the United States. The patriotism of immigrants is naturally fragile, if not purely utilitarian. There may exist some flaws that prevent one's unconditional love for a stepmother or stepfather. It is natural for immigrants to exaggerate the love of their non-native home. It was long ago ascertained by Tocqueville (1835:197), "While the Americans are thus united together by common ideas, they are separated from everybody else by one sentiment, namely, pride." He also noted (1835:330), "In their relations with strangers, the Americans are impatient of the slightest criticism and insatiable for praise." No guest should be truly at home; but the guest can easily feel at home if the homeowner is forgotten and the guest perceives himself as the owner.

Bertrand Russell (1872–1970) made it plain why freedom of speech is practically difficult: "Freedom of opinion can only exist when the government thinks itself secure."

Men naturally love to freely take advantage of other people and the environment. Power in various forms (political, institutional, economical, physical, spiritual, respectable, or knowledge...) is admired and desired or despised and neglected by different people. The law of scarcity and inborn nature of unlimited desire imply that freedom is the most valuable and fragile asset in human society.

If America is admired and loved, it is, as Grunwald (1976:36) attested, for "its constant, difficult, confused, gallant, and never finished struggle to make freedom possible. One loves America for its accomplishments as well as for its unfinished business — and especially for its knowledge that its business is indeed unfinished." The Japanese empire builder Tokugawa Ieyasu (1643–1616) told the Japanese people: "Destruction is caused by oneself." His prescription has been influencing Japan till today.

Whether America can maintain a consensus on political ideology, liberty and equality is determined by itself. The 33rd president of America, from 1945 to 1953, Truman described the trustfulness of the government in the following way: "You want a friend in Washington? Get a Dog." "Bad politicians are sent to Washington by good people who don't vote," W.E. Simon (1927–2000) suggests.

A society selects its boss through the process of evolution of selection specific to that culture. Globalization implies the necessity of selecting global leaders, possibly using alternative methods as yet unidentified. The Greeks instituted democracy by peaceful voting among the members with high status and secure economic conditions. Noam Chomsky (1928–) described American democracy, saying: "Governments regard their own citizens as their main enemy, and they have to be — to protect themselves. That's why you have state secret laws. Citizens are not supposed to know what their government is doing to them."

Today, traditional politic strategies are losing efficiency for maintaining social order and justice. This can be seen in changes in levels of trust with regard to the U.S. protection of personal freedoms by people from its five most friendly countries (France, Germany, Poland, Spain, and the UK); each of which has sent a large number of immigrants to America over centuries.

The survey below was conducted for the period of 2008 to 2018. The percentages in the table are the five country medians based on these countries, surveyed by Pew Research Center. The countries displayed an increase in distrust of America since 2008. It is reasonable to argue that this is natural as the world is more informed about what is happening within each country. America has taught other countries to respect freedom but without improving its own performance. Freedom does not mean only the freedom to mock the government. By 2018, in these countries more people said that the U.S. government did not respect personal freedoms of its people than it did before.

Table 6.2 Dynamics of Europeans' Distrust of the U.S. Government

Do you think the U.S. government respects the personal freedoms of its people?

	2008	2013	2014	2015	2016	2017	2018
No in %	26	18	30	46	42	45	57
Yes in %	69	76	65	52	53	50	40

A dream may be beautiful or horrifying, but is fairly free. Millions of new, highly educated immigrants to America in last few decades have had their dreams broken. In its golden time, diligence and talent fairly reliably led to a prosperous life. But good laws and well-established institutions do not automatically bring greatness to a nation if it does not enjoy some good luck in global conditions.

When a disciple asked Confucius about government, he (12:7) replied: "The requisites of government are that there be sufficiency of food, sufficiency of military equipment, and the confidence of the people in their ruler." When his disciple asked which of the three should be forgone first, if one of these must be dispensed with, Confucius answered, "The military first." And second, if necessary: "Part with the food. Since olden times, death has been the lot of all men; but if the people have no faith in their rulers, there is no standing for the state." He went on to explain (12:14) how to obtain this trust: "The art of governing is to keep its affairs before the mind without weariness, and to practice them with undeviating consistency." American politicians are not much concerned either with the confidence of the people in the government or with relieving the economic difficulties of the poor. Being pushed by big companies and wanting quick money, the American government was busy strengthening its national military advantages without any real enemy around. Guns and weapons are now required by big corporations rather than to meet national needs.

The traditional role of time and space in cultural formation is changed. Growing globalization has brought about a new dynamics of nationalist, ethnic, and linguistic struggles for recognition and survival. Before a new world order is established with still fast-evolving technologies, loyalties to racial, national, regional, and linguistic identities might go through an epoch of rapid change with great confusion, or "rational chaos," or even isolationists from the rest.

Cultural differences can be explored as sources of knowing, imitating, understanding, improving, self-examining, or sources of conflicts, or fatal action. "When I walk along with two others," said Confucius (7:22), "they may serve me as my teachers. I will select their good qualities and follow them, and their bad qualities and avoid them." Confucius (4:1) taught people to choose by foot: "It is virtuous manners which constitute the excellence of a neighborhood. If a man in selecting a residence does not fix on one where such prevails, how can he be wise?" "When we see men of worth," he advised (4:17), "we should think of equaling them; when we see men of a contrary character, we should turn inwards and examine ourselves." *The Great Learning* (505–435 BC) teaches: "Men are partial where they feel affection and love; partial where they despise and dislike; partial where they stand in awe and reverence; partial where they feel sorrow and compassion; partial where they are arrogant and rude. Thus it is that there are few men in the world who love, and at the same time know the bad qualities of the object of their love, or who hate, and yet know the excellence of the object of their hatred." This is perhaps a proper way for peaceful co-existence in the global village.

The ancient Chinese dreams were approximately realized on American cultural soil, rather than in mainland China. Loving one's own dwelling and its surrounding territory is a survival strategy of many social animals. Before modern times, man's emotional identity was used to protect one group's profit and to harm the outsider when necessary. Most Americans have never lived in a village very long and have little idea yet about village civilization. One needs time to adjust to new situations. Once a great power has no money or favors to offer, its small obedient friends will disobey and betray it.

The global economy, global environment, global education, global sports, global beauty, global body, global entertainment, global knowledge and technology, global literature and arts, global potential destructiveness of national wars, global sentiments, and global sufferings are simultaneously displayed on some billion screens connected with many hundred types of equipment. Tocqueville (1835:332) had already talked about the convergence of cultures: "Variety is disappearing from the human race; the same ways of behaving, thinking, and feeling are found in every corner of the world." He saw convergence not only due to intensified connections with each other and learning from each other, but also due to completely discarding the ideas and feelings peculiar to one caste, profession, or family. They are "all the same getting closer to what is essential in man, and that is everywhere the same. In that way, they grow alike, even without imitating each other."

Many countries no offer more upward mobility than the U.S., while America has now less social order and property security than some other industrialized, not to say industrializing economies.

Poor Europeans immigrated to America and soon dropped country-of-origin to adopted race as a new identity. White peoples united to discriminate against the native Americans and people of color, irrespective of the complexity of conflicts among themselves back in Europe. Sometimes, cultural movement is well directed, while sometimes it may wander a long time before it is sure what to do. There is no simple progression from traditional to modern.

Dynamic mechanisms of human nature drive civilization. An emphasis on deep learning and moral improvement tends to irritate uneducated rich and uncultivated people in power. They have a natural inclination to mock scholars and devalue wisdom, as this makes it easier for (some of) them to appear superior to others. Diligence and broad and deep knowledge would be perceived as "inferior" goods in a declining stage of civilization. Watching the adult world, one might think young people would grasp the importance of moral improvement and virtue. Sigmund Freud (1856–1939) distrusted the sustainability of freedom among masses: "Most people do not really want freedom, because freedom involves responsibility, and most people are frightened of responsibility." Man may grow amiable and agreeable but cannot become respectable through playfulness alone, without seriousness and dutifulness.

The course of life is to complete an unstoppable process from the greatest constructiveness towards the final self-destructiveness. The American civilization is built on the assumptions necessary to an open economy. But Western civilization has almost no history of peaceful co-existence of rational civilizations in a village-like world.

Is America at the end of its rope? Even if it is not great again, as in its golden time after WWII, America has a decisive influence on the future of mankind, as portrayed by White (1996:438): "What mattered was what was remembered and emulated, not what was resisted, by nations that progressed, not by ones in decline. What mattered was creation in philosophy, science, agriculture, industry, medicine, art, song, architecture, writing, morality, and chemistry, in which lay something of the immortal that lives on after the civilization itself is gone. For even if America should finally fail, it might pass on as a legacy its techniques of commerce, communication, and democracy to others who valued them, the way it once profited from earlier civilizations.

In those connections lie the continuation of human history and the emergence of global civilization."

America is faced with new necessities; it needs to make some changes in its values in the globalizing village in whose formation it has played the key role. When the rules in a game change, it brings about unforeseen results for players. America is still an economic powerhouse and a technologically (and militarily) advanced country. But this kind of greatness can be replicated by others, such as Europe, China, India, and Africa. American civilization has been linearly and joyfully growing, with a few elements for protracted melancholy.

America can destroy the world overnight, and fortunately some other nations have that capacity as well. If America started WWIII, the war might reduce the world's population by a third. The earth might become a safer and more beautiful home for future generations. The 1/3 estimation is a much more optimistic number than what Albert Einstein came up with: "I do not believe that civilization will be wiped out in a war fought with the atomic bomb. Perhaps two-thirds of the people of the earth will be killed." The tragedy of human life is that man so easily loses himself in modern man-made complexes. There is always an easier way to look a bit more beautiful: hang out with the ugly. But quarrels with barbarians do not make a civilized person look better. Many talented men consciously spend much time and energy falsifying their public personas just to appear decent. Le Bon (1876) depicted this trend in *The Crowd*:

> With the definite loss of its old ideal the genius of the race entirely disappears; it is a mere swarm of isolated individuals and returns to its original state — that of a crowd. Without consistency and without a future, it has all the transitory characteristics of crowds. Its civilization is now without stability, and at the mercy of every chance. The populace is sovereign, and the tide of barbarism mounts. The civilization may still seem brilliant because it possesses an outward front, the work of a long past, but it is in reality an edifice crumbling to ruin, which nothing supports, and destined to fall at the first storm.

To pass in pursuit of an ideal from the barbarous to the civilized state, and then, when this ideal has lost its virtue, to decline and die, such is the life cycle of a people.

Gustave Flaubert (1821–1880) observed: "The more humanity advances, the more it is degraded." Contemporary American society is practically organized with profit and pleasure as the main motivations of individuals and the nation. Sigmund Freud (1856–1939) predicted, "America is the most grandiose experiment the world has seen, but, I am afraid, it is not going to be a success."

Human society — if one wants to wriggle out of the boredom associated with controlled order and forced conformity — prospers through variety and change. A Chinese proverb says: "Ripe fruit falls by itself — but it does not fall in your mouth." The end of the Cold War is the ending of a half-civilized and half-barbarian human history. The world is on its way towards an unprecedented type(s) of civilization, much due to the great success of American civilization. The creative processes of structures are always characterized by structural uncertainties, sudden changes, and chaos. Man is now in the stage of changes in chaos before a new structure and order are born. No one can know exactly what this unexperienced order would look like. History and the future are a set of partial differential equations. No one has that set of equations. It will take one or a few generations to have a useful set of equations, or formulas or mechanisms, tested with historical data, to enable a robot to simulate history and the future.

I wind up my endeavor by recollecting the closing part — written two decades ago — of my *The American Civilization Portrayed in Ancient Confucianism*:

Even while concerned for the future of civilizations, we can draw inspiration from Confucius: "When a man's knowledge is sufficient to attain, and his virtue is not sufficient to enable him to hold, whatever he may have gained, he will lose again. When his knowledge is sufficient to attain, and he has virtue enough to hold fast, if he cannot govern with dignity, the people will not respect him. When his knowledge is sufficient to attain, and he has virtue enough to hold fast; when he governs also with dignity, yet if he tries to move the people contrary to the rules of propriety: — full excellence is not reached." Wealth and social recognition (power) give man satisfaction but do not necessarily ennoble man. Confucius once declared: "It is all over!" But perhaps it is not — not the end of rational civilization, but only the beginning of a truly humanistic, multi-culturally meaningful, globally peaceful, and (hopefully) non-mediocre, tolerably equal, rational civilization.

REFERENCES

Allison, G. (2018) *Destined for War: Can America and China Escape Thucydides' Trap?* Boston: Mariner Books.

Alterman, E. (2020) *Lying in State: Why Presidents Lie – And Why Trump Is Worse.* New York: Basic Books.

Alvaredo, F., Atkinson, A.B., Piketty,T., Saez, E. and Zuckman, G. (2015) The World Wealth and Income Database. *http://www.wid.world*

American Community Survey (2018) Retrieved from https://en.wikipedia.org/wiki

Aristotle (2009) *Nicomachean Ethics*, rev ed., translated by Ross, W.D. Oxford: Oxford University Press.

Arnold, V.I (1992) *Catastrophe Theory*, 3rd rev ed. Berlin: Springer-Verlag.

Bancroft, G. (1855) *Literary and Historical Miscellanies*. New York.

Baptist. E.E. (2016) *The Half Has Never Been Told – Slavery and the Making of American Capitalism*. New York: Basic Books.

Beckert, S. and Rockman, S. (2018, edited) *Slavery's Capitalism: A New History of American Economic Development*. Philadelphia: University of Pennsylvania Press.

Bell, D. (1960) *The End of Ideology*. Glencoe, IL.: The Free Press.

Bell, D. (1978) *The Cultural Contradictions of Capitalism*. New York: Basic Books.

Bell, D. (1996) Afterword: 1996, in *The Cultural Contradictions of Capitalism*. New York: Basic Books.

Bell, D. (2010) John Stuart Mill on Colonies. *Political Theory* 38(1), 34-64.

Bell, D.A. and Jayasuriya, K. (1995) Understanding Illiberal Democracy: A Framework, in *Towards Illiberal Democracy in Pacific Asia*, edited by Bell, D.A., et al. New York: St. Martin's Press.

Benedict, R. (1974) *The Chrysanthemum and the Sword*. New York: Plume.

Bennett, W.J. (1994) *The Index of Leading Cultural Indicators: Facts and Figures on the State of American Society*. New York: A Touchstone Book.

Bernays, E. (1928; 2004) *Propaganda*, with introduction by Miller, C. Singapore: Ig Publishing.

Bloom, A. (1987) *The Closing of the American Mind: How Higher Education Has Failed Democracy and Impoverished the Souls of Today's Students*. London: Penguin Books.

Bon, L.G. (1876) *The Crowd – A Study of the Popular Mind*. London: T. Fisher Unwin LTD.

Bourdieu, P. (2001) *Masculine Domination*. Cambridge: Polity Press.

Brogan, D.W. (1941:116-7) *USA – An Outline of the Country, Its People and Institutions*. New York: Oxford University Press.

Brunozzi, S. (2018) Why is US GDP Growth so Weirdly Constant? Oct 25, 2018, Retrieved from *https://medium.com/datadriveninvestor/why-is-us-gdp-growth-so-weirdly-constant-c73024d56103*

Butler, J. (1997) Religion in Early America. *The William and Mary Quarterly* 54(4), 693-94.

Camarillo, A.M. (2013) Navigating Segregated Life in America's Racial Border-hoods, 1910s-1950s. *The Journal of American History* 100(3), 645-62.

Cavanagh, S.R. (2019) *Hivemind: The New Science of Tribalism in Our Divided World*. New York: Grand Central Publishing.

Capra, F. (1982) *The Turning Point - Science, Society, and the Rising Culture*. New York: Simon and Schuster.

Chan, S. (2020) *Thucydides' Trap?: Historical Interpretation, Logic of Inquiry, and the Future of Sino-American Relations*. Ann Arbor, Michigan: University of Michigan Press.

Chan, W.T. (1963) *A Source Book in Chinese Philosophy*. Princeton: Princeton University Press.

Chomsky, N. (2002) Conversations with History. https://www.youtube.com/watch?v=8ghoXQxdk6s.

Collier, J.L (1991) *The Rise of Selfishness in America*. New York: Oxford University Press.

Commager, H.S. (1951) *Living Ideas in America*. New York: Harper & Row.

Confucius (1992) The Confucian Analects, in *The Four Book* translated by James Legge and revised and annotated by Zhongde Liu and Zhiye Luo, Hunan: Hunan Publishing House.

Cott, N.F. (2000) Public Vows: A History of Marriage and the Nation. Mass., Cambridge: Harvard University Press.

Cowan, R.S. and Hersch, M.H. (2017) *A Social History of American Technology*, 2nd. Cambridge: Oxford University Press.

Davenport, S. (2004) Liberal America/Christian America: Another Conflict or Consensus? *Journal of the Early Republic* 24(2), 190-97.

Davis, D.B. (1988) *The Problem of Slavery in Western Culture*. New York: Oxford University Press.

Deresiewicz, W. (2005) *Excellent Sheep: The Miseducation of the American Elite and the Way to a Meaningful Life*. New York: Free Press.

DiNunzio, M.R. (1987) *American Democracy and the Authoritarian Tradition of the West*. New York: University Press of America.

Ede, A. (2019) *Technology and Society: A World History*. Cambridge: Cambridge University Press.

Ellis, J.J. (2020) *Founding Brothers: The Revolutionary Generation*. New York: Vintage.

Epstein, D.J. (2019) *Range: Why Generalists Triumph in a Specialized World*. New York: Riverhead Books.

Fischer, W.C., Gerber, D.A., Guitart, J.M., and Seller, M.S. (1997, eds.) *Identity, Community, and Pluralism in American Life*. Oxford: Oxford University Press.

Foner, P.S. and Rosenberg, D. (1993) *Racism, Dissent, and Asian Americans from 1850 to the Present – A Documentary History*. Westport: Greenwood Press.

Formisano, R.P. (2015) *Plutocracy in America - How Increasing Inequality Destroys the Middle Class and Exploits the Poor*. Baltimore: Johns Hopkins University Press.

Foroohar, R. (2017) *Makers and Takers – How Wall Street Destroyed Main Street*. New York: Crown Business.

Freedman, E.B. (1982) Sexuality in Nineteenth-Century America: Behavior, Ideology, and Politics. *Reviews in American History* 10(4), 196-215.

Freud, S. (1951) *Civilization and Its Discontents*. London: Hogarth Press.

Fukuyama, F. (1992) *The End of History and the Last Man*. New York: Free Press.

Fukuyama, F. (1995) *Trust – The Social Virtues and the Creation of Prosperity*. London: Hamish Hamilton.

Fukuyama, F. (1999) *The Great Disruption: Human Nature and the Reconstitution of Social Order*. New York: Free Press.

Galbraith, J.K. (1972) *The New Industrial State*. New York: Penguin Books.

Galirndo, S.M. (2018) *Inequality in America – Race, Poverty, and Fulfilling Democracy's Promise*. New York: Westview Press.

Gilbert, D. (2002) *The American Class Structure: In an Age of Growing Inequality*. CA., Belmont: Wadsworth.

Goffman, E. (1963) *Stigma: Notes on the Management of Spoiled Identity*. N.J., Englewood Cliffs: Prentice-Hall.

Graebner, N. (1959) Abranham Lincoln: Conservative Statesman. In Basler, R.P. (ed.) The Enduring Lincoln: Lincoln Sesquicentennial Lectures at the University of Illinois. Champaign Illinois: University of Illinois Press.

Great Learning, translated by James Legge and revised and annotated by Zhongde Liu and Zhiye Luo, published in the Chinese English bilingual series of Chinese classics. Hunan: Hunan Publishing House, 1992.

Greenhouse, C.J. (2006) Separation of Church and State in the United States: Lost in Translation. *Indiana Journal of Global Legal Studies* 13(2), 493-502.

Greenspan, A. (1996) The Challenge of Central Banking in a Democratic Society, the speech delivered at *AEI's Francis Boyer Award* on December 5, 1996.

Greenspan, A. (2013) *The Map and the Territory: Risk, Human Nature, and the Future of Forecasting*. New York: The Penguin Press.

Greenspan, A. and Wooldridge, A. (2018) *Capitalism in America: An Economic History of the United States*. London: Penguin Press.

Grimes, A.P. (1983) *American Political Thought*. New York: Michigan State University.

Grunwald, H. (1976) Loving America. *Time*, 35-6.

Guelzo, A.C. (2004) *Lincoln's Emancipation Proclamation: The End of Slavery in America*. New York: Simon and Schuster.

Harrington, J.L. (2008) *Technology and Society*. Mass., Sudbury: Jones& Bartlett Learning.

Hawking, S.W. (1988) *A Brief History of Time – From the Big Bang to Black Holes*. New York: Bantam Books.

Hayek, F.A. (1991) *The Road to Serfdom*, published in 1944. London: Routledge

Heidegger, M. (1993) *Basic Writings of Martin Heidegger*, edited by D.F. Krell. San Francisco: Harper.

Herrnstein, R.J. and Murray, C. (1996) The Bell Curve: Intelligence and Class Structure in American Life. New York: Free Press.

Hilfer, T. (2003) Marriage and Divorce in America. *American Literary History* 15 (3), 592-602.

Hochschild, J. (1995) *Facing Up to the American Dream: Race, Class, and the Soul of the Nation.* Princeton: Princeton University Press.

Hoffmann, F., Lee, D.S., and Lemieux, T. (2020) Growing Income Inequality in the United States and Other Advanced Economies. *The Journal of Economic Perspectives* 34(4), 52-78.

Hofstadter, R. (1972) *The American Political Tradition.* New York: New Vintage Edition.

Hudson, W.S. (1981) *Religion in America – An Historical Account of the Development of American Religious Life.* New York: Charles Scribner's Sons.

Hughes, J. and Cain, L.P. (1998) *American Economic History.* New York: Addison-Wesley.

Huntington, S. (1996) *The Clash of Civilizations and the Remaking of World Order.* New York: Touchstone.

Johnson, H.B. (2006) *The American Dream and the Power of Wealth: Choosing Schools and Inheriting Inequality in the Land of Opportunity.* New York: Routledge.

Jones, G. (2015) *Hive Mind: How Your Nation's IQ Matters So Much More Than Your Own.* Stanford: Stanford Economics and Finance.

Jung, C.G. (1930) Your Negroid and Indian Behaviour. *The Forum* 83 (4), 193-9.

Jung, C.G. (1989) *Memories, Dreams, Reflections.* New York: Vintage.

Kallen, H.M. (1970) *Culture and Democracy in the United States.* New York: Arno Press and the New York Times.

Keynes, J.M. (1936) *The General Theory of Employment, Interest Rate and Money.* New York: Harcourt, Brace.

Kiely, R. (1999) From Monticello to Graceland: Jefferson and Elvis as American Icons. In Garber, M. and Walkowitz, R.L. (Eds.) *One Nation Under God? Region and American Culture.* New York: Routledge.

Kim, Y.Y. (1999) Unum and Pluribus: Ideological Underpinnings of Interethnic Communication in the United States. *International Journal of Intercultural Relations* 23, 591-611.

Kimmel, M. (2018) *Manhood in America – A Cultural History.* New York: Oxford University Press.

King, Jr.M.L.(1992) In Washington, I. (Ed.) *I Have a Dream: Writings and Speeches That Changed the World.* San Francisco: Harper Collins.

Klinenberg, E. (2013) Going Solo: The Extraordinary Rise and Surprising Appeal of Living Alone. Richmond: Duckworth.

Kostyal, K.M. and Rakove, J.N. (2014) *Founding Fathers: The Fight for Freedom and the Birth of American Liberty*. Washington, D.C.: National Geographic.

Lao Zi (Lao Tzu), *Tao Te Ching*, translated with an Introduction by D.C. Lau, 1963, London: Penguin Books.

Lawrence, W. (2008) Did Hayek and Robbins Deepen the Great Depression? *Journal of Money, Credit and Banking* 40(4), 751-68.

Lee, J.B. (2008) *The Fortune Cookie Chronicles: Adventures in the World of Chinese Food*. New York: Twelve.

Leibniz, G.W. (1994) *Writings on China*, translated by D.J. Cook and H. Rosemont. Chicago: Open Court.

Leiserson, G., McGrew, W., and Kopparam, R. (2019) The Distribution of Wealth in the United States for a Net Worth Tax. *The Washington Center for Equitable Growth*, March 21, 2019. Retrieved from: https://equitablegrowth.org

Levine, L.W. (2009) *Highbrow/Lowbrow: The Emergence of Cultural Hierarchy in America*. Mass., Cambridge: Harvard University Press.

Lind, M. (1996) *The Next American Nation: The New Nationalism and the Fourth American Revolution*. New York: Simon & Schuster.

Lipset, S.M. (1996) *American Exceptionalism – A Double-Edged Sword*. New York: W.W.Norton & Company.

Lipset, S.M. (1998, ed.) *Democracy in Europe and the Americas*. Washington D.C.: Congressional Quarterly INC.

Liu, H.M. (2015) *From Canton Restaurant to Panda Express: A History of Chinese Food in the United States*. New Jersey, New Brunswick: Rutgers University Press.

Locke, J. (1689) *Two Treatises of Government*. 1960, Cambridge: Cambridge University Press.

Locke, J. (1946) *The Second Treatise of Government and a Letter Concerning Toleration*, edited by J.W. Gough. Oxford: Basil Blackwell.

Ludwig, G. (2020) *The Vanishing American Dream: A Frank Look at the Economic Realities Facing Middle- and Lower - Income Americans*. New York: Disruption.

Mainzer, K. (1996) Thinking in Complexity – The Complex Dynamics of Matter, Mind, and Mankind, 2nd edition. Berlin: Springer.

Malthus, T.R. (1798) *An Essay on the Principle of Population*, in two volumes, the 7th edition, 1967. London: Everyman's Library.

Manson, R.S. (1981) *Conspicuous Consumption – A Study of Exceptional Consumer Behavior*. Hampshire: Gower Publishing Company Limited.

Marshall, A. (1890) *Principles of Economics*, 1990. London: Macmillan.

Maslow, A.H. (1943) A Theory of Human Motivation. *Psychological Review*, 50(4), 370-97.

Maslow, A.H. (1987) *Motivation and Personality*, 3rd ed.. Delhi, Pearson Education.

Mauk, D. and Oakland, J. (1997) *American Civilization – An Introduction*. London: Routledge.

Mayfield, D.L. (2020) *The Myth of the American Dream: Reflections on Affluence, Autonomy, Safety, and Power*. London: IVP.

McClosky, H. and Zaller, J. (1984) *The American Ethos: Public Attitudes toward Capitalism and Democracy*. Mass., Cambridge: Harvard University Press.

McLeod, S.A. (2018) Maslow's Hierarchy of Needs. Retrieved from

Mencius (1992) The Works of Mencius, in *The Four Book* translated by James Legge and revised and annotate ed by Liu and Zhiye Luo, Hunan: Hunan Publishing House.

Merton, R.K. (1957) *Social Theory and Social Structure*. New York: Free Press of Glencoe.

Mills, C.W. (1951) *White Colllar: The American Middle Classes*. Oxford: Oxford University Press.

Mills, C.W. (1956) *The Power of Elite*. Oxford: Oxford University Press.

Mungello, D.E. (1977) *Leibniz and Confucianism - The Search for Accord*. Honolulu: The University Press of Hawaii.

Murray, C. (2020) *Human Diversity: The Biology of Gender, Race, and Class*. New York: Twelve.

Myers, H.A. (1982) *Western Views of China and the Far East - Ancient to Early Modern Times*. Hong Kong: Asian Research Service.

Niebuhr, R. (1996) *The Nature and Destiny of Mn: A Christian Interpretation*. KY., Louisville: Westminster John Knox Press.

O'Connor, A. (2001) *Poverty Knowledge: Social Science, Social Policy, and the Poor in Twentieth-Century U.S. History*. Princeton: Princeton University Press.

Okun, A. (1975) *Equality and Efficiency, The Big Trade-Off*. Washington, D.C.: Brookings Institute.

Olzak, S. (1992) *The Dynamics of Ethnic Competition and Conflict*. California, Stanford: Stanford University Press.

Olzak, S. (2006) *The Global Dynamics of Racial and Ethnic Mobilization*. California, Stanford: Stanford University Press.

Ortiz-Ospina, E. and Roser, M. (2020) Marriages and Divorces. Retrieved from: 'https://ourworldindata.org/marriages-and-divorces'.

Peitgen, H.O. Jörgens, H., and Saupe, D. (1992) *Chaos and Fractals - New Frontiers of Science*. Heidelberg: Springer.

Piketty, T. (2017) *Capital in the Twenty-First Century*, translated from the French by Goldhammer, A. Mass., Cambridge: Belknap Press: An Imprint of Harvard University Press.

Pluckrose, H. and Lindsay, J. (2020) *Cynical Theories: How Activist Scholarship Made Everything about Race, Gender, and Identity - and Why This Harms Everybody*. North Carolina, Durham: Pitchstone Publishing.

Postman, N. (1985) *Amusing Ourselves to Death – Public Discourse in the Age of Show Business*. New York: Penguin Books.

Prigogine, I. (1997) *The End of Certainty - Time, Chaos, and the New Laws of Nature*, written in collaboration with I. Stengers. New York: The Free Press.

Prigogine, I. and Stengers, I. (1984) *Order out of Chaos: Man's Dialogue with Nature*. Boulder: New Science Library.

Putnam, R.D. (2016) *Our Kids: The American Dream in Crisis*. New York: Simon & Schuster.

Redenius, C. (1981) *The American Ideal of Equality – From Jefferson's Declaration to the Burger Court*. London: Kennikat Press.

Reilly, M. (1974, edited) *Play as Exploratory Learning – Studies of Curiosity Behavior*. London: Sage Publications.

Rhea, J.T. (1997) *Race Pride and the American Identity*. Mass., Cambridge: Harvard University Press.

Ricks, T.E. (2020) *First Principles: What America's Founders Learned from the Greeks and Romans and How That Shaped Our Country*. New York: Harper.

Rodgers, H.R.Jr. (1996) *Poor Women, Poor Children – American Poverty in the 1990s*. New York: M.E.Sharpe.

Rooger, H. (1994) *Masculinities in Crisis: Myths, Fantasies, and Realities*. New York: St Martin's Press.

Ross, D. (1991) *The Origins of American Social Science*. Cambridge: Cambridge University Press.

Ross, I.S. (1995) *The Life of Adam Smith*. Oxford: Clarendon Press.

Roosevelt, F.D. (1944-1945) *The Public Papers and Addresses of Franklin D. Roosevelt*, 1928-45. 13 vols. New York: Random House, 1938-50.

Rothchild, J.A. (2020) *Introduction to Athenian Democracy of the Fifth and Fourth Centuries BCE*. Retrieved from:

http://homepages.gac.edu/~arosenth/265/Athenian_Democracy.pdf

Safire, W. (1992) *Lend Me Your Ears*. New York: Norton.

Samuel, L.R. (2012) *The American Dream: A Cultural History*. New York: Syrcause University Press.

Schlesinger, A.M.Jr. (1998) *The Disuniting of America – Reflections on a Multicultural Society*. New York: W.W.Norton & Company.

Schor, J.B. (1998) *The Overspent American – Upscaling, Downshifting, and the New Consumer*. New York: Basic Books.

Schultz, K.M. (2006) Religion as Identity in Postwar America: The Last Serious Attempt to Put a Question on Religion in the United States Census. *The Journal of American History* 93(2), 359-384.

Schumpeter, J.A. (1934) *The Theory of Economic Development*. Mass., Cambridge: Harvard University Press.

Schumpeter, J.A. (1942) *Capitalism, Socialism, and Democracy*. New York: Harper.

Sechiyama, K. (2014) Japan, The Sexless Nation. Tokyo Business Today, by Toyokeizai Online, 19,December, 2014. Retrieved from *https://toyokeizai.net/articles/-/56360*.

Sen, A. (1999) Democracy as a Universal Value. *Journal of Democracy* 10(3), 3-17.

Shapiro, B. (2020) *How to Destroy America in Three Easy Steps*. Broadside e-Books.

Shklar, J.N. (1995) *American Citizenship: The Quest for Inclusion*. Mass., Cambridge: Harvard University Press.

Shklar, J.N. (1998) *Redeeming American Political Thought*, edited by S. Hoffmann and D.F. Thompson. Chicago: The University of Chicago Press.

Simler, K. and Hanson, R. (2020) The Elephant in the Brain: Hidden Motives in Everyday Life. Oxford: Oxford University Press.

Smith, A. (1776) *An Inquiry into the Nature and Causes of the Wealth of Nations*, edited by E. Cannan, 1976. Chicago: The University of Chicago Press.

Smith, D.B. (1982) The Study of the Family in Early America: Trends, Problems, and Prospects. *The William and Mary Quarterly* 39(1), 3-28.

Smith, R.M. (1997) *Civil Ideals: Conflicting Visions of Citizenship in U.S. History*. New Haven: Yale University Press.

Soh, D. (2020) *The End of Gender: Debunking the Myths about Sex and Identity in Our Society*. New York: Threshold Editions.

Sowell, T. (2019) *Discrimination and Disparities*. New York: Basic Books.

Stiglitz, J. (2013) *The Price of Inequality*. London: W W Norton & Co Inc.

Spence, J.T. (1985) Achievement American Style: The Rewards and Costs of Individualism. *The American Psychologist* 40, December.

Stanley, T.J. and Danko, W.D. (1996) The Millionaire Next Door: The Surprising Secrets of America's Wealthy. Ga., Marietta: Longstreet Press.

Stein, Z. (2019) *Education in a Time Between Worlds: Essays on the Future of Schools, Technology, and Society*. London: Bright Alliance.

Striner, R. (1995) Political Newtonianism: The Cosmic Model of Politics in Europe and America. The William and Mary Quarterly 52(4), 583-608.

Thelin, J.R. (2019) *A History of American Higher Education*. Baltimore: Johns Hopkins University Press.

Thoreau, H.D. (1910) Walden or, Life in the Woods, reprinted in 1992 with introduction by V. Klinlenborg. London: David Campell Publishers.

Thorley, J. (2005) *Athenian Democracy*. London: Routledge.

Tocqueville, A.de. (1835) *Democracy in America*, translated from the French origin by Lawrence, G, 1990. Chicago: Encyclopedia Britannica, INC.

Tocqueville, A.de. (1988) *The Ancient Regime*. London: J.M. Dent & Sons.

Tsuda, Y. (1986) *Language Inequality and Distortion*. Philadelphia: John Benjamin.

Turner, F.J. (1986) *The Frontier in American History*. Tucson: The University of Arizona Press.

Twiss, S.B. (1998) A Constructive Framework for Discussing Confucianism and Human Rights, in *Confucianism and Human Rights*, edited by De. Barry, W.T. and Tu, W.M. New York: Columbia University Press.

Veblen, T. (1899) *The Theory of the Leisure Class*, reprinted in 1949. London: George Allen & Unwin Ltd.

Vitz, P.C. (1989) Religion in School Textbooks, in *Education & the American Dream – Conservatives, Liberals & Radicals Debate the Future of Education*, edited by Holtz, H. et al. Mass., Granby: Bergin & Garvey Publishers, Inc.

Wallerstein, I. (2001) *The End of the World as We Know It – Social Science for the Twenty-First Century*. Minneapolis: University of Minnesota Press.

Walter, K. (1994) *Tao of Chaos - DNA & the I Ching*. Shaftesbury: Element.

Weber, M. (1904) *The Protestant Ethic and the Spirit of Capitalism*, translated from the German by T. Parsons, 1991. London: Harper Collins Academic.

Weber, M. (1951) *The Religion of China - Confucianism and Taoism*, translated from the German original by H.H. Gerth with an introduction by C.K. Yang. New York: The Free Press.

Weber, M. (1991) *The Protestant Ethic and the Spirit of Capitalism*, translated from the German by T. Parsons. London: Harper Collins Academic.

Wechsler, H.S. (1984) The Rationale for Restrictions: Ethnicity and College Admission in America, 1910-1980. *American Quarterly* 36, 643-67.

White, D.W. (1996) *The American Century: The Rise and Decline of the United States as a World Power*. London: Yale University Press.

Williams, D. (2014) Adam Smith and Colonialism. *Journal of International Political Theory* 10(3), 283-301.

Williams, R.M. Jr. (1960) *American Society: A Sociological Interpretation*, 2nd ed., rev., New York: Knopf.

Williams, W.E. (2011) *Race &Economics: How Much Can Be Blamed on Discrimination?* Washington DC: Hoover Institution Press.

Williamson, J.G. and Lindert, P.H. (1980) *American Inequality: A Macroeconomic History*. New York: Academic Press.

Wolfe, A. (1998) *One Nation, After All*. New York: Viking.

Wright, G.G. (1998, edited) *Ludwig Wittgenstein – Culture and Value*. Oxford: Blackwell.

Xun Zi (1999) *Xunzi*, in Chinese-English Library of Chinese Classics, translated into English by Knoblock, J. and into modern Chinese by Zhang Jue. Hunan People's Publishing House.

Yi Jing (I Ching, Book of Changes, 1993) translated by James Legge and revised and annotated by Qin Ying. Hunan: Hunan Publishing House.

Zinke, F.B. (1868) *Last Winter in the United States*. London: John Murray.

Zweigenhaft, R.L. and Domhoff, G.W. (1991) *Blacks in the White Establishment? A Study of Race and Class in America*. London: Yale University Press.

Zweigenhaft, R.L. and Domhoff, G.W. (1998) *Diversity in the Power Elite: Have Women and Minorities Reached the Top?* New Haven: Yale University Press.

Internet sources for the figures

Figure 1.1 GDP per Capita in the USA, 1878–2012, in 1990 dollars https://www.rug.nl/ggdc/historicaldevelopment/maddison/releases/maddison-project-database-2018

Figure 1.3 The Dynamics of Population of the United States, 1610–2020 https://en.wikipedia.org/wiki/Demographic_history_of_the_United_States

Figure 2.1 U.S. GDP Growth Rate, 1961–2019, in 2010 U.S. https://www.macrotrends.net/countries/USA/united-states/gdp-growth-rate

Figure 2.2 Dynamics of American Income Distribution from 1968 to 2018 https://www.pewresearch.org/fact-tank/2020/02/07/6-facts-about-economic-inequality-in-the-u-s/

Figure 2.3 Household Income Distribution due to Education Degree https://en.wikipedia.org/wiki/Household_income_in_the_United_States

Figure 2.4 Ethics-Based Household Income Distribution https://en.wikipedia.org/wiki/Household_income_in_the_United_States

Figure 2.7 Growth Rates (%) of Productivity and Worker's Hourly Compensation https://www.epi.org/productivity-pay-gap/

Figure 2.8 The Compensation Ratio of CEO and Worker, 1965-2019

https://www.statista.com/statistics/261463/ceo-to-worker-compensation-ratio-of-top-firms-in-the-us/

Figure 2.9 Poverty and Poverty Rate of America, 1959-2016 https://en.wikipedia.org/wiki/Economy_of_the_United_States

Figure 2.10 Gross National Saving Rates of U.S., Japan, and China, 1980-2018

Source for U.S.: https://www.quandl.com/data/ODA/USA_NGSD_NGDP-United-States-Gross-National-Savings-of-GDP

Source for Japan: https://www.quandl.com/data/ODA/JPN_NGSD_NGDP-Japan-Gross-National-Savings-of-GDP

Source for China: https://www.quandl.com/data/ODA/CHN_NGSD_NGDP-China-Gross-National-Savings-of-GDP

Figure 2.11 Dynamics of Personal Saving Behavior in America, 1960-2019

Source: https://www.statista.com/statistics/246234/personal-savings-rate-in-the-united-states/

Figure 2.12 College Degrees Awarded in US, 1987-2009

Source: https://en.wikipedia.org/wiki/History_of_higher_education_in_the_United_Statescite_ref-39

Figure 2.13 The Government Budget for R&D in the United States, 1953-2013

Source: http://www.proposalexponent.com/federalprofiles.html

Figure 2.14 Convergences of R&D Structure Between America and China

Source: https://itif.org/publications/2019/08/12/federal-support-rd-continues-its-ignominious-slide

Figure 2.15 China is Catching up America in Total R&D Expenditures

Source: https://itif.org/publications/2019/08/12/federal-support-rd-continues-its-ignominious-slide

Figure 3.1 The Eligible Voter Turnout Rate in the US Presidential Elections https://en.wikipedia.org/wiki/Voter_turnout_in_United_States_presidential_elections

Figure 4.4 Dynamics of US Births Outside of Wedlock in Percentage, 1964-2014 https://yaleglobal.yale.edu/content/out-wedlock-births-rise-worldwide

Figure 4.5 U.S. Crime Rate per100K Population, 1990-2017 https://www.macrotrends.net/countries/USA/united-states/crime-rate-statistics

Figure 4.6 Incarceration Rates of the World May 1, 2018 https://www.pewresearch.org/fact-tank

Figure 4.8 Ethnic Media Household Income in US in 2018, US$ https://en.wikipedia.org/wiki/List_of_ethnic_groups_in_the_United_States_by_household_income

Figure 6.1 Falling Share of U.S. Economy in the Global Economy

Source: https://en.wikipedia.org/wiki/Economic_history_of_the_United_States

Figure 6.2 Falling Share of U.S. Economy in the Global Purchasing Power

Source: https://www.statista.com/statistics/270267

Figure 6.3 U.S. Arms Exports, 2000 to 2019, in 1990 million U.S.D.

Source: https://www.statista.com/statistics/248521

Figure 6.4 The Top 6 of Average Annual Arms Exports, 2007 to 2017

Source: https://www.cnbc.com

Figure 6.5 Original Countries of American Immigrants

Source: https://courses.lumenlearning.com/boundless-sociology/chapter/race-and-ethnicity-in-the-u-s/

Figure 6.6 Ethnic Population Components across Ages

Source: https://courses.lumenlearning.com/boundless-sociology/chapter/race-and-ethnicity-in-the-u-s/

Figure 6.7 Dynamics of American Population Components

Source: https://en.wikipedia.org/wiki/Immigration_to_the_United_States

Figure 6.8 Origins of the U.S. Immigrant Population, 1960–2016

Data based on: https://en.wikipedia.org/wiki/Immigration_to_the_United_States

Internet sources for the maps

Map 1.1 Contemporary Map of the United States https://www.mapsofworld.com/usa/usa-state-and-capital-map.html

Map 1.2 Landscape of the United States https://i.redd.it/r8euj7tftfz01.jpg

Photo 1.1 Moses, Confucius (left), and Solon at Supreme Court of the United States.   Source: https://hermonatkinsmacneil.com

Internet sources for the tables

Table 1.1 Some Indicators in Singapore and America https://www.world-data.info/about.php; https://data.worldbank.org/indicator/NY.GDP.PCAP.CD

https://en.wikipedia.org/wiki/World_Happiness_Report

Table 6.1. Average IQs, GDP per Capita, Happiness Indexes, and Sex Times

Sources: Table 6.1 http://durexnetwork.org/SiteCollectionDocuments/Research%20-%20Face%20Of%20Global%20Sex%202005

Table 6.2 Dynamics of Europeans' Distrust on the U.S. Government https://www.pewresearch.org/global/2018/10/01/americas-international-image-continues-to-suffer/

Printed in the United States
by Baker & Taylor Publisher Services